Serendipity

To my son Francesco,
eldest of the three.
He's setting out on a fascinating
new work adventure.
I have a feeling
he'll find himself dealing
with more than one case of serendipity.

He's the one
who gave me the idea for this book.

CONTENTS

SERENDIPITY

The beauty of making mistakes

We make a lot of mistakes, and often we take the wrong path. Sometimes we're looking for something we've lost and instead we find something else we were searching for. It happens because we're imperfect. But that's not a bad thing.

Anyway, there's no such thing as perfection. And if there were it would be boring and there'd be no incentive to grow. Imperfection spurs us on to become better; to become better we have to put in the hard yards, and make mistakes along the way. Then there are accidents, events outside our control that we have to live with and adjust to, possibly taking us in a new direction.

Sometimes things happen that actually change the course of history. Think of the meteorite that shattered near Yucatán in Mexico sixty-six million years ago. Basically, it caused the extinction of the dinosaurs. If that meteorite hadn't smashed into Earth, we human beings probably wouldn't exist. Or at least we wouldn't be who we are today.

In short, for about three and a half billion years—ever since life first appeared on Earth—a vast number of accidents, mistakes and adaptations have led to the result we have today. We humans are the product of a series of imperfections that have had some degree of success, you might say, considering that of all the living beings we're the ones who have taken charge of the planet. At least that's how it looks to us. We got to this point thanks to our inventions—a multitude of discoveries, from fire right up to the internet.

In order to invent you need to do research. Sometimes you set off in the right direction and get where you wanted to go, or you happen to take the wrong path and you fail. But there are times when you take a particular direction to reach a given goal and stumble on another one you weren't expecting. Which might be even better. Spectacular examples include Christopher Columbus, who went looking for the Indies and "discovered" America. Penicillin and X-rays were both created by mistake, as were the microwave oven, cellophane, Teflon, dynamite and Post-it Notes.

In 1754, Horace Walpole coined the word "serendipity" to describe a discovery you make by accident when you were looking for something else. His inspiration was an old Persian fable about three princes, the sons of King Giaffer of Serendip (modern-day Sri Lanka). The princes traveled the world, continually (and always accidentally) discovering things they weren't looking for.

But the word "serendipity" is not just used for inventions. There's serendipity in love (you miss your train, get the next one and find the person of your dreams), in literature ("Serendipity is common when you're writing a poem: you're aiming to conquer the Indies and you get to America," wrote Andrea Zanzotto) and in film (think *Sliding Doors*).

In this book I tell the great serendipitous stories relating to my area of work: food. I've been involved with food and wine as a professional for nearly twenty years, but as an amateur for more than double that. In studying the history of various foods, I've come across some amazing cases of serendipity. A good many of the stories I tell in this book are conventional, in the sense that they're about hugely successful and well-known dishes or drinks, like Coca-Cola and gorgonzola. Others are about great things that have come from trying to fix a mistake, an oversight or an accident; for example, panettone, Russian salad and Guinness. Others are about dishes, ingredients or drinks worth including just because their origins are so bizarre, such as chili, Barolo and Milanese risotto.

While I was writing these stories it occurred to me there's an "absolute" serendipity, the most important of all—humankind—and so, with the help of a scholar, I have included that story too.

In order to tell these stories, I had a conversation with people who know a lot more than I do about the inventions in question. Producers, bon vivants, cooks, pastry chefs, artists, scientists—a varied slice of humanity I think provides crucial added value to this book. A book by someone who meets people with more talent than himself every day, and would like to pass on what he's learned. I hope you enjoy the read.

PS: A suggestion for all of you who enjoy good food and drink: as you're reading, I recommend sampling the product that's the subject of the chapter. Our enjoyment is doubled when we know more about what we're tasting. I've done this experiment with friends and, trust me, it works!

OSCAR FARINETTI

1

ANCHOVIES FROM
THE CANTABRIAN SEA

A timely shipwreck

WITH JOSÉ MARINO

"The anchovy is a dangerous and vindictive animal. Many people who've tried to feather their nest at the anchovy's expense have ended up ruined and destitute, and a few have committed suicide. Sometimes if there's an abundance of fish at the end of the season, prices crash, so anyone who foolishly bought them at high prices at the start of the season suddenly finds they're losing a lot of money. This can be so overwhelming that nothing seems worthwhile anymore. It's the revenge of the little silver fish!"

This is my great friend José Marino, an awesome guy. José was my first supplier of *acciughe alla vera carne*, the name given to anchovies from the Cantabrian Sea that are caught before the eggs are laid, when the flesh has just the right amount of fat. He splits his time between Genoa and Biarritz in French Basque Country on the Atlantic Coast near the Spanish border. I've been there with José and watched the Basque women hand-select the anchovies one by one according to size, dividing them into at least four categories numbered 0 to 3. It's done with efficiency, speed and precision that no machine could hope to match.

"José, all I'll say to you is this: *Serendipity* is not a book all about anchovies. So please, do try to be brief." He looks at me for a moment. He's casting his mind back in time, and after a few seconds we're at the end of the 1800s. Am I ready? Sure. Is he ready? Silly question: getting him to talk won't be hard, but stopping him will be.

"My uncle Antonino, who was my grandfather's uncle, although they were the same age, told me that around 1880 a few Palermo locals from the Terrasini area were in a merchant vessel that was wrecked in the Cantabrian Sea near Euskal Herria, the land of the Basques. It was spring. They were rescued and fed by the local fishermen, and over the next few days they watched as the *traineras*—big fishing boats with oars—unloaded vast quantities of anchovies, more than could be eaten fresh or even sold at the local markets, no matter how low the price.

"That's when the Sicilian shipwreck survivors realized that the Basques didn't know about the art of salting. Salted fish had been processed in Sicily and the Mediterranean since the time of the Phoenicians, who had to spend long periods at sea. So instead of going home straight away, the Italians shipwrecked at Euskal Herria stayed and taught the locals how to salt the fish they caught. A few started families and set up businesses and got rich.

"Is this a myth? I don't know. Maybe I put it out there myself," José chuckles to himself.

There's another story he wants to tell me—another tale bordering on the truth. It's the story of some Sicilians on Basque whaling boats who spotted vast schools of young anchovies and sardines, known in Italian as *bianchetti* or whitebait. They're a delicacy for cetaceans. Up to the beginning of the twentieth century the Basques were great whale hunters, sailing from Greenland to Terranova and farther south to the Cantabrian Sea. On these journeys they used the expertise of the Sicilian mariners, and they were the ones who spread the word about the indescribable, wondrous treasure trove of anchovies in those waters.

And what really happened?

José shrugs. "I prefer to believe the first version, but however it went the point is they discovered there was this wealth of poor man's fish in the Cantabrian Sea, and anchovies were considered the poorest of the poor. Even the sardines had more taste! And the mackerel too. The local companies were already preserving mackerel and tuna."

He goes on to explain that the best anchovies are the *Engraulis encrasicolus*, fished in both the Mediterranean and the temperate waters of the Atlantic. But it's the *Engraulis encrasicolus* in the Cantabrian Sea that are the world's finest anchovies, found during the costera, the period between March and June when they come in to the shore to deposit their eggs.

The anchovies in other areas like the American Atlantic and the Pacific and Indian Oceans belong to different families—*Engraulis ringens* and *Engraulis japonicus*—and José seems perfectly sincere when he says their quality and taste is barely passable, if not awful.

The time machine revs up again and he continues his story.

"The Sicilian salters needed funding to set up in the new areas, to lease spaces for salting and to buy the necessary equipment, so they asked their main clients for help. That's how this Italian community in the north of the Iberian Peninsula started. It was mainly Sicilian, and most of the Sicilians were from Palermo—from Porticello and Sant'Elia in Santa Flavia, or from Terrasini. Later there were companies set up by Genoans from Darsena, by Livornese and a few Piedmontese. The first Italian company was in Bermeo in the Basque Country, financed by Genoans with Sicilian salters."

It's as if José was part of that Sicilian, Genoan, Italian and Basque dynasty where the link is not blood, but experience, technique, a specific kind of knowledge, and especially the recognition of all those ancestors brought together by just one thing. He calls it the art of salting. It's a technique of preserving in salt "so simple that it's difficult to learn." The details are what make the difference.

It's simple to buy the anchovies, take them to where they're processed and give them an initial salting in special containers; it's simple to remove the heads and intestines in a single movement and halve them lengthwise. The trickier part comes when the men are at sea, and the women are required to place the anchovies meticulously in tins, sprinkling a good handful of salt between one layer and the next. José explains that the layering must continue well beyond the limit of the tin.

"How far?"

"The women make that decision depending on the size of the anchovies. They put a heavy weight on top of the layers, and over a few months the anchovies lose fat and become leaner, until the last layer is level with the top of the tin."

"And then?"

"Then every three days (or five at most) they have to be washed with a saturated brine solution at 25 degrees Celsius [77 degrees Fahrenheit]. But I'm not going to explain it to you because you'll think our work is too easy."

He chuckles, knowing exactly where he will steer the conversation. "The difference is in the details," he repeats. "It's in the experience of the salter. It's in knowing how to choose the best specimens when you're making the purchase. It's in knowing how to clean them with the right brine solution, accurately assess their size and salt them correctly, taking into account the different conditions of each fish. Has it come a long distance? It needs lots of hours. Was it caught close to home? Just a few hours. Has it been refrigerated on the boat? Are the females full of eggs? Are they fat or thin? And so on. It's about knowledge with a capital 'K' which you learn with experience."

Maybe you also need to be born into it, or at least practice it every day. José has worked hard to honor his family name and carry it forward. His history testifies to this, so here's the short version. His maternal grandfather, Don Liborio Orlando, a native of Terrasini, went to Getaria in the Basque Country in 1895 aged fourteen and settled there. His paternal grandfather, Don Santo Marino, set out for the United States as a boy, around 1885, and headed west. They called him

4

"cave devil" because he came from Porticello, famous for its pumice caves. When his son Vincenzo Marino, José's father, was born they were living in Louisville, but Don Santo Marino became fed up with the violence in America and eventually returned to Italy. He had heard about his countrymen emigrating to Spain for the anchovies, and although he had zero expertise in the trade he moved his family to Orio, near San Sebastian.

Years later, when Vincenzo (now called Vicente) married Carolina Orlando, it was as if all the Sicilian families involved in producing anchovies had united: on the maternal side the Terrasini family (Orlando, Cusimano and Tocco), and on the paternal side the Porticello and Sant'Elia branch (Marino, Dentici, Billante, Zizzo, Tarantino, Corrao and Scardina).

The first Sicilians who moved to Spain were people who'd never been outside their village, completely underprepared and some of them illiterate (as was the local population, incidentally). In a few cases when they made a bit of money it went to their heads and they frittered it away on women, gambling and the high life. Many ended up ruined, while the more responsible struggled on and succeeded in the end. José's father was one of these. Today, the family's anchovies still carry the brand name Vicente Marino, "with the rooster image my grandfather chose," José adds. But the precious anchovies did have their moment of crisis.

At the end of the twentieth century, the world had such an insatiable appetite for these little silvery fish that the anchovies of the Cantabrian Sea were on the brink of extinction. Then, after a five-year biological rest period, with no exemptions, they were back in large numbers. The biomass had shrunk to nine million metric tons, but today it's ten times that. Catches have been restricted to a quota of twenty-five thousand metric tons, and a few Sicilian companies buy millions of kilos for processing in Albania, Tunisia and Morocco. The businesses in northern Spain, with much higher costs, are looking to secure the PGI (Protected Geographical Indication) for anchovies caught and processed in the Cantabrian zone. All's well that ends well, right?

But my friend doesn't seem convinced.

"You see, Oscar, generational change in the fishing boat crews is a big problem. Economic conditions are great in northern Spain, especially the Basque region, and the fishermen earn good money, but it's the same as everywhere else—the young people don't want to do the work their parents did. This means employing migrants, but when the second generation comes along we're back to square one. There's a risk these magnificent boats will be scrapped and never replaced."

*

Biarritz, with its waves and surfers and the smell of the sea, is the backdrop for our nostalgic conversation about a lucky discovery. Behind José's expression lies the experience of someone who has battled all their life to bring Cantabrian anchovies to tables. His eyes are those of a tired but ever-confident fighter. There's a reason for this. When the Spanish Civil War broke out in 1936, the Marinos were in Laredo, where the Basques fled after the taking of Bilbao. When fascist Italy brought in its army to support Franco's revolutionaries, the family suddenly found itself in danger. José's parents and his older brothers were given shelter in a small hotel to save them from execution. Outside, people were shouting: "Fascist Italians, shoot them!" They were evacuated, escorted to Santander, taken out to sea on a fishing boat and shepherded aboard the famous *Deutschland* class "pocket battleship" along with other Italians and Germans from the area. They disembarked at Saint-Jean-de-Luz on the French Basque coast and returned to the family in Sicily.

But it didn't end there.

José's father wanted to go back to Spain and left as soon as the North fell to Franco's forces in 1938. What he found was not the place he remembered: the entire production of Orio and Laredo anchovies was gone, confiscated for the army.

So Vicente had to start again more or less from scratch.

His wife, Carolina, José's mother, said that from their house in the

Basque Country, at dawn they'd often hear the weeping and prayers of people condemned to death, even many years after the war.

The wheels of the time machine seem to jam up unexpectedly in José's mind.

"You tell me, Oscar, how can I not be anti-fascist with a story like that weighing on my shoulders!"

We part, while the Cantabrian Sea laps the strip of golden sand, and a few old fishing boats can at last go back out to sea.

2

TRADITIONAL BALSAMIC VINEGAR OF MODENA

Silence, do not disturb!

WITH MASSIMO BOTTURA

Massimo Bottura always gets emotional when he's talking about the traditional balsamic vinegar of Modena. Although he's one of the world's greatest chefs, he's still incorrigibly a son of his native Emilia Romagna, a region in northern Italy.

He feels (and shows) deep attachment to many gastronomic products from the Emilia Romagna region, but for this intense liquid condiment aged over decades, it's a consuming passion.

In Massimo, the marks left by centuries of work, struggle and tradition are almost visible: the stories of peasants and dukes that lie behind the excellence. When he's holding a bottle of balsamic he resembles a hero, a cavalryman of the Risorgimento bearing the Italian flag aloft. He'll sometimes say to a diner, "Do you realize what it is I'm pouring onto your plate?"

He loves balsamic so much that he makes it himself, and one day he takes me to see his barrel storage room in the attic at Casa Maria Luigia, his new accommodation and dining venue in the Modena countryside.

This is it: the mysterious shining sepulchre of Modena's gold. As you enter, you lower your voice instinctively so as not to disturb the silent play of molecules that leads slowly—ever so slowly—to something marvelous.

This is an attic, mind you—not a cellar—because making great balsamic vinegar calls for big hikes in temperature—up to 122 degrees Fahrenheit. It needs time, lots of it, and a set of barrels in decreasing order of capacity: at least five different sizes that the cooked grape must pass through, year after year, on its way to becoming the traditional balsamic vinegar of Modena. Of Modena, but also of Reggio Emilia, where it's made using exactly the same method and so it's equally good.

There was a time when these two consortia fought over the origin of balsamic, but in the end everyone knows it was born in the court of the Este family, dukes of Modena and Reggio Emilia as well as Ferrara. However, its roots go back much further than the fifteenth and sixteenth centuries, and we need to go a very long way into the past to find the first instance of serendipity.

We know for certain it started with a natural fermentation of saba, a sweet syrup derived from cooking fruit, which was part of peasant culture thousands of years ago. But there are no specific stories about who first noticed that mixing saba and vinegar could create an excellent preservative, as well as a sweet condiment.

Evidence suggests that as early as 3000 BC, vinegars and grape musts were widely used in Mesopotamia for preserving and seasoning. The practice came to the Mediterranean with the Egyptians around 1000 BC. The passage from the pyramids to the Roman Empire was inevitable considering that every table in Rome had its *acetabulum*, an ampoule filled with vinegar, and it was often special vinegar mixed with cooked grape must. It's well known that the Romans loved their food. Then in the Middle Ages, when many practices in agriculture and Roman cuisine were abandoned, must and vinegar were perfected largely thanks to the monastic communities.

So, we come to 1046. The special Emilian vinegar must have already been revered because Duke Henry II of Franconia specifically requested it when he passed through Emilia on his way to Piacenza. It had been recommended, and it was made just eleven miles from Reggio Emilia in the castle at Canossa.

In the Renaissance, when multiple-course meals rich in flavors came back into fashion, the famous sweet-sour vinegar of Reggio and Modena naturally appeared in all the European courts. When Cesare d'Este was forced to hand over Ferrara to the Papal States in 1598, he retreated to Modena, which then became the capital of the Este duchy. He took with him the Ferrara vinegars, and from then on they complemented the cooked musts of Modena and Reggio. The fusion of these traditions led to balsamic more or less as we know it today, although the term "balsamic" didn't feature in the ducal palace records until the end of the eighteenth century.

Then came the last two events of the story.

The first concerns Napoleon Bonaparte. Arriving in Modena in 1805, he decided to dismantle the magnificent ducal vinegar cellars and sell them to local wealthy families. The aim was to replenish the French army's coffers, but one beneficial side effect was the spread of balsamic culture among humbler social strata than the ducal circles.

The second involves the kingdom of Savoy, and as a native of Piedmont I'm a bit embarrassed about this, but it falls into the category of serendipity, so I'm obliged to tell you about it.

At the time of Italy's unification, King Victor Emmanuel II arrived in Modena and decided to stop there for some good food and wine. Modena was famed for its food and the good king was something of a glutton. After his umpteenth compliment on balsamic vinegar, the people of Modena decided to present him with a complete *acetaia*—a set of barrels filled with the precious vinegar, and of course plenty of suggestions on how to manage it.

But once they'd installed the *acetaia* in an attic at the court in Turin, the Piedmontese forgot all about the instructions. The precious blending process fell by the wayside and the *acetaia* remained unused.

Luckily there was a nobleman in the Savoy entourage who was a big fan of balsamic, and he wrote to Francesco Aggazzotti, a citizen of Modena and the leading balsamic connoisseur of the time. The reply to that letter, written over a century and a half ago, is now the most important historical and scientific document on balsamic.

Aggazzotti's letter became the cornerstone of today's production specifications for the traditional balsamic vinegar of Modena. At least it's comforting to think that those distracted Piedmontese were useful to the cause, albeit unwittingly.

Now here I am, speechless, in the vinegar room in the attic at Casa Maria Luigia with Bottura, the Aggazzotti of the third millennium. Here you breathe in the aromas of time, wood and thickened must and acknowledge the tremendous patience required to produce the vinegar. And there's also a bit of serendipity about the creation of this room. During the restoration of the villa, some abandoned barrels were found in this attic. The vinegar and the appearance of the barrel sets didn't impress Massimo and his team, and they certainly didn't suit the atmosphere of the place. But with the help of the Consortium of traditional balsamic vinegar in Spilamberto they were replaced. Legendary coopers Renzi provided a new set of barrels, the space regained its dignity and its wonders came to light.

The great chef continues the story: "We wanted to lovingly restore this place as we'd done with the garden. For me it's a pleasure and an honor to be looking after an *acetaia* that already existed and gave this house a soul long before we came here."

So is it love for balsamic or a greater love that motivates Massimo and makes him so emotional? Is the desire to restore honor and respectability to forgotten traditions part of his mission?

At the foot of the stairs on the first floor, the aroma of the vinegar envelops you and invites you to come on up. The vinegar room is hidden away among the guest rooms in the attic. It's a jewel to be kept safe: just as creating balsamic isn't simple, getting to the treasure chest shouldn't be simple either. The suffused light falls sideways on the casks, and in the semidarkness time seems to stand still.

"This is a place of silence, it's almost sacred. But we like to come here with our guests to sample something that seems to interpret the essence of our DNA in a few drops."

I give him a sneaky grin: "Massimo, Massimo ... I knew you'd get to the DNA!" Now he knows he can't avoid the last essential question. His shadow on the wall begins to speak: another leap into the past. Up here it seems very fitting.

"As a kid I loved watching those ancient movements of our elders among the barrels. Something magical was happening in the semi-darkness of the vinegar room, and the aroma intoxicated me. Here in Emilia it's balsamic, not blood, running through our veins: it's part of us from the moment we come into the world until our last breath. In a profound sense balsamic vinegar represents the identity of this territory. It symbolizes our way of living: soaring, dreaming and never getting lost in the mundane, making the most of life every day. It's also the perfect metaphor for the approach my team and I take to the job. *Festina lente*, hasten slowly. It means knowing how to proceed slowly to reach your goals, one step at a time. Think about it. Within that slow process there's the propensity for change and at the same time there are gradual transformations and interactive connections. In other words, proceeding slowly becomes evolving. Toward a precious end result."

The shadow falls silent. The time has come for us to taste the splendid, long-awaited end result.

3

AMARONE

Bungled wine

WITH MARILISA ALLEGRINI

To understand the story I'm about to tell, it's important to know that west of the city of Verona there's a hilly region bordered by the Adige River and extending north to the Lessini mountains. This strip of land in the Veneto Region is called Valpolicella.

It covers eight municipalities and ninety-three square miles of hills and lush green foothills, bordered by rivers and fertile valleys. In Roman times Valpolicella was renowned for its wines, derived from three main native vines: Corvina, Rondinella and Corvinone. Two wines the ancient Romans were making still survive: Valpolicella, a fresh red for drinking young, and Recioto, a sweet *passito* wine that lends itself to aging.

It was much later, just over half a century ago, that the mistake occurred, resulting in a new beverage, now more famous than the others: Amarone.

*

Marilisa Allegrini is a friend of mine. She's the daughter and grand-daughter of two major Amarone producers and is now responsible for making a great Amarone and selling it all over the world. Her predecessors were the original creators of the "bungled wine" that's become a worldwide success, much to everyone's surprise.

"Amarone is a wine which, along with just a few others, has come to symbolize 'brand Italy.' As you know, Oscar, life is full of surprises, sometimes good and sometimes not so good. What we've learned is that we must accept them and be able to turn them into opportunities, even when what we're seeing are problems or bumps in the road."

She gives me a wink. We share an unshakeable belief in the human capacity to convert misfortunes into strengths. It only takes three moves: accept the imperfection, learn to manage it and never give up. We're united in our faith in serendipity. And I want to hear her serendipitous story.

"The story of Amarone starts with its ancestor, a completely different wine from an organoleptic viewpoint but made with the same technique." This is Recioto, a name derived from *recie*, which means "ear" in the Venetian dialect. People have been drinking it since Roman times when it was made from the Corvina grape, which is shaped like a body with two lateral wings that do in fact look exactly like ears.

Since the *recie* are the grapes that are most exposed to the sun when the clusters are on the vine, they have the highest level of sugar ripeness. The small artisan wine producers in Valpolicella worked out that putting this part of the bunch out to dry would result in a delicious nectar. Calling it Recioto came naturally. This was the wine that graced the sumptuous tables of the Roman emperors.

In 1500 AD, when Verona was already a major logistical and commercial center, a statesman named Cassiodorus serving in the administration of Theodoric the Great, king of the Ostrogoths, described the production of Recioto in a letter to the senate.

We wish to describe the unique method used to make it: The grapes are selected in autumn from the vines in the pergolas of the houses, hung upside down, preserved in their jars, and kept in the usual repositories. They harden over time, not becoming liquid, then exuding their insipid humors, gently sweetened. This continues up to the month of December, until winter causes it to flow, and wondrously the wine is new when all other wine in the cellars is already old.

Then there's a lovely organoleptic description of Recioto:

This is also singular in taste and royal in color; so you may think it is colored purple at the source, or its liquor squeezed from the color purple itself. You taste the sweetness in it and its incredible softness, its density invigorated by I know not what steadfastness, and it swells in contact with the mouth in such a way that you would say it's a meaty liquid, or a drink to be eaten.

I wonder if Recioto is still made the same way.

"It sure is. The method remains the same more or less, although we get a lot of help from modern technology. First, we don't just select the *recie* anymore, but the best clusters on the vine. Then the grapes are put into wooden crates and taken to well ventilated rooms where they're left to dry over winter. We call this the active hibernation period, where they lose about 40 percent of their original weight. The water in the grape is 'breathed out' and thus evaporates, and when it comes to the crushing stage, the sugar content is very high. During fermentation, the yeasts are only able to change a portion of the sugars into alcohol, so very high residual sugar content is a mark of the wine."

So, Amarone is the result of a mistake made during the ripening of grapes for Recioto. What happened was that in some vintages the winemakers couldn't fully meet the overripening criteria, the grapes failed to reach a high enough sugar content to halt fermentation, and so the transformation to that intense sweetness didn't happen. Instead all the sugars became alcohol, so what they got was a dry wine rather than a sweeter, mellow one.

The bungled wine was no longer Recioto; they saw it as the wine that got away and initially they called it *Recioto scapà*, escaped Recioto. The name Amarone came later. In Italian *amaro* is the opposite of sweet—it means bitter.

"Actually there's nothing *amaro* about it—no bitterness, it's simply dry," my friend explains. "Anyway, at first there was no market for it. It was a wine for family drinking, like the amaro we have at the end of a meal as a digestive, you know? My father, Giovanni, was always telling me that every time we got the Amarone instead of the Recioto it suggested disaster to my grandfather Valentino. 'A disaster as terrible as hailstones!' he'd say, and you can well imagine what an enemy those are to a farmer. Each time the Amarone emerged, the family saw their income from an entire vintage disappearing into thin air."

Then came the Eureka moment.

Around the mid-1950s, a few producers sensed a business opportunity: Amarone might have some appeal beyond the family table. Giovanni and Valentino Allegrini were among them, and time proved them right. Amarone has enjoyed great commercial success in recent years because it stands out among the great Italian reds for its unique and unmistakable sensory characteristics.

Also, the drying technique has evolved and been optimized over time to produce two distinct wines: Recioto and Amarone. The naming regulations have changed too: the DOC guarantee of quality and origin set up in 1968 established that Recioto Classico della Valpolicella and Amarone Classico della Valpolicella were two distinct and equally valid wines.

Today, Amarone is consumed all round the world. Fourteen million bottles are produced annually—more or less the same as the well-known Barolo (see p. 25), though it has a much longer history.

"That's happened partly because our commitment to research was aimed at developing the tradition respectfully." Marilisa tells me modestly that the Allegrini family were the innovators: in 1998 a plan was drawn up for Terre di Fumane, a modern drying center to optimize production spaces and preempt risks from excessive moisture. "Because the humidity that persecutes us right through autumn in some vintages can also cause molds to form."

Not exactly ideal.

Amarone is the expression of a unique terrain. It's also one of the Italian wines with the greatest longevity. "In our cellar it's normal—necessary in fact—to offer a rigorous interpretation and make it pleasurable at the same time. I love the intense Amarone: it's full-bodied but at the same time beautifully balanced and it never lapses into excess during extraction. The high alcohol content is one of the natural consequences of the drying process, but the complex and powerful structure …" (Marilisa pauses for a moment) "… must never mean the loss of elegance."

This story with its happy ending would almost have you thinking good old Recioto has been forgotten. It hasn't. Every instance of serendipity only adds to the range of possibilities; it certainly doesn't destroy what was there before. The Allegrini family's Recioto remains a jewel in their crown, and it's dedicated to Marilisa's father, Giovanni. It was his job at dinners with the extended family to uncork the wine between the main course and dessert. And yes, he always had his fingers crossed that there'd be a Recioto, his favorite wine. And no hailstones!

4

THE NEAPOLITAN BABA

From France, with love

WITH GENNARO ESPOSITO

I first met Gennaro Esposito fifteen years ago. Eataly was in its early days and I was traveling often to Campania—a region blessed with sun, sea and breezes—looking for the products it offers every season. Sure, I loved Naples and also the hinterland with its dairy delights, but my heart longed for the coasts. Amalfi on one side and Sorrento on the other. Those narrow curves worming their way round the sheer rock above the Tyrrhenian Sea were my favorite part of the trip.

Along the Sorrento seaboard between Castellammare di Stabia and Massa Lubrense is where I found the best places for fabulous feasts with my great friend Pasquale Buonocore. His very name is a guarantee of Neapolitanism.

Pasquale and I both like to compensate for our very long working days with memorable dinners. On the trip in question, we'd already tried many dining venues along the Sorrento coast and decided we had two favorites. As luck would have it they both had the same name: La Torre in Massa Lubrense and La Torre del Saracino in Vico Equense. Dancing around the tables in Massa Lubrense was Tonino, known by the English moniker "On Fire" because he's always on fire, while his wife, Maria, sweltered over the stove. In Vico, the great chef Gennaro Esposito led the team in the kitchen. One restaurant offered top-class but simple dishes; the other, research and innovation, using produce from Sorrento's sea and mountains, without losing respect for tradition.

What did they have in common to make us fall in love with them? They might have seemed like chalk and cheese, but as soon as you stepped through either door you had the same feeling of well-being, welcome, complete harmony with the surrounding area, and authenticity. So whenever we were in the vicinity, we chose either Tonino or Gennaro.

One night, when we'd opted for Gennaro in Vico, we were joined by Bruno Fieno, one of my long-time partners in my businesses Unieuro and Eataly, and Corrado Colli, a great bloke who'd recently been appointed my successor at Unieuro. We sat down and I said to Gennaro, "You decide what we'll have tonight. We trust you." He made us such a superb dinner that here I am still talking about it fifteen years later. The aroma, the colors, the flavors of the sea, the taste of citrus and so much more. It was like being drugged. On the way back to Castellammare, Pasquale was at the wheel and we drove those nine miles at an average speed of six miles per hour in first or second gear, never touching third. I remember we were singing Neapolitan songs at the top of our lungs. I also remember that before we left La Torre del Saracino, Corrado was sinking his teeth into his sixth baba. That's how crazy he was about it: one bite and he was a goner.

I thought this made a good starting point to write about the baba, in the context of coastal roads, catchy songs and that legendary evening. I ask Gennaro if he can help me tell the true story of the baba.

"Well, Oscar, the origin of the baba is controversial."

"Why?"

"There's no one story we can trust about who invented our famous beloved traditional dessert."

"Didn't it come from Naples?"

"Absolutely not!" Gennaro laughs and explains: "There are two legends about the origin of the baba, but both started the same way. It's the middle of the eighteenth century. Stanislaus, Duke of Lorraine and former King of Poland, was very fond of *babka*, the Austrian Kugelhopf, a cake made with saffron and candied fruit. He loved it so much that when it turned dry and hard he was sad, so he ordered his cooks to douse it in liqueur. Here the story takes two different directions.

"According to the first version, there were possibly various trials and Stanislaus himself might have experimented by dunking the *babka* in whatever he was drinking, until he found it tasted good with Madeira. Later, when it reached the court of Versailles with the French Revolution, the Madeira was replaced with rum."

"Basically, the baba was created by a deposed king with plenty of time to devote to his culinary pleasures. So where's the serendipity?" I ask.

"The serendipity is in the second story," Gennaro tells me, "and it's my preferred take because it shows that steeping the baba in liqueur was purely accidental." That's the one I favor too.

It seems that one day the *babka* got drenched when Stanislaus was fed up with the same old court dessert and hurled it down the lunch table. It happened to hit a bottle of Madeira, which fell over and drenched it.

"An involuntary act, a mistake if you will. But sometimes errors lead to the sublime." And the sublime came to Naples after meandering around Europe. Gennaro gives me a summary of the baba's long journey. "Stanislaus's daughter, Maria, married King Louis XV of France and took her father's Polish pastry cook, Nicolas Stohrer, with her to Versailles. He was the one who replaced the Madeira with Jamaican rum, much to the horror of the king's father-in-law who had invented the dessert. Anyhow, the baba with rum was very popular throughout the reign of the next king as well, the unfortunate Louis XVI. But if you have your staff at Versailles making babas for you while Paris has no bread, sooner or later they're going to hang you.

"Long before the pitchforks arrived, the baba had a huge fan at the court of Versailles in Maria Carolina of Austria, sister of Queen Marie Antoinette. She married Ferdinand IV of Bourbon, King of Naples, and so at the end of the eighteenth century, the baba went to Naples with her and came into vogue big-time. You know what we Neapolitans are like when we fall in love, Oscar. By the mid-nineteenth century it was the ultimate Neapolitan dessert: wiped out by the French Revolution and adopted by the Neapolitan bourgeoisie."

This is a treat that moved from one place to another and found a home a long way from where it was born. For pastry chefs it has become the classic litmus test: a cake everyone tries their hand at but also a mandatory test and a very hard one at that. There are multiple coefficients contributing to the difficulty, Gennaro explains: leavening, technique, elasticity of the dough. . . .

"Manual skill and sensitivity are indispensable to making a good baba, which is why it commands respect. The rules I learned as a boy still hold: taking care to soak the baba at the right temperature, leaving it to drain and then delicately squeezing it are crucial. The danger of getting it wrong lurks around the corner. At La Torre del Saracino we have a little secret. We soak it when we're about to serve it, so that the aroma of the batter and the density of the rum are just right. The bathing syrup is quite hot, and at the end we add custard and wild strawberries to enhance the taste even further."

My mouth is watering. Gennaro gets the message without me uttering a word. He knows better than I do that talk never filled anyone's belly.

"Come on, sit down," he says with a grin, and asks with an accent that's emphatically Neapolitan: "What'll you have to drink with this?"

5

BAROLO

Call me a madman

WITH CARLO PETRINI

It's dawn on Friday, October 22, 1841. The Italian Royal Navy frigate *Des Geneys* is setting sail from Genoa under its captain, Giorgio Mameli.

Destination: Rio de Janeiro, Brazil.

The cargo includes 141 barrels of red wine from the 1840 vintage, plus a few bottles of the '38. It's wine produced in the cellars of the royal estate in Pollenzo from Nebbiolo grapes sourced in Roddi, Verduno, Santa Vittoria d'Alba and Serralunga d'Alba. But this is not a sale: the bill of lading reads: *Test transport to America*. After crossing the Atlantic, tackling the waves and the arduous wintry weather, enduring the heat shock of the equator and then spending two years in Brazil (subjected to the obligatory tastings, of course), this wine would return to Genoa and from there to the estate of King Charles Albert of Sardinia, halfway between Bra and Alba, to the cellar where it was made. An experiment.

So, in the winter of 1843, the *Des Geneys* returns to the Ligurian port carrying the same barrels it had on board when it left.

The Pollenzo wines returned from America not only un-
damaged, but much improved ... In brief, this is the full secret to
achieving a safe way of sending our wines on very long journeys
without the slightest detriment to them; moreover the discredit
that has debased our wine for centuries compared to many
others coming from abroad is now also removed. Piedmont is
qualified to distribute it, and it can be transported from one
end of the Earth to the other without undergoing any harmful
change whatsoever.

So wrote General Paolo Francesco Staglieno, the mastermind behind the mission.

He's the one who opened the barrels and rejoiced, as you can well
imagine. He's the one who made that Nebbiolo wine and apparently
added a bit of Barbera. He's the one who introduced two innovations he
judged essential for it to keep—adding sulphates and clarifying. General
Staglieno, backed by the military and political traditions of his noble
Genoan family, had completed his military career and then commanded
the Forte di Bard in Valle d'Aosta. But his natural inclination veered
toward wine. Not only as a connoisseur—he also liked to make it and
innovate. He was an oenologist before his time, before wine schools
existed and even before the word had any meaning. After the result of
the experiment on the *Des Geneys*, the king didn't hesitate to trust him
with the Pollenza Royal Estate, which he'd purchased and equipped for
the specific purpose of conducting research to improve Piedmontese
agricultural products. Especially wine.

Staglieno didn't let him down. There's a power and determination
in his words that's disarming:

Call me a madman, as many have, say that presuming to
change the method of winemaking in Piedmont is like expecting to heal the lame. His Royal Highness has allowed me to
practice my winemaking method in his unique estate and you

should all have patience and leave me to it, even if I ruin all
the wine.

According to the general, the Nebbiolo would be very different
from the one normally produced in the areas around Barolo at that
time. Up to the mid-nineteenth century, the wine from the Langhe was
sweet, cloudy and sparkling. Staglieno wanted it "dry, clear, transparent;
it should be full-bodied, alcoholic, pleasing to the palate, a delicious and
healthy wine retaining a fragrant aroma. At this point we'll be able to
send it even to the most distant countries and it will hold its own with
the Bordeaux and the Burgundies."

He imagined that with the marvelous Nebbiolo grape at his disposal,
he'd be able to create a wine with more or less the same characteristics
that make Barolo one of the most esteemed wines in the world today.
He studied, experimented and revolutionized wine to reach that goal.

General Paolo Francesco Staglieno is probably the person we're
most indebted to for the overwhelming success of Barolo, now known
almost everywhere in the world. If not for his idiosyncratic venture in
sending those 141 barrels to the other side of the planet and back, Barolo
would probably be a different, and perhaps less appealing, wine. In my
opinion, he's not sufficiently remembered for the good he did for all of
us in the Langhe and for Italians in general.

*

Juliette Colbert, great-granddaughter of the Colbert who was finance
minister to the Sun King, came to Barolo as the bride of Count Falletti,
whose lands included most of the vineyards as well as the magnificent
Barolo castle with cellar attached. Juliette came from the Loire, a region
of France where they knew how to make great wines. After tasting the
Nebbiolo made in Barolo, she decided something better could be done
with those grapes. She engaged her great friend Louis Odart, one of
France's leading oenologists and wine traders who was already working

with Camillo Benso, Count of Cavour. Together they introduced a series of innovations on the land and in the cellar with the goal of improving the wine.

Countess Colbert Falletti's most sensational move came in 1845: she had arranged for 325 carts (one for each day of the year excluding Lent, because she was deeply religious) pulled by six hundred oxen to leave Barolo for Turin. Their destination was the Royal Palace. A barrel of red wine was lashed to each cart, and the aim was to convince the court that the wine produced at Barolo was the "wine of kings and the king of wines."

A cunning marketing ploy? Sure, but an effective one: it's impossible to count the number of descriptions of this epic journey published in documents and newspapers of the time, both domestic and international.

Brava, Giulia (as they called her in Barolo)! That's what it takes to bring some things to the world's attention! Those innovative ideas contributed to the success of a wine now found on the best wine menus around the world, more than 150 years later.

*

Carlo Petrini is not only the founder of the Slow Food movement and the brains behind the University of Gastronomic Sciences in Pollenzo (yes, the town where Staglieno made his wine), he's also one of the people who worked hardest and most effectively to restore the reputation of wine from the Langhe region after the 1986 Narzole scandal, when high amounts of methanol added to low-quality wines caused poisoning and the deaths of twenty-three people.

Perhaps now, decades later, there's a need for change and innovation.

"That need is clear to everyone," Carlo agrees. "Not just in food and wine circles but across the entire industry. Earth is asking us to recognize it."

Carlin, as we call him, father of the Slow Food philosophy, explains that the Earth's loss of biodiversity and fertility show how urgent the issue is. The current climate crisis forces us to ask ourselves questions and come up with answers. And there's only one possible answer: "The productivist approach is only about maximizing profit. We have to abandon that in favor of agriculture that puts the protection of ecosystems and people first."

It's easy enough to say, but doing it is a lot more complicated. However, Carlo seems to have carved a path through the forest of improbabilities and the obstacles of our time. A major industry like wine can start the engine of the revolution: specifically, Barolo wine and the people associated with it.

"Because of the place it had, and still has, in the market and in people's hearts, the Barolo industry has a huge responsibility. In order to respect the history it carries, and to honor the visionary personalities we've talked about, we must ensure Barolo continues to be not only 'the wine of kings and the king of wines' but also, and most importantly, a promoter of change."

"So you think we're facing a new 'year zero' for the Langhe? You think the choices we make in the next few years can strongly influence the future?"

Carlo nods. This is the real challenge of our time. General Staglieno's courage and perseverance and Countess Colbert's creativity and vision should inspire today's winegrowers and oenologists, who have (and should feel) a moral obligation to free Barolo from synthetic chemistry once and for all. Respect for the vine, respect for the grape and more generally respect for the territory of the Langhe. That's what we need first and foremost if we're going to pass it on to future generations intact.

The banning of herbicides and synthetic fertilizers is the utopia of organic farming, and it's becoming an imperative. Already many winegrowers are trying it.

But as Carlo agrees, it would be great if the Consorzio di Tutela (the consortium responsible for protecting the origin and authenticity of the wines) was the one asking for Barolo to be made only where chemicals are banned. It's true the world's first organic designation might look like a marketing strategy, but as Giulia or Juliette (take your pick) teaches us, when, and if, there is substance, communication is essential to ensure it provides an example and driving force for the rest.

But that's not the end of it. There's another challenge my friend hopes the producers will take to heart—defending biodiversity. Their role in ensuring it survives will be fundamental.

"At one time here in the Langhe they made eight million bottles of Barolo; today we've reached fourteen million. The producers ought to have what I call 'limit control,' giving space not to Nebbiolo mono-cultures but to other traditional local varieties, like the *dolcetto* that's becoming forgotten. After all, there'd be no reason for the Langhe to go on existing without its native vine stock and its biodiversity, and Barolo would be one of the first to suffer."

Carlo always sees things before anyone else does. I feel a bit like his ally in this vision of our future, which could be reality in just a few years. I would also add that all the Langhe's farm machinery should function on renewable natural gas. Every farm business has the poten-tial to produce that for themselves. As soon as this thought pops into my head, my mind wanders to faraway places and possible futures, and I imagine how much we could increase sales and the average price if only we explained this philosophy to the world. It would be the first consortium to force all producers to grow their crops without chemi-cals, respect the biodiversity of its territory and create circular energy with zero impact. It's a dream. Carlo smiles.

"In the meantime, *dumse da fé*, Oscar, let's get to work. But if you think about it, what should be pushing us toward this choice is the com-mon good. That's more important than the good of the individual, and never more so than now."

A wise man is my friend Carlin, a visionary with faith and tenacity who knows his dreams can come true.

6

JUJUBE BROTH
The joy of "broth"

WITH ANDREA BERTON

Actually jujube broth isn't a broth. It's a liqueur.

There's a small town in the province of Padua, framed by the Euganean Hills, called Arquà Petrarca. Jujubes have been harvested there for centuries, and the farmers use them to make a low-alcohol liqueur. This infusion has been known forever as *brodo di giuggiole*, jujube broth.

The small red berries have a sweet flavor a bit like dates, and the drink tastes great. The best way to enjoy it is by heading to Arquà Petrarca between the end of September and early October for the Jujube Festival, because specialties usually taste better in their place of origin.

In Italian we say "*andare in brodo di giuggiole*," literally to go into jujube broth, when we mean we're over the moon, in a state of delight, utter joy and unexpected well-being. Why do we refer to jujubes and not strawberries, for example, or cherries, or truffles, or even the capon broth that I am crazy about?

This is exactly the question (about the metaphorical use of the term, not how it was created) that brought about the jujube broth's serendipity. As usual, the story branches off with different versions criss-crossing the timeline.

First, there's the story told in Arquà Petrarca, where they believe the metaphor comes directly from Ancient Greece. When Odysseus went ashore on the island of the lotus-eaters, north of Africa, the inhabitants offered the crew the only food they had—lotus fruits. The Greeks made a feast of it, but as Homer tells us it sent them out of their minds and made them oblivious to everything in the past and the future.

Odysseus forced all his men back onto the boat and set sail imme-diately, so they wouldn't forget their homeland, their relatives and their roots, and lose the desire to return home at all. Some argue that the lotus Homer mentions was none other than the Ziziphus lotus—in other words, the wild jujube—and that they didn't in fact eat the fruit but drank the alcoholic beverage made from it. It was essentially a drinking spree, leading like all drinking sprees to a loss of memory. But this is only the oldest theory: the Treccani encyclopedia tells another story, not quite so old but still dated.

In the 1612 edition of the dictionary *Vocabolario degli Accademici della Crusca*, the phrase "*andare in brodo di succiole*" appears for the first time. Note: *succiole*—not *giuggiole*.

A *succiola* is a boiled chestnut, so it was chestnut soup that gener-ated well-being. The transition from *succiole* to *giuggiole* seems to have happened suddenly when the consonants were mistakenly changed in an attempt to make pronunciation easier.

*

Some time ago I went to Andrea Berton's restaurant in Milan, in the Porta Nuova area. The restaurant is also called Berton. Andrea is one of those chefs who can truly cook creatively. No improvising. His way of being creative stems from his thorough knowledge of raw materials and his skill in combining them. I've always loved his food, but I hadn't yet tried the broth section of his menu. So many broths! All matched with extraordinary and surprising ingredients, with the broth served either in a glass or directly on the plate coating the other ingredients. Ten different variations and every one of them excellent. And of course the jujube broth is there too.

The precious amber liquid, nonalcoholic and with just the right degree of sweetness, is poured into a glass and served with the dessert. It's incredible, transparent like a meat broth, and it surprises the palate with an acidic and aromatic aftertaste.

Andrea tells me it contains rosemary, thyme and mint, and a touch of honey as well to balance the acidity.

This "special" jujube broth was also created by accident. "Do I really have to tell you the truth?" He smiles before revealing his misdeed. "The truth is that when I created it, I really wasn't planning for this result at all. I was looking for one thing and something else came out of it, but in my opinion it's actually better. I was cooking jujubes in a pressure cooker with the seasoning I told you about earlier. I left it to cook and then glaze, and I realized I was extracting the juice from the jujubes. With the extraction I got a liquid that I left on the heat until the jujubes were fully glazed, and then I poured them into a sieve. As far as I'm concerned, that's the moment the nonalcoholic jujube broth was born."

So that's the most recent instance of serendipity around this product—the last bit of the story. But I still want to know how he came up with the idea of creating a menu of broths and nothing else. A menu he offers in summer as well.

My favorite broth is the one at Carrù, made with fattened ox and served steaming hot in December. If you mention broth, people think of a hot one made with meat. That's very appealing as a comfort food, but this chef has managed to turn the idea on its head. Whether it's cold or hot, mixed with other ingredients or served to complete a particular dish, broth now plays an unprecedented leading role, like a good actor able to interpret any character. The prosciutto broth paired with flaked cod is one example. The cod has a delicate but pronounced flavor, and Andrea says the prosciutto broth is what makes the fillet succulent and the dish well balanced. A candied radish adds acidity, and *voilà*, a masterpiece is served.

At the end of the menu is a chocolate broth, which Andrea explains is made with just chocolate, cocoa beans and water.

"We dissolve them together and put them in a blast chiller at a temperature of minus 40 degrees Celsius [or Fahrenheit]. Then they have to be liquefied and decanted, like the jujube broth."

It's the decantation that allows the chef to obtain liquids from all those products that are mostly solid and difficult to make transparent. That's how his broths are born; he believes they represent our origins, as well as letting us taste the flavors even in the liquid part of a product.

"After all, water is part of our nature. And creating a water that tastes the same as the main ingredient I think gives completeness to what you'll be eating."

Undoubtedly, his philosophy is ultra-modern. I picture endless years of Italian kitchens with the greasy broth slowly simmering in a stockpot. The healing food par excellence, and the interlude that prepares the stomach for a hearty meal. But Berton is a chef of the third millennium. Research is the future, and the future can only be read in the residue of a broth like his.

7
___

BROWNIES

When forgetting means good fortune

WITH KATIA DELOGU

"A saint!" That's how my wife always refers to Katia Delogu when we go into Eataly in New York and see her busy filling the counter with Italian sweet treats. Katia is our pastry chef for North America. She's the one who supervises the making and selling of cakes and confectionery in all of the Eataly stores in the United States and Canada, from New York to Boston, Chicago, Los Angeles, Las Vegas and Toronto. The Big Apple is her HQ, but she's always on the move around the continent and we see her less and less in our center opposite the Flatiron Building, where it all started.

We can never go past the confectionery window without my wife exclaiming, "She's a saint!" Indeed, it's all so beautiful, so colorful, so inviting and well displayed even when Katia isn't there—it really does look like the work of a divine hand.

Not only does she put in twenty-five hours a day with an unfailing sense of duty, she's also a true master of the art of pastry. Bless Luca Montersino who introduced us to Katia in 2010. We asked her to come to New York to give us a hand when we opened the first Eataly in

America. The idea was that she'd stay a few weeks and give the local pastry cooks a bit of training—teach them to make tiramisu, panna cotta, Sicilian cannoli, the Neapolitan *pastiera* and plenty more. But she never went back to Italy. Now she's the boss.

When I wanted to tell the story of brownies, I immediately thought of her and ran into one case of serendipity within another.

Actually it involves not just a recipe but Katia's life as well, and how she encountered brownies years ago when she was in junior high school. To earn a bit of cash she would babysit the children of an English lady. Her eyes still light up when she talks about it: "Their names were Orso and Rowen, lively kids but so adorable, Oscar! I'll never forget them."

The mother of these two kids would make sweets for snacking and there was one very dense, soft one made with chocolate, walnuts and coconut: "It was like eating a block of chocolate! It was obviously a special brownie. I can't describe the taste but it was scrumptious. I had to restrain myself so there'd be some left for the children."

"I can imagine! But where's the serendipity in this story?"

"The first time I tasted it I wanted to make some myself straight away. And that thought grew stronger whenever I ate one. I think it's what influenced my life choice, at least partly; now I spend my time cooking sweet things—in the homeland of brownies, as fate would have it."

Katia has the enthusiasm typical of those who love their work beyond measure. The things close to her heart are research, doing the job well and the absolute precision you need for working with pastry and cakes. But she has a particular fascination for things created accidentally. When something unexpected is brought to life by a mistake or an accident, it never ceases to amaze her.

"Brownies are the result of a sensational mistake. It's as if they'd always been there just waiting to be invented, don't you think?"

As the story goes (it's Katia who tells it to me but it's common legend for anyone who works with pastry and cream fillings), a slightly absent-minded pastry cook was tasked with making a chocolate cake but forgot to add yeast to the dough.

"First of all it's just as well he wasn't working here with me. I'd have sacked him on the spot and goodbye brownies!" She bursts out laughing as she reflects on the fact that brownies are like pieces of a particularly delicious cake that failed to rise. In terms of texture, a brownie vaguely resembles the Italian *tenerina* cake, or maybe a soft chocolate filling.

But here's the more accurate story. Brownies first appeared on a large scale around 1897 in the famous Chicago department store Sears. But they'd been invented a few years earlier at the Palmer House Hotel in that city, a bit farther north near Lake Michigan. The hotel's owner, Bertha Palmer, asked her pastry cook to make a cake that would be easy to eat in small mouthfuls, and most importantly without getting one's hands dirty.

It was 1892, just before the World's Columbian Exposition dedicated to the four hundredth anniversary of Columbus's voyage to America. Miss Palmer didn't want a small treat to mean the ladies who'd be visiting would need to run to the bathroom to clean their fingers afterward. The result was the Palmer House brownie with walnuts and apricot glaze. To this day, 130 years later, the brownie is still served in the same hotel and made to the original recipe. Unfortunately, we don't know the name of the pastry cook who invented it. We hope they got at least some of the glory for their delicious creation and not just a lecture for forgetting the yeast.

The earliest written recipe appears in the 1896 *Boston Cooking-School Cook Book*, and in 1907 new versions began to emerge, like the much denser and more chocolatey Bangor brownie, named after the city in Maine where it was created. The Blondie, made with vanilla, is another old version, and since then plenty more variations have been developed. Brownies might come served with whipped cream, icing sugar or different types of sprinkles and chocolate, but the most popular way of eating them in the United States is as a snack with a glass of milk.

Now, in the United States you can find brownies at every turn. On display in bakeries, in little bags, in the supermarkets and in cafés.

"Can we call it America's national cake?" I ask. Katia nods: "You sure can! It's the most commonly eaten cake in the United States and there are so many variations you'll always find one you like."

Its popularity has me a bit worried. "Recently I've seen a lot of them in Italy. We've already got pubs instead of *osterie* and Halloween instead of Carnevale. Let's hope we're not going to find ourselves eating brownies instead of cannoli or *canestrelli* (butter biscuits), *crumiri* (cornmeal cookies), *pastiera* (Neapolitan tart), *bonet* (baked pudding) or tiramisu?"

As if she'd read my mind, Katia is ready with a convincing and rational answer: "Look, Oscar, the reason it's so successful worldwide is undoubtedly that it's simple to make and there are all sorts of ingredients you can add if you want. Like so many other things from America, brownies first appeared in Italy in the years after World War II. You're right to say we're seeing more and more of them in our country, but that's normal: it's called globalization. On the other hand, here in America typical Italian sweets are going gangbusters. And we've done our bit," she adds with a wink. "I'm one of those people who think that instead of going on the defensive we need to attack. And we have weapons, that's for sure!" She's probably right—we're better off thinking of how to attack than defending ourselves from the sweets invasion.

She tears a page from a notebook and recites the recipe aloud as she writes. I follow her one step at a time.

"First I'll give you the basic one that's the most popular here in New York."

INGREDIENTS:

5 tbsp butter	1/2 cup flour
1-1/2 cups sugar	2-1/2 tbsp cornstarch
2 eggs, plus 1 extra yolk	1 tsp salt
1/3 cup extra virgin olive oil	1 tsp baking soda
3/4 cup cocoa powder	5 oz chocolate flakes

METHOD:

1 Melt the butter, add the sugar and then the eggs, oil, and cocoa.

2 Use a spatula to mix in the flour, cornstarch, salt, baking soda, and finally the chocolate flakes.

3 Bake for 30 minutes in a preheated oven at 350°F.

―――――

"And this one is the original Palmer House Hotel recipe from 1892."

―――――

INGREDIENTS:

14 oz chocolate	8 eggs
2 cups butter	1 cup chopped walnuts
2 cups sugar	apricot jelly
3/4 cup flour	

METHOD:

1 Melt the chocolate and butter together.

2 Mix the sugar and flour together and add them to the chocolate and butter, mix well and then stir in the eggs.

3 Pour the mixture into a baking tin, sprinkle the chopped nuts over the top, and bake at 350°F for 30 to 40 minutes.

4 To finish, brush the surface with apricot jelly.

―――――

"Which is your favorite?" I ask. Katia gives me a sly smile: "I like the third version best." So she gives me the last one, her most successful brownie recipe. There's always a hint of nostalgia when she talks about what she loves most, and now all her memories of the Piedmontese walnuts come to the surface.

So here's the recipe for Katia Delogu's brownies.

==

INGREDIENTS:

4 eggs	1-1/4 cups flour
1-1/4 cups cane sugar	1 tsp baking soda
12 oz chocolate flakes	1 cup roughly chopped
3/4 cup butter	toasted walnuts
1/4 cup cocoa	

METHOD:

1 Beat the eggs with the sugar (just to dissolve the sugar—they don't need a lot of beating) and add the chocolate and butter melted together.

2 Add the dry ingredients and finally stir in the chopped toasted walnuts with a spatula.

3 Bake in the oven at 350°F for 30 minutes.

==

You can add whatever ingredients you like to this (the expert assures me). Just don't overcook the brownie. It must be a little bit dry only at the corners, and beautifully soft in the rest of the tray.

Anyone can experiment without ever having to throw out what they've made. It's a big advantage, especially over waste. Katia herself has tried thousands of versions, and in the course of her long sessions in the kitchen she has attempted to recreate the one with coconut and walnuts the Englishwoman who hired her as a babysitter used to make.

And the result? She's never managed it. "Sweets are not made just with ingredients: love, emotions and memories of particular moments come into it as well. But I'm not giving up, Oscar. I'll keep trying. Every now and again I think about that woman. I'd like to thank her given that it's because of the brownie that I'm here now in the city that's the center of the universe, doing this job."

What did I tell you? Nostalgia, the past, everything that happens in life comes back in a dish, in a baking tray that's still a tad warm, filled with aromas that remind you why you can feel you're finally in the place that's right for you.

8

CAESAR SALAD

Something spectacular from almost nothing

WITH VIVIANA VARESE

Today in Britain if they want to identify ancient Roman sites, they search the fields and woods for wild lettuce plants. Usually, where there's lettuce the archaeologists know they're on the right track.

When the Roman legions were conquering the island, they'd set up camp with a *castrum*, a fortified camp site, and the first thing they did was create a large garden for growing lettuce. They were gluttons for it. They credited lettuce with having digestive properties, so every meal for the Roman soldiers would have a few green leaves in it. Hence the name "Romaine lettuce," although its origins are probably Siberian. Anyhow, from those desolate lands began a journey that took lettuce first to the Sumerians in Mesopotamia, then to the Egyptians and all over the Middle East, finally landing in Italy. In Rome they called it "Turkish," like everything that came from the distant Orient. It was the Eternal City that made lettuce famous, and as it mutated naturally and adapted to its location it became known as Romaine lettuce.

We still call it that, although now it's grown in every Italian region from Puglia to Piedmont and Campania to Liguria. The latter is my favorite, grown organically on the Albenga plain where the favorable winds from the North Tyrrhenian meet the breezes of the Maritime Alps to create the ideal microclimate for growing vegetables. The leaves are long and straight with a large juicy central rib full of latex, the white liquid that leaks out when you strip off the leaves: it's what gives the lettuce its generic name, *lattuga*.

I'm talking about lettuce because it's the core ingredient of the Caesar salad.

I love this salad. I discovered it in America and that's where I usually eat it, as an antipasto or on its own if I'm in a hurry—but not too much of a hurry to add in chicken or crisp bacon. A basic Caesar salad has neither of those: it's simply a salad of Romaine lettuce (also known as cos) with cubes of fried bread added. It's dressed with Italian-style mayonnaise enriched with Worcestershire sauce, a splash of vinegar and freshly ground black pepper, and garnished with small shavings of Parmigiano Reggiano. Other variations have emerged over time, such as with anchovies or fried pancetta or pieces of roast chicken breast, or sometimes even prawns.

The last time I ate a Caesar salad, I wasn't on the beach in California or in New York City. I was in Piazza XXV Aprile in Milan, at the ViVa restaurant in the Eataly building. ViVa is the restaurant of Viviana Varese, a Michelin-starred chef heading a cosmopolitan kitchen with a great range of influences and creative new discoveries. So why a Caesar salad in a menu full of innovative offerings? Viviana sat down next to me as I ordered her Ave Cesare from the menu and she explained the name. "It's my favorite salad; I've been offering it in my restaurant for years, changing the form and adding to it. But I try to keep the taste as close as possible to the original."

I stab my fork into another lettuce leaf, trying not to be distracted from the conversation by thinking only of the sublime taste of this dish, as the chef tells me the story of the Caesar salad. Everything new and nothing new, as always. Again, nobody quite knows which is the original story.

Everybody thinks it was invented in the United States, but it was actually in Mexico, by an Italian cook in 1924. His name was Cesare Cardini, a tall man with very little hair and a persuasive smile. He's no longer with us, but his photo is displayed in his old restaurant along with the story of how the dish was created.

Viviana admits the story might have been romanticized, just a tiny bit. "My Mexican friend Zahie, an exceptional cook, took me to that restaurant to taste the salad. To be honest it could have been better, but we consoled ourselves with an excellent old Gavi di Gavi white wine that wore its age well and brightened up our evening. I should explain that Cesare Cardini's family no longer manages the place, although his photo is still there on the wall and the restaurant proudly carries the name of his creation—it's called Caesar's. It's in Tijuana, on the Pacific coast, only separated from San Diego by the US border."

The story's getting interesting: a dish invented by an Italian working in Mexico ended up flying the stars and stripes? How did that happen?

Cesare Cardini was born in 1896 in Baveno on the Piedmontese shore of Lake Maggiore and emigrated to America as a twenty-year-old, first to Sacramento and then to San Diego where he opened a restaurant. He was an excellent cook and the restaurant did well. But in the 1920s, Prohibition meant that many Americans bypassed San Diego to go to Tijuana a few kilometers farther on. There they could drink as much alcohol as they liked without having to defy the US police. Bars and restaurants proliferated as never before and they were always packed to the gills, so Cesare seized the opportunity to move his restaurant from San Diego to Tijuana. It immediately got the good fortune it deserved. Italian cuisine was very trendy and his restaurant was among the most popular. Even Hollywood stars went to eat at Cardini's restaurant, Viviana tells me, joining the crowd crossing the border to enjoy a glass or two.

So we get to a fateful night in 1924. All day the flow of customers had been busier than usual. Cesare was in the kitchen checking the last of the supplies and nearly everything was finished. There was no meat, and no fish, just as a group of VIPs came in. The kind that would leave generous tips at the end of their meal and pass the word around. There was no way our chef could disappoint them.

He approached their table pushing two carts decked out with lettuce (he never ran out of that) and a few other ingredients. Imagine their puzzled faces at the sight of a well-dressed Italian coming toward them with nothing but salad to offer! But Cesare knew what he was doing. He would surprise them by inventing a dish with what little he had left, assembling it in front of them and explaining the ingredients step by step.

As she tells this story Viviana gets caught up in the enthusiasm of the moment: "The truth was he didn't really know what the result would be! But I'm sure his ability to combine the ingredients in his mind first would have given him courage. It's a skill only great chefs have, and he was truly one of those. So right there in front of the diners, he prepared a rich mayonnaise with dual nationality—no, actually, triple."

Let me explain what that means: he poured Californian lemon juice (nation no.1) into a large transparent bowl, followed by two very fresh Mexican eggs (nation no.2), a little Italian white wine vinegar (nation no.3), a splash of American Worcestershire sauce, chopped garlic, salt and pepper. Then he started whisking in Italian extra virgin olive oil a little at a time, all the while constantly talking—talking on and on until he was about ready to faint, celebrating the origin and quality of the ingredients as he whipped up a magnificent, very special mayonnaise.

Viviana resumes the story. "So Cesare took the croutons of bread he'd toasted in the kitchen, mixed them in with the lettuce and poured over some of the freshly made mayonnaise. Finally, he sliced a generous amount of Parmigiano Reggiano paper-thin and sprinkled it liberally on top. All the while singing the praises of this rare Italian cheese he was somehow able to import in large quantities! Some say he added a few anchovies as well, but I'm not sure about that. The nameless dish was a resounding success. Those customers came back to eat it time and again and talked about it; word spread around town and Cesare Cardini was obliged to put it on his menu. It wasn't hard to settle on a name—Caesar salad. And then people made more elaborate versions, like what happens in Italy with pizza."

But the stories always take unexpected directions, and often it's the direction of the prevailing wind. Prohibition was abolished. Tijuana steadily lost its attraction. Chef Cardini, who not only managed operations around the burners but also managed them very well in business terms, decided to move to Los Angeles. It was 1935 and his salad, with dozens of variations, became the central dish at his new restaurant in California. It was such a success that after a few years Cesare began marketing it and produced bottles of ready-made sauce to sell. He set up a factory and a commercial chain, and in 1948 registered the Caesar salad trademark for the whole of the United States.

"That's why everyone now thinks it was born in the US," Viviana concludes.

Meanwhile, I've finished the last mouthful of her Ave Cesare. I want to order another and I beg her to tell me what makes it so good. I'm still licking my lips and the empty plate makes my mouth water. "Give me one minute, Viviana: just one minute."

"I don't want to see you disappointed, Oscar. Just quickly, I put two sauces in my Caesar: the original with a bit of mustard added, and one made with yogurt. And then along with the usual ingredients—but no garlic—I add cubes of chicken, fried mustard greens, chicken-skin crisps, wild fennel, marjoram and edible flowers. I serve it with a small glass of skimmed chicken broth on the side and I suggest the patrons drink it while they're eating the salad. The flavor of the original Caesar salad predominates, but it's blended harmoniously with other tastes that go well together—for me at least."

"Not just well, wonderfully well!" I say.

Viviana gives just a hint of an embarrassed smile: that's the way she is, modest and generous, and she manages to surprise me every time. Her dishes aren't overly experimental but they make every ingredient stand out—tangible, perceptible and authentic. It's as if she conjures the complete dish in her mind each time before she actually creates it. She said it herself: it's the talent of the great chefs.

9

COFFEE

Caffeinated goats

WITH FRANCESCA LAVAZZA

There is a legend about coffee that automatically places it in the ranks of the serendipitous.

Although most Italians sip coffee from an espresso cup every morning, possibly every day for their entire lives, it doesn't mean they know its history, which began in antiquity.

The story goes that one day a shepherd named Kaldi, who took his goats to graze in the highlands of Kaffa, noticed they were accidentally eating the red berries from a luxuriant flowering plant. After munching and digesting them the flock seemed much friskier than usual. At first he was merely surprised, but then he became curious and thought he'd try them himself. He enlisted the help of a monk to roast the berries, and the aroma they released was so appetizing he thought he would grind them to a powder and mix that with hot water. And so he drank the first cup of coffee in history. Like his goats, he felt a burst of unfamiliar energy, and that's how coffee was born.

*

Francesca Lavazza is the daughter of Emilio, who was the son of Beppe, who was the son of Luigi Lavazza, who founded Lavazza coffee toward the end of the nineteenth century. Together with her brother and their cousins, she is the fourth generation to head up the family company. It's the largest in Italy and one of the most important family-owned companies in terms of volume and quality but also because it's Italian, and the world largely regards Italy as the land of coffee. This is odd because coffee came to Italy relatively late and Italians are certainly not heavy consumers (for a start, in Finland they drink twice as much on average as Italians do).

So I ask Francesca: "Why Italy, exactly?" The question presupposes a leap thousands of years into the past, to the origins of the coffee plant. But again another question springs to mind: why don't people know where it came from?

Brazil? No, the Portuguese introduced it into South America early in the eighteenth century.

Central America? No, the French took it down there more or less at the same time.

The Orient? No—the Dutch transported it to Indonesia, specifically the island of Java.

"So can you tell us where coffee originated, Francesca?"

"The shepherd Kaldi took his goats to graze in the highlands of Kaffa in Ethiopia. Coffee comes from the place where everything started: Africa. The name comes from the region, Kaffa, where they celebrate the oldest coffee ceremony of all time."

She proceeds to describe this curious ritual. It's celebrated only by the women, who are responsible for harvesting, drying and roasting the coffee and then grinding it. Once crushed it goes into a pot called a *jebena* and onto the brazier. The ritual involves drinking four cups of coffee, each with its own meaning. But there's one peculiarity about this custom: the coffee cups must not have handles, because that would mean distancing the drink from the heart—you need to have the coffee in your hands and be able to keep it warm, held close to the body.

Like Homo sapiens, it's widely believed that coffee originated in Ethiopia and then spread to every corner of the planet.

"Coffee was confined to Africa for thousands of years, but at a certain point it took off northward and never stopped." Francesca explains the different stages of the journey with an imaginary map of the world in front of her.

First of all, in 1300, coffee reached Sana'a in Yemen, a place that connected Asia, Persia and Africa and so was an epoch-making junction on the coffee route. In those countries it was known as "the black wine of the prophet," and one particular city here is the origin of the name *moka*, the ubiquitous Italian stove-top coffee pot. Mocha or Al-Makha, a port city in western Yemen, was one of the earliest and best-known production areas, especially for the prized Arabica. And the export of Yemen's coffee to the rest of the world began there.

The second stage Francesca tells me about covers a large geographic area as coffee spread throughout the Muslim world.

"The forerunners of coffee shops existed as far back as the fifteenth century: shops set up in the oriental fashion, places for men to meet and exchange ideas. Mainly they drank coffee to stay awake through the evening prayers. Initially its export was banned, to protect the secret of a plant that was considered magic and precious, and was used for medicinal purposes as well. But people quickly realized that it had great social value. Let's say that while in the Far East tea was the preferred 'thought stimulator,' in the Middle East and later in the West it was coffee."

And so it came to Italy on the great ships. Third stage of the story: Venice. "But it wasn't a straightforward voyage," Francesca explains, "because first they had to overcome resistance from the Church. In the late sixteenth century Pope Clement VIII (he who cruelly sent Giordano Bruno to the stake) was asked to ban consumption of a drink made by Muslims, which the clergy believed was a perverse black liquid initially introduced by the devil himself!" Fortunately, Pope Clement VIII wanted to taste this coffee himself. He was so taken by the flavor and the aroma that he pronounced it "a sin" to leave the privilege of enjoying it to the pagans. So he bestowed the sacrament of baptism on it and the doors of Europe opened to coffee.

The first cargo blessed by the Pope was unloaded at Venice, the gateway from the Orient for all manner of exotic merchandise: spices, silk, perfumes, dyes and now coffee. Thus the first Italian to drink coffee was a Venetian. From that moment on, the key terms relating to coffee (like the terminology of music) would be Italian.

From Venice, coffee reached France courtesy of the people of Marseilles, where Europe's first literary cafés emerged coinciding with the coming of the Enlightenment. By the end of the eighteenth century, there were around three hundred cafés in Paris alone—places where dozens of young intellectuals would gather to discuss art, books, history, current affairs, music.

Then it was England's turn, with coffee houses bringing together writers, poets and businessmen in conversations covering new investments, books, art and scientific discoveries.

"But Italy didn't lag behind." Francesca pauses for a moment. I know she's going to talk about Piedmont, and she knows that when she talks to me about Piedmont I puff up with pride.

"We were part of the Enlightenment as well, Oscar, especially here in Turin. The nineteenth century, and even more so the twentieth, saw lots of literary cafés come onto the scene. Pietro Verri founded Italy's most famous Enlightenment magazine and called it *Il Caffè*. Balbo, D'Azeglio, La Marmora and Cavour planned the Italian nation in the cafés of Turin."

I'm surprised. "So we could say Turin is Italy's capital of coffee? What about Naples?"

"Yes, we can safely say that without taking anything away from Naples, where they do an excellent espresso. The reason for this is simple: the first espresso machine was invented and developed in Turin fifteen years before the beginning of the twentieth century."

Ten years after that Francesca's great-grandfather Luigi Lavazza, along with his family and a promissory note duly honored, bought an old grocery store in the city center. He began trading in coffee as many others were doing, but he also did something nobody had done before, mixing different varieties. At the time, coffee was sold and consumed as single origin; in other words, each packet contained ground coffee from a single country. Luigi had the idea of creating blends by mixing coffees from different places, which was already happening with tea. It gave him a product with a distinctive and completely new taste that made it instantly recognizable.

But this was only the first great idea. Years and decades passed, and the custom of drinking coffee during the day became more and more deeply entrenched among Italians.

"Keep in mind we're talking about the end of the fifties, Oscar, the years of the economic boom and the beginnings of mass consumption. And what could be more iconic of that time than *Carosello*? Italians would sit down in front of the TV with full stomachs after a family dinner and watch those little advertising tales—can we call them that? Stories publicizing particular products. Then my grandfather Giuseppe, Luigi's son, had the second great idea."

Giuseppe put himself in the hands of the greatest Italian cartoonist of the time—probably of all time—Armando Testa, who came up with two fabulous characters for Lavazza's advertising called Caballero and Carmencita. They came into every Italian home via TV, and Lavazza coffee followed them.

Now, thanks to the Lavazza family and other good Italian producers, Italian coffee is enjoying a time of great popularity. The next step for coffee producers needs to be a commitment to sustainability, not only environmental but also in terms of working conditions for the farmers. It's an idea we share; we both want to see Italian producers become world leaders in this space. Lavazza began that journey several years ago and is sincerely committed to it.

"It's not just a marketing operation, it's a matter of valuing those who work to make it possible for this high-quality product to exist. That's our approach in developing ¡Tierra!, a blend that's sustainable throughout the production process and takes us back to the places of origin, to the heart of coffee and the land, responsibly, with all the care and attention the product deserves."

10

CHAMPAGNE
Terroir is not just geography

WITH BRUNO PAILLARD

"Bruno, what's the origin of champagne?"

"Do you want the Dom Pérignon fairytale or the real story?"

Bruno Paillard was born in Rheims, where he still lives, is about the same age as I am, and his father was one of the leading brokers and traders in grapes and wines in the Champagne region. He studied oenology, and now he not only runs the business bearing his name but also heads the giant Lanson-BCC Group: eight prestigious brands, including Lanson and Philipponnat, with an annual turnover of over $300 million. But that's not the point. Bruno Paillard is truly a master of this prestigious wine. He has studied it and knows it well, so naturally he's the man to talk to on this subject.

He cuts straight to the chase. "Champagne was born from a series of accidents."

Champagne has ennobled our toasts for decades, but its serendipitous story goes back to the days of ancient Greece, if you can imagine that. Paillard goes into the detail: "First we must remember that champagne is a wine and in France the history of wine began twenty-six centuries ago, when the Greeks founded Marseilles and planted vines in Provence. The Mediterranean is a natural environment for wine, the quintessential region for growing hundreds of different grape varieties. But France is continental as well, and vines came to the rest of the country much later, when Julius Caesar conquered Gaul in 58 BC. The wine growing tradition gradually spread from there."

Mind you, it wasn't like that in Italy. France is not exactly a peninsula surrounded on three sides by a gentle sea. It's largely attached to the continent, but it's bordered by the Atlantic Ocean and its climate certainly isn't as dry and mild as ours in Italy. It wasn't possible to grow vines everywhere and, as Bruno tells me, they proceeded by natural selection. "Large vineyards only emerged in the most favorable areas. We know the Romans went much farther up to the north and the northwest, but the vines wouldn't grow there in any case. Mother Nature sets the limits, and our ancestors believed that too. The grapes never reached a ripe and healthy condition, perhaps due to the influence of the ocean with the Gulf current bringing too much rain."

Champagne is the most northerly area in France planted with grapevines and it has some specific characteristics, being far enough from the Atlantic to moderate its influence but also far enough east to benefit from a continental (or more accurately semi-continental) climate. Bruno explains these things like a technical expert, with precise answers and cause-effect relationships between the elements he's talking about.

"I appreciate that you started with the terroir, as you call it in France, but the point is something else. The efferves—"

"Hold on, Oscar, I'll get to the effervescence too, don't worry. Be patient."

I want to tell him it's not impatience, it's curiosity, but Bruno goes on: "First we need to consider the terroir, Oscar."

The French word *terroir* encompasses three different elements: soil, climate and know-how.

"Let's talk about the first. By good luck the subsoil in Champagne consists of white limestone, derived from the sedimentation of marine life between forty and eighty million years ago. That's the first essential element for the unique character of our wines."

We've already discussed the climate but the third point, the human contribution, is perhaps the most interesting. Over centuries, humans have selected different varieties of grapes and they've been adapted and domesticated over the centuries. It was in the meeting between variety and climate that the first case of serendipity occurred.

In terms of climate France is on the border between two influences: oceanic and continental. And you know what that means? Short but hot summers, resulting in a rather late ripening of the grape and consequently a late harvest.

So where's the serendipity? We have to take a big leap backward to find it, this time to the seventeenth century and the earliest champagne. After wine grapes were crushed, the juices would be put into barrels to ferment, and that's what the French did for this wine. But the winter chill froze the juice before fermentation was complete, and the producers faced a dilemma: keep them or throw them out? Many opted for the former. In those days they didn't have today's methods of analysis or microfiltration, so there were often residual sugars and yeasts that could cause another fermentation as soon as the wine thawed. That's what happened to the earliest champagnes in the old seventeenth-century cellars. The barrels were filled up again with the partly fermented wine, and sold in Paris or exported to England on the boats that plied the Marne and the Seine.

It was normal for the cork in the keg to come under pressure because the wines "revived" in spring or summer with the rising temperatures. The transporters would put the stopper back into the barrel, muttering unhappily and bellyaching because even if it didn't affect the quality of the wine, the double fermentation was considered a defect. This went on for many hundreds of years—mainly because the phenomenon was temporary, what we might call an ephemeral effervescence, only lasting for the few weeks of really hot weather before the wine returned to its usual silence. Essentially there was an incomplete fermentation due to the cold climate and then a re-fermentation caused by the softening of the climate; however, this second change was seen as flawed.

"So there are two incidents? The cold weather and the subsequent fermentation?" I ask.

"Yes, exactly. These 'incidents' are replicated in the bottle. Modern champagne is the result of effervescence in the bottle, which happens the same way as it does in the kegs but it causes more of a disturbance because of the greater compression. This characteristic comes from the geography: a northern vineyard, seasons marked by sudden temperature changes, cellars less isolated than they are today and no filtration method or accurate measuring of the residual sugars."

Bruno explains that it took a technological revolution to capture this natural effervescence, preserve it over time and be able to commercialize the champagne wines in this form. Years of research and finessing were fundamental to realizing the principle of fermentation inside the bottle, developing a bottle with a stopper that would resist the pressure, coming up with the notion of *perlage* (fizziness), and removing the yeasts from the second fermentation.

That's the reason research is included in the factors that led to the creation of champagne. The initial studies were carried out during Louis XIV's reign, around the mid-1600s. The king was rather austere and consequently this wine was frowned upon as frivolous. It was further developed during the Regency period from 1715, while the nation waited for Louis XV to reach maturity. It was he, the "much-beloved" king, who in 1728 agreed to the free circulation and sale of bottled wine, and that's when modern champagne was anointed. Before he finishes Bruno mentions the two oldest brands of this marvelous product, coincidentally both founded immediately after the king's decree: Ruinart, established in Rheims in 1729, and Canon, established in Epernay in 1730.

"So what about the legend of the monk Dom Pérignon?" I ask. If you've been paying attention you might have wondered the same thing.

The legend of Dom Pérignon is just that, Bruno explains: a legend. No single individual could have been responsible for inventing all of that. There were a large number of abbeys in the Champagne region, all producing the eponymous drink with the same "defects," and the monks shared opinions and knowledge as they experimented together.

"We owe the creation of the most famous wine in the world to them, all of them together, and to the research that continued for centuries after them. Although, history tells us the growth of champagne was slowed twice: during the revolution in 1789 and amid the destruction of World War I."

"Can we say, as a great English historian once did, that champagne invented itself?"

Bruno screws up his nose. Obviously the cause of the error was a natural and spontaneous process, but it needed humans to bring it under control so the real magic would emerge.

Nowadays, French champagnes are imitated in every respect, but they have no equal because of that specific terroir. This is where French greatness comes in, *la grandeur de la France*.

11

CHARTREUSE

Elixir for a long life

WITH MARCELO BARBERIS

Ask Marcelo Barberis anything at all to do with distillates and he'll leave you spellbound.

He knows everything. Not only is he a technical expert, but his explanations take you on a virtual tour of the world, hearing stories that only someone with deep knowledge of local traditions can tell.

Distillates are his job; he's based an entire career on them. For thirty years he's been working with Luca Gargano at Velier in Genoa, importing the rarest distillates from every corner of the world to distribute in Italy. Over time they've become the leaders in the field.

Every so often I have a drink with him. It's pure enjoyment. I find the pleasure of tasting exceptional food or drink is doubled when you're doing it with someone qualified to talk about it. Besides, what I call a "food orgasm" is an essential component of life. That pleasurable sensation is amplified when we're eating or drinking something of the highest quality, and if we know the fundamentals behind it, it becomes sublime.

Before we get to the serendipity of Chartreuse, I ask Marcelo to tell me how the art of distilling came about.

"It's quite a recent practice, almost modern," he says. "But the seren-dipity started way back. We know that wine is at least seven thousand years old and beer six thousand. The alcohol in them is diluted with a mixture of water and vegetable and mineral elements. But alcohol on its own can only be obtained through distillation, and that was discov-ered much later.

The Arabs, and before them the ancient Egyptians, were masters of distillation, but they only used it to obtain medicines, perfumes and cosmetics.

"Then the monks learned the technique from the Arabs in the early years of the eleventh century—the Dark Ages. The Church was intent on stopping the practice, so it was done in secret; a progressive intellec-tual and alchemist named Cecco d'Ascoli was roasted on a pile of wood for demonic practices."

"However," Marcelo continues, "the monks were able to demonstrate the humanitarian aspect of their alchemic activity as they used it to obtain medicines and healing substances. Once they had the imprima-tur of the Church, distillation could officially proceed.

"Through distillation, the monks extracted the active and curative ingredients of herbs, plants, leaves, flowers, fruit and roots and sealed them in bottles and test tubes. This was the beginning of pharmaco-poeia. The medicines made in the monasteries would be given to the villagers in exchange for chickens or eggs. But for the moment, still no alcohol."

I interrupt him here because there's something I don't understand: if herbs, plants, leaves, flowers, fruit and roots already contain healing elements, why distill them? Tisanes made with herbs are as old as the world; distillation seems to me to be a wasted effort. I ask the question.

Marcelo tells me about his mother. In May every year, she would get him to stick out his tongue for a health check, and often she'd exclaim, "There you are, full of inflammation—too much salami!" Then she'd hand little Marcelo a basket and say, "Go and pick some mallow!" He would run and get some of the mallow growing upstream from a freshwater spring and bring it home for his mother to boil with two or three apples. She'd sweeten the mush with honey to remove the bitterness. This would happen two or three times a year before the mallow blossomed into pink flowers amid the green of the woods, when it was no longer needed.

"After two or three treatments I'd already be feeling better, Oscar!" he continues enthusiastically. "But if mallow does have active anti-inflammatory ingredients, it's only for twenty days of the year, thirty at most. So what about winter? What would we have done if the inflammation happened when the remedy wasn't there? That's where the alchemist comes in: extract the active agents when they are available, isolate them and seal them in a jar so they'll be on hand in winter as well. But again, no alcohol."

This continued for a few more years. It was a period of supreme confidence and the conviction that sooner or later they'd distill the elixir of eternal youth, the universal panacea, the remedy for all ills. In the end they didn't find any of that, but by distilling wine or beer—they got alcohol.

It was a major triumph, and it had a huge impact in times when wounds from weapons or rusting farm machinery were the order of the day. Marcelo puts it like this: "The greatest disinfectant ever to emerge in nature, aqua vitae. Not drinkable, of course, but how many lives would it save from recurring septicemia? And then came the first case of serendipity: after a few years in a keg, alcohol changed completely. It tasted good and it generated energy, warmth and conviviality. People discovered its benefit as a digestive: good for the stomach and restorative."

On the table our glasses are giving off an exotic aroma of herbs and spices. This is Chartreuse VEP, a superb green chartreuse, and the story that goes with our sipping gets better and better—fascinating, if not mysterious.

"It started with Saint Bruno: Bruno of Cologne, who studied and taught theology in Germany and later in France. But as an adult, in

1080 or thereabouts, he chose the path of contemplation and asceticism. He found six companions of like mind, and they set off to find a suitable location for a monastery. The Bishop of Lyon gave them a piece of land at the foot of the Chartreuse massif in the Haute-Savoie, and there they built the first abbey and established the strictly closed Carthusian monastic order."

The story goes on. One of Bruno's disciples was the particularly gifted Urban, who soon became Pope Urban II. He invited Bruno to move to Rome, but Bruno wasn't comfortable in the papal environment. He was searching for asceticism, so he set off again for Calabria and found a place in what is now the municipality of Serra San Bruno, where he would build another abbey. He died there in 1101.

The Carthusian order grew substantially, and Marcelo tells me they still own some amazing real estate: today there are seventeen Carthusian monasteries scattered around the world, housing around 280 monks. There's a waiting list of more than one thousand applicants, nearly all of them business executives prepared to give up all their possessions once they're admitted to the order.

But it wasn't all sunshine and roses for the Chartreuse abbey where the order started. It was twice destroyed by floods and mudslides, and the order was dissolved during the French Revolution (the monks dispersed mainly in Switzerland, resurfacing in Italy in 1903 thanks to a new law) and a second time when World War II broke out, turning up later in Spain.

"Two genuine diasporas calling for the tenacity and the patience of ... a Carthusian." Marcelo sighs and presses on: "These monks had the joys of alcohol available to relieve the sorrows of the spirit. In 1605, François-Annibal d'Estrées, a Marshal of France and Knight of the Order of the Holy Spirit, gave them a parchment with the formula for an elixir of longevity. Almost a mission impossible, with 130 ingredients including herbs, spices, roots and flowers, some found in the mountains of Savoy and the rest from around the world."

At this point the word "serendipity" strikes Marcelo as somewhat out of place in a religious context. Better to talk about a miracle, he thinks.

Supported by their strong international relations and determined to increase the lifespan of humans, the monks found the ingredients they needed. All 130 of them! The Elixir Végétal was born in 1637: a 69-per-cent-alcohol "bomb" and the world's oldest liqueur. Incredibly, it's still being sold today in a little 100 mL bottle packed in a wooden container.

Along with the Elixir came a new color, chartreuse green, the natural result of infusing the ingredients in the purest alcohol and re-distilling them in traditional copper stills.

The 69-percent-alcoholcontent was a bit much for the market though. So in 1764 they produced green Chartreuse, the same color as the Elixir but with 55 percent alcohol, and then in 1838 the yellow Chartreuse with distillations of honey, sugar and saffron, in direct com-petition with the great 40-percent-alcohol liqueurs of the time, such as Benedictine and Strega. Yellow Chartreuse quickly became popular: it spawned a great international cocktail, the Alaska, and in 1963, rid-ing the wave of this success, came the first version of Chartreuse VEP (Vieillissement Exceptionnellement Prolongé), a favorite of leading con-noisseurs today.

During the second diaspora, production was moved to Tarragona in Spain, but in 1990 it returned to Voiron in Savoy where it had all started. These days, the few remaining bottles from Tarragona are price-less and are sought by collectors all over the world.

Anyone wanting to visit Chartreuse should know they're in for a double surprise. First, the closed nature of the order means you can't visit the abbey; you can only observe it from the scenic road above. It looks beautiful, monumental, with thick white walls and dark roofs with a steep pitch because of the snow. On a Monday afternoon the monks socialize in pairs for four hours (never the same two), and people watch them through binoculars from the road above as they chat amiably, serene and smiling. A museum outside the abbey is open to the pub-lic, with a collection of artefacts dating from the year 1100 onward and an example of a monastic cell identical to the ones the monks live in.

Because of the enforced solitude, lunch is passed through a peephole. Beneath each cell there's a workshop, accessed via an internal staircase because each monk has chosen a job to do, once more in solitude.

The second surprise is the production plant. After passing the wonderful copper stills you enter the aging cellars, and it's just like going into the real Fontanafredda cellars in Serralunga d'Alba: the same big oval barrels where the Jaune and the Verte are aged for three years and the VEP for more than ten years.

Marcelo goes on: "This is one of the very rare cases in the world, because nobody ages liqueurs anymore—they use heat, alcohol, sugar and flavorings for the transformation, and off they go to be sold straight away!" That's today's imperative, unfortunately, in a world where Carthusian patience is exclusive to Voiron.

And to the two of us, at least for this evening. Like true Carthusians we've been sipping a Chartreuse VEP for more than half an hour as we chat. We drink one last toast. To Marshal d'Estrées and to all those solitary monks and their search for the elixir of longevity.

Our glasses touch lightly. Marcelo smiles, proud of what he's about to savor: "This is a superb liqueur. It won't make our lives longer, that's for sure, but it won't shorten them either. But there's another truth, which is that this liqueur makes life better."

12

COCA-COLA

Good medicine, that!

WITH MUHTAR KENT

Muhtar Kent was CEO of The Coca-Cola Company from 2008 to 2017. I was fortunate to meet him in 2013 and we became good friends. I visit him whenever I go to the United States and we have a meal together, and it's the same when he happens to be in Europe.

Born to Turkish parents in New York City, where his father was Turkey's consul general, Muhtar is an absolute genius (university-educated in the UK with an MBA from London's Cass Business School) and a champion, as his career shows; in fact it's like a fairytale. He started working with Coca-Cola in 1978 after answering an advertisement for drivers (without telling his father) and was hired to drive those red open trucks that delivered the drinks all over America. He'd drive in, unload the crates and leave.

Muhtar went on to become not only CEO of the company but also its president from 2009 to 2019—the two main positions in the largest worldwide soft-drink company. The board was rewarded with excellent results.

In my life I haven't met many people as likable as he is, extroverted and erudite, so naturally I looked to him to learn about one of the most sensational cases of serendipity in history—Coca-Cola.

"You know, Oscar, I've been asked to write a book too. There's a publisher who wants an autobiography. I don't know if I'll do it; we'll see. But we're not here to talk about me—you want me to tell you about the birth of Coca-Cola. I worked there for over forty years and I've heard this story, and had to tell it myself, many times. In Atlanta there's even a museum that illustrates the story with beautiful images and lots of items from that time. I've invited you over and over again but you've never come. Bad man!"

I'll go, I think, I swear I'll go. Muhtar comes straight out with what he thinks and doesn't beat about the bush, and it's one of the reasons I like him. As for his autobiography, one volume might not be enough: he was a witness to the entire history of the most famous fizzy drink in the world and a lead actor in it to boot. He knows it deep down. He starts talking.

Coca-Cola was created for an entirely different purpose. On May 8, 1886, when Atlanta pharmacist John Stith Pemberton completed his formula for "wine coca," he believed he'd invented an excellent syrup to remedy headaches and tiredness—essentially a medicine. In reality, he had more or less copied a mix of wine and coca leaves called "coca wine" that was experiencing some success in Europe as a medicinal syrup.

Pemberton took a carafe of his invention to a fellow pharmacist to taste. This colleague declared it was effective but more importantly tasted good, and he put it on sale straight away at five cents a glass.

However, there was a problem.

Muhtar pauses for a second to see if I can guess what it was, and then smiles: "The problem was some customers couldn't tolerate alcohol."

"So, what did he do about it?"

"Our inventor tried replacing it with an extract from the nuts of the cola, a tropical plant that was thought to be very good for health. The resulting taste was something unexpected. And that's how we got the combination of coca leaves and cola-nut extract, which is what gives our drink its inimitable taste."

Even Pemberton didn't take long to realize that as well as being a medicine, the infusion could become an excellent nonalcoholic beverage to drink purely for pleasure. So (and here our pharmacist surprises us with his intuition) he tried adding sparkling water. But this time he kept the result to himself, as he had no clear idea how to sell it. It was his bookkeeper, Frank Mason Robinson, who gave the new drink an identity. Taking inspiration from the Spencerian script in vogue at the time, he put the names of the two ingredients together and emphasized their twin initials, making the two Cs giant capitals. So, essentially, Robinson invented the trademark that's still used today with a few light finishing touches.

"Two great guys, Pemberton and Robinson," I remark. "Imagine if they could see the colossus their invention has become today."

"Ah, no," responds Muhtar, "Pemberton died just two years later, in 1888."

At that point the company and the product were already out of his hands: before his death he'd been forced to sell nearly all he owned, including the pharmacy and the Coca-Cola formula and trademark. The buyer was Asa Candler, a businessman who shook poor Pemberton's hand for $2300, more or less the amount of debt he'd accumulated in developing his invention.

At that time Coca-Cola was only sold by the glass in kiosks. The kiosk managers would buy the syrup from the pharmacy and serve it to their customers, adding a small amount of water. Under Candler's guidance, distribution was expanded to kiosks beyond Atlanta, then in 1894 growing demand and a desire to make the drink transportable led Joseph Biedenharn to install bottling machinery at the back of his soda kiosk in Mississippi. He was the first person to bottle Coca-Cola. But large-scale bottling only began five years later, when three far-sighted entrepreneurs in Chattanooga, Tennessee, secured the exclusive rights from Asa Candler to bottle and sell Coca-Cola. They paid one dollar.

Those three, Benjamin Thomas, Joseph Whitehead and John Lupton, can take the credit for developing what would become the world bottling system for Coca-Cola. But as with all highly successful products, imitators sprang up everywhere. It dawned on them then that an exclusive beverage needed a special and distinctive bottle, which is what makes a drink original, aside from the taste.

In 1916 the bottlers—now in the hundreds and expanded into all states—agreed on a bottle with an odd shape, easy to hold and instantly recognizable. It's the one in our fridges and on the table at pizza restaurants today.

That's also when the first marketing operations started, first with coupons for free Coca-Cola samples and then with lots of newspaper advertising and the slogans that passed into history.

What I recall from their advertising in the '60s is an imperative that didn't concern itself with the niceties: "Drink Coca-Cola." I ask Muhtar if he remembers it.

"Of course, but in the beginning they were much more timid and polite: 'The pause that refreshes,' 'Coke adds life,' 'Have a Coke and a smile.' And you know one of the earliest slogans was 'The Great National Temperance Beverage.'"

Meanwhile, in 1919 the Woodruff family came onto the scene, and with other partners took over The Coca-Cola Company for $25 million, sparking a period of fantastic growth with the first exports going out to conquer the world.

The whole story is too long to tell even for Muhtar. So he tells me a single episode about the spread of Coca-Cola during World War II. "In 1941 when America entered the War, the company president, Robert Woodruff, wrote: 'We must make sure every man in uniform can buy a small bottle of Coca-Cola for five cents, wherever he is and whatever the cost to the company'. Two years later a cablegram arrived from general command in North Africa. General Dwight Eisenhower wanted an urgent shipment of machinery to set up ten bottling plants, and an immediate supply of three million bottles of Coca-Cola. It's said the pilot of the plane that took off with that cargo risked his life because it was crammed so full that it struggled to lift off from the dunes.

Meanwhile, a few of the company's experts set off for Algiers to establish a bottling plant, the first of the sixty-four set up overseas during the war."

Apparently the drink was just the thing to cheer up the troops. In fact it raised everyone's morale: those soldiers and airmen, and then subsequent generations in living rooms, restaurants and bars.

The rest is more recent history: Coca-Cola became a public company listed on the stock exchange and took over the world. Today we consume more than 110 billion bottles of it every year.

There's one uncomfortable question to ask Muhtar before I go, and maybe he's expecting it: "110 billion. You don't think that's too many?"

"When I came to the company in 1978 its value was less than $2 billion. When I retired in May 2019 it was capitalized at over $200 billion. Clearly that's an enormous increase in value, due to the growth in sales and profits. But I do know what you mean, Oscar. The social responsibility of a successful company like that is enormous. Coca-Cola is very much aware of the ecological problem facing humanity. Under my leadership it started a research program aimed at respecting the environment, and now it's following through with big investments and seeing the first results."

The goal they've set for themselves is to reach 100 percent packaging recycling and reuse. Muhtar believes Coca-Cola will once again surprise the world and show that it's not just aware, but it's part of the collective effort to save the planet: something that's now beyond urgent.

Nothing is now more important, for every one of us.

13

THE ICE-CREAM CONE

A democratic and sustainable treat

WITH ARNALDO MINETTI

There are so many successful products created by accident or mistake that when it was time to decide which serendipitous stories to tell in this book, I was spoiled for choice.

The ice-cream cone might seem minor in comparison with champagne, for example. After all, isn't the cone simply the humble holder of the much nobler ice cream? On the contrary, the wafer-like holder is what made ice cream a democratic treat, by enabling the common people to enjoy it. In this sense it's a symbol of social equality.

Another reason why the ice-cream cone is so important, especially at this moment in history, is because we eat all of it, from the rim to the pointed end. That's why it might also be regarded as a symbol of environmental sustainability: it doesn't produce waste or trash. It needs no cutlery, just your hands, and it replaces crockery that requires washing with detergents after use. So the crunchy fawn-colored wafer that children and adults of all ages have held in their hands for over a century is a consummate example of how to keep the planet clean!

Never undervalue the simple things. But even simplicity often involves an inventor. To find out how the ice-cream cone was invented, I went to an Italian company that's been making high-quality cones in Bergamo since 1938.

Ostificio Prealpino has grown in size during its more than eighty years, but it remains a company deeply rooted in artisan culture and many young workers there are third-generation employees. Arnaldo Minetti, the son of its founder, has been running it for nearly four decades. He's a special character, one of those people who is in business first and foremost because they love what they make. As soon as I asked if he'd like to chat about the story of the cone, I knew I'd found the right person.

"Ah, my friend, first I should talk about ice cream itself, why it's become known far and wide and has acquired prestige and devoted consumers. That's true more or less everywhere in the world now."

It seems there is a pattern emerging in this book. To talk about any product we have to delve into the origins of something else related to it. Without those roots our understanding is incomplete and distorted, as it often is when we attempt to understand people as well. Talking about ice cream will help explain how the cone has contributed to its universal success.

"The first gelati were made many centuries ago using snow, honey and fruit, for the rich banquets of the powerful aristocrats of imperial Rome and then later for the Florentine aristocracy with milk, butter and eggs added, and finally at Le Procope café in Paris, with chocolate and granitas.

"The 'common people' wanted to eat and enjoy gelato like the wealthy, but they couldn't afford to sit at the illustrious tables of cafés and restaurants adorned with exquisite plates, glasses, cups and goblets and be served by liveried staff. This is where the cone comes in to do its job of democratization."

"Hang on a second, Minetti. If the origin of gelato is to be found in Roman banquets, you have to admit it took an awfully long time to become a popular product."

That much is obvious. As Arnaldo explains, there was no substantial change in the situation until the beginning of the twentieth century. Rumors spread about how good ice cream was, and curiosity grew: the general population wanted to eat it but didn't know where or how. In the few cafés where it was served in cups at tables? Too expensive! In the gardens of restaurants with glasses and spoons? Too chic! The ordinary people wanted ice cream to be accessible to all.

So ice cream and granitas began appearing at local festivals and at fairs, but still served in cups and glasses that needed to be washed and brought with them the risk of breakages and the associated costs. Minetti tells me somebody even suggested using fig leaves or paper wraps, but mass consumption was still a long way off.

At that point the milk shops got busy, serving ice cream to take home in cups or bowls or other impractical containers. Then, at the end of the nineteenth century, there was a breakthrough. Rather chaotically, an early version of wafers emerged, cooked on small hotplates. The ingredients? Milk, sugar, flour and sometimes flavorings. The wafer was either round and flat or in the form of a roll, the so-called *cigarette russe*, and then ... a stroke of genius! Somebody thought of making them conical.

Our enthusiastic expert continues: "There's a curious story about this that makes the ice-cream cone a true case of serendipity. On July 23, 1904 the Louisiana Purchase Exposition in St. Louis, Missouri, a.k.a. the St. Louis World's Fair, was packed with visitors. It was a scorching day and the ice-cream stand, still a novelty at the time, was overrun. There were no serving plates left but lots of people still waiting in the queue. At this point a Syrian pastry cook named Ernest Hamwi, who was in the next booth selling *zalabia*, a wafer dough cooked in a red-hot press, had a brilliant idea. He would help the desperate ice-cream seller out by rolling the *zalabia* into a cone shape to hold the ice cream. In no time he had made enough of them to satisfy all the customers."

It's a lovely story of serendipity, but it smacks a bit too much of legend. We know for certain that Italo Marchioni, an Italian migrant from Vodo di Cadore (Belluno) who moved to New York, was the first to register the patent for making ice-cream cones, with a small machine for artisan ice-cream makers and separate machinery for commercial producers. This was on December 13, 1903, before the incident with the Syrian pastry cook in St. Louis. Thanks to Marchioni, not only dairies, ice-cream shops and bars but also kiosks and pedal carts, and even motorbikes and small vans, could offer ice cream simply, quickly and for eating on the move.

Ice cream had found its perfect holder at last: informal, for everyone and edible to boot. Thanks to this innovation the consumption of artisan ice cream went through the roof and, predictably, the ice-cream industry jumped on the ice-cream cone bandwagon. Manufacturers began producing cones in a wrapper and delivering them to areas with supermarkets, to kiosks, to the freezer section of the local bar ... and for decades now we've had commercially produced "cornettos." Still, the cone that's close to Arnaldo Minetti's heart is, and always will be, the traditional one for artisan ice creams, with the batter mix and quality constantly improving over the years.

"The shape has evolved as well—for instance, with the introduction of a ring at the mouth, making it easy for ice-cream sellers to put the various flavors in place with a spatula."

"Let's look at its other feature," I suggest, "nothing is thrown away, everything is eaten, no waste, no rubbish."

"Maybe this is the food product most in harmony with the well-being of the planet: ice cream in a cone! But to persuade everyone to eat the holder as well, it has to be good. An artisan cone must not be too sugary and has to be made with natural, high-quality ingredients without artificial flavors or colors. All this so as not to overwhelm the taste of the ice cream itself. I love the cone in all its shapes and forms, mainly the traditional one with the ring but also the rolled-up one without it, big or small, as long as it's made in accordance with certain standards. First the cone won a democratic battle; now it can be a prime example of respect for the environment," says Arnaldo.

I couldn't agree more. From now on forget bowls and paper cups, let alone glasses short or tall. Whether I'm walking or sitting, I'll be eating my ice cream in a cone! Then I'll eat that as well: crunchy and tasty but not too tasty. It will bring back old memories.

"You know what the taste of a cone reminds me of, Arnaldo? The time long ago when I was still taking communion. I always loved the wafers."

14

KELLOGG'S
CORN FLAKES

A family feud

Apparently the exact date was April 14, 1894, a Saturday. John Kellogg, aged forty-two, a doctor and manager of the sanatorium in Battle Creek, Michigan, along with his thirty-four-year-old brother, Will, was cooking the usual amount of corn for the tasteless soup he would serve to his patients.

All of a sudden they were called urgently to the hydrotherapy department, where a machine had gone haywire. When they got back to the kitchen after an hour or so, they found the corn had gone completely hard. Trashing it was out of the question, so they tried pushing it through rollers to crush it, hoping it would form a sheet, like dough. What they actually got was a large quantity of small separate pieces of cooked corn: in other words, flakes. Then they came up with the idea of toasting them, and when the flakes cooled they decided they'd invent a new form of breakfast. They fed the toasted flakes, steeped in a large cup of warm milk, to all their patients and they loved it.

But for a better understanding of the Kellogg brothers' incredible story, we need to go back a few decades. John was born in Michigan in

1852 into a family that belonged to the Seventh-day Adventist Church. Basically, they believe universal judgment is nigh and Jesus will return at any moment. But again and again the dates of His return are predicted and then moved when He fails to appear, so new streams of the Church are constantly forming. Its worshippers are vegetarian and lead a life of sacrifice, don't trust education or traditional medicine, and the only learning they provide for their children is about their religious beliefs.

John was illiterate (and sickly) as a child. But at the age of eleven he began reading Adventist religious texts, and from then on nobody could stop him. He turned out to be a champion at learning, quick and intuitive; he read voraciously and even became a good writer. He forged a career in the editorial office of the town newspaper in Battle Creek, owned by the White family. Mr. and Mrs. White were the leaders of the Adventist church, and John began working at the paper as an apprentice. Within a few years he was editor-in-chief, and was sent to university to complete his studies. He chose medicine, with the express intention of inventing an alternative type of medicine in line with the precepts of his church. He studied first in New Jersey and Michigan and then went to Europe to specialize, taking courses in nutraceutical medicine and hydrotherapy in particular.

After graduation he returned to Battle Creek, and the Whites sent him to work in a clinic they'd recently established: a sanatorium where people of different classes, mostly of the Adventist faith, would go for brief periods if they were sick or just looking to improve their physical (and mental) fitness. John soon became manager and transformed it into a kind of luxury clinic, a healing spa of sorts, open to everyone. In some ways—taking account of the times and the United States as it was then—he could be considered a forerunner of Mességué, a father of modern herbal medicine. His sanatorium was amazingly successful, with clients including VIPs such as Henry Ford and US president Grover Cleveland.

Nonetheless, John Kellogg didn't take a step back from his principles of austere living and in fact delved further into them. He didn't eat meat or sugar, didn't drink tea or coffee, didn't smoke, didn't take alcohol, and refrained from sex. Naturally, he imposed the same rules on his patients. He wrote many books, including *Plain Facts about Sexual Life* where he explains why, in his view, sex is bad for you. It sold 1.5 million copies. Then in 1879 he married Ella Eaton, and lived with her for over forty years without ever consummating the marriage; instead, they adopted forty-two orphaned children.

His brother, Will, was entirely different, apart from the outstanding intelligence that must have run in the family. Eight years younger than his brother, he was not attracted by the values of the Adventist Church: quite the opposite. As an adolescent he started smoking, eating steak, drinking alcohol, and above all taking an interest in girls. He abandoned his studies as soon as it was allowed and went to work in his father's small broom factory, where he soon showed an uncommon entrepreneurial streak. So his older brother brought him into the clinic. It needed somebody with managerial skills, and John preferred to concentrate on creating new recipes and innovative health and anti-sex treatments rather than bothering with costs and profits and management.

And here we are back to that Saturday in April 1894.

Following their accidental discovery of corn flakes, Will realized the product had huge marketing potential, way beyond its use in the clinic. So he begged his brother to patent the invention and allow him to create a plan for making the flakes of corn in quantity and launching them all over America.

No way. John was dead set against the idea. The corn flakes had to be and forever remain exclusive to the Battle Creek clinic. In the years that followed, Will tried again and again to persuade him, especially as news had spread of the toasted corn flakes for adding to the breakfast bowl of milk, and others were trying to imitate them. But John was immovable, and so the time came for Will to break free. He founded a company to produce corn flakes, called it Kellogg's, and patented the recipe created by mistake with his brother but with one powerful innovation: the addition of sugar. Of course, like a good brother, he offered

John a 50 percent share in the company, but John (as well as flying into a rage over the sweet and sinful extra ingredient) responded by taking the matter to court. How dare Will use their family name for the corn flakes without his permission?

Cut to 1906. From that time on the two brothers were never to meet again; not a word, not a single greeting was exchanged for the rest of their lives. And to think that both lived to exactly ninety-one years of age.

They spent many years in courts until the definitive judgment came down in favor of Will: Kellogg's Corn Flakes could be made and sold with that name and using that recipe.

Will achieved the worldwide success we're all familiar with today. He soon became a multimillionaire, went on drinking and smoking and gorging himself on food, married no less than three times and fathered eight children. There were also various lovers.

John continued his work in the clinic until it closed, bankrupt as a result of serious management failures. Undaunted, the elder Kellogg opened another clinic, wrote a few more books and continued his research into nutrition for lengthening life expectancy and repressing sex.

And so ends the strange and serendipitous story of the Kellogg brothers and their Corn Flakes. Now I ought to question an expert friend as I have for all the other stories.

But this time, as a one-off, I'll hand this over to the legendary brothers themselves and imagine them meeting at least once after 1906.

I should mention that of all the human activities I happen to participate in my favorite is making peace or, even better, contributing to peacemaking. I'm well aware it isn't a very fashionable pursuit in recent times, but that doesn't matter. Believe me, it's not in the spirit of contradiction, but I'm convinced that while making peace is much harder than making war it definitely leads to better results, always.

John: "Perhaps if you hadn't added the sugar I might have thought about going into business with you."

Will: "My dear brother, believe me, the sugar was crucial to the mass-production of our Corn Flakes! The truth is you were never enamored of the market. For you the market began and ended in your beloved sanatorium. Maybe it was just me who was wrong—I should have seen this sooner and gone my own way at least five years earlier. But I put all my efforts into trying to persuade you. See what you've lost?"

John: "I haven't lost anything of importance. Only money and fame, but the values close to my heart are very different ones."

Will: "You've always pocketed the royalties from your books, though. You didn't turn up your nose at that money. I've tried to uphold important values while doing business. Meanwhile, I've created lots of jobs, and in 1929 during the Depression I invented six-hour shifts to keep enough work for everyone."

John: "True, I acknowledge that. And thank you for always admitting the recipe is mine ... It's a shame about that damned sugar, though. Nothing to do with my recipe!"

Will: "I've never stopped thinking of you, my dear brother. If you knew how many times I've been on the point of coming to talk to you."

John: "I've missed you too. We were wrong to avoid each other all these years."

Will: "No regrets, John. I never understood your life of sacrifice but I went overboard in the opposite direction. Okay, I've made a lot more money than you have, for sure, but as you can see in the end you're the one history remembers."

John: "Oh come on, our family name is famous around the world and it lives on thanks to you."

Will: "But the Kellogg's brand would never have seen the light of day if you hadn't been so stubborn. Thank you brother. Let's give each other a hug. It's never too late."

You'll have to excuse me, that's how I am. I like to imagine that those two brothers would've met again in the future. So that they could make peace. At least it's happened in this book over a hundred years later. Now I'm getting emotional. I'd like to hug them myself.

15

THE NEAPOLITAN
CUTLET

The burnt crumb cover-up

WITH EDOARDO BENNATO

When someone talks about *cotoletta*, I immediately think of the Milanese-style cutlet. It's famous, and not just in Milan. When done well it's a great dish. There's no serendipity around its origin, because despite various paternity claims there's actually no doubt it was born in Milan. The Austrians maintain it was copied from their famous Wiener schnitzel. That's good too, for sure, but there's a fundamental difference: the traditional Lombard recipe calls for a thickish cut with the bone in, whereas the Wiener schnitzel is a thin, tenderized fillet.

But it's not only a question of the cut. It's about historical fact. In the mid-nineteenth century, the Austrian general Radetzky of Radetz mentioned in a letter that during a sojourn in Milan he'd tasted a crumbed cutlet for the first time. And if that's not enough, it's described in recipe books from the twelfth century. So for me, there's no doubt about the Milanese origins of the crumbed cutlet, and there are no stories of accidental mistakes involved in creating it or Milanese legends like the ones around risotto (see p. 205) and panettone (see p. 179).

Instead, there's a cutlet that's similar to the Milanese version (but let's just call it "enriched"), the origin of which is especially serendipitous. Firstly, it's named after a city where it wasn't created, and secondly, it really does appear to have been the result of a mistake. It's the *cotoletta napoletana*, and it doesn't yet have the fame it deserves. I recommend that you try it if you're lucky enough to visit Naples, even if it isn't all that easy to find. I know there's a powerful distraction in pizza and pasta—both spectacular dishes that taste special when you eat them in their birthplace—and the fish specialties in Naples are hard to refuse as well. Even so, next time you're there in the shadow of Vesuvius, I respectfully urge you to do as follows: order a quarter of a pizza, maybe as an entrée (I recommend the original margherita), followed by a half portion of *pasta alla genovese*, and then get them to make you a *cotoletta napoletana* and enjoy it with a glass of Taurasi. You'll thank me for it.

The special thing about this cutlet is that it's originally from Argentina. Yes, created in Jorge La Grotta's restaurant in Buenos Aires, called El Napolitanu because the original owner and cook were Neapolitans. Their patrons were mainly Italian migrants who'd done well in Argentina, but even the locals in that most Italian city in Latin America loved it. This was toward the end of the 1940s; Perón had triumphed in the recent elections and his wife, Evita, was entering into legend as the embodiment of two great myths: beauty and power.

One evening, Jorge La Grotta's cook was preparing a cutlet ordered by an important customer. He got distracted and burnt the crumb coating, which was a disaster because it was the last slice of meat they had. The customer would be sure to complain. What to do? The imaginative cook scraped off the burnt part, covered the rest with a little tomato sauce, and topped it with a slice of cooked ham and a slice of mozzarella. Basically, he made a ham pizza with the cutlet instead of dough as the base. He put it in the oven until the mozzarella had melted, sprinkled on some fresh oregano and called the waiter: "Serve him this and tell him I cooked my new specialty just for him. It's called *la milanesa a la napolitana*."

The customer looked askance at this strange multicolored cutlet, but eventually, cautiously, he took a small bite. One mouthful convinced him he'd made a marvelous discovery. He lavished compliments on the cook and left a hefty tip. That day the "Neapolitan Milanese cutlet" went straight onto Jorge La Grotta's menu. In no time it became his specialty. Word spread and many other restaurants adopted it.

What happened next? Someone returned to Naples and a miracle occurred: a delicious specialty that had never really left had returned home. To Naples from Argentina, an invention born of the best Neapolitan traditions.

Now, there are people who describe that cutlet as a *cotoletta milanese* decorated with a bit of Neapolitan flair. But it isn't: the differences are noteworthy and crucial. First the meat: the real Milanese cutlet is made with a slice of veal with the bone in, while the Neapolitan version is inspired by the Buenos Aires (or Viennese) one calling for boneless beef. The second difference is in the frying: in Milan they use clarified butter, whereas in Naples it's extra virgin olive oil. Third difference: the Milanese version begins and ends in the pan, while the Neapolitan one starts in the pan and ends in the oven. This is an indispensable finishing touch to combine the ingredients with the meat and allow the mozzarella to melt. Those three details make the two cutlets totally different. For the Neapolitan version, I suggest frying in a pan for no longer than two minutes on a fairly high heat (a minute on each side) so the finishing in the oven doesn't overcook it.

*

One day, Edoardo Bennato took me to eat a fantastic Neapolitan cutlet. "The best in Naples," he said, and I have no reason not to believe him; it was really good. I love spending time with Bennato. I remember perfectly what we discussed as we were eating that wonderful cutlet—something he calls "latitudinal conflict," meaning the different relationships people have with life, work and society depending on their geographic location relative to the Poles. In other words, how much the prevailing climate and geomorphology of any given country affects behavior and habits.

He divides the world into the "adult" and the "child" human families. He believes a grim violence is developing: a destructive, deadly escalation caused by the worldwide imbalance between rich and poor according to the latitudinal parameter. The first step toward finding a new world harmony is an awareness of this parameter, according to him.

He's a great artist of the Italian south skilled in poetic analysis, and an entrepreneur of the north who's fanatical about solutions. "You're asking an acrobat like me for a solution?" As we ate that cutlet most of the talking was done by Edoardo, who had long been reflecting on this vast theme, has written immortal songs about it and painted beautiful pictures. I remember I also said my bit, despite the distraction of that great food, but I have to admit I took home more than I'd contributed. I went looking for him to reminisce about that day and the *cotoletta* in particular. Now I only have to report what he told me word for word. His reasoning is fantastic.

"The joy of my life is my daughter, Gaia. She's fifteen and very good at school, and she's also an athlete. She went to an American school from the age of three so to all intents and purposes she's a native English speaker. She likes England and Ireland and she's at home in northern Europe, although she loves Naples and her Neapolitan roots. She lives her role as a citizen of the world with spontaneity and she has problems like global warming and caring for the environment at heart. She loves Neapolitan cuisine but she's open to the flavors of the world, and she's constantly updating her personal ranking of pizzerias and restaurants from Sorrento to Dublin, Romagna, Rome, Milan and Naples. The *cotoletta* in all its versions is one of her favorite dishes and she has diligently drawn up a ranking for that as well. She's decided after thorough investigation that first place goes to the *cotoletta* they make in Naples. The best."

16

CRÊPES SUZETTE AND TARTE TATIN

A tale of two unexpected treats

WITH GINO FABBRI

On a Monday in June 2015, teams of pastry cooks—the best in the world—from twenty-two countries were gathered in Lyon at the International Trade Fair for Hospitality, Restaurants and Catering (Horeca). They had ten hours to make a given number of desserts and compete for the World Pastry Cup.

After eighteen years of unchallenged domination by the French, the Italian team led by the master Gino Fabbri of Bologna won.

So, in order to tell the story of two very important French desserts, I'm going straight to the world champion pastry cook. He's Italian to his bootstraps, but he won that title on French soil.

*

Gino Fabbri is a fantastic pastry chef who's always worked in his own business in Bologna, but he also teaches young people wanting to become *chefs pâtissiers*.

We met one day at Fico in his hometown, and I watched him maneuver two classes of students dueling with tiramisu at two paces. He was explaining how to make a good *savoiardo* or sponge finger, how to recognize whether an egg is fresh and how to make a great mascarpone cream. I saw the students' expressions as they gazed at him like some god. His character, his jovial nature and his humility impressed me.

At the end of the lesson, as he was clapping his hands to clean them (or perhaps to say, "That's it, done," as chefs often do), I went up to talk to him.

"Thank you for agreeing to have a chat about crêpes Suzette and tarte tatin," I said. "You know every dessert on Earth, and obviously you know all about these two monuments to French pastry making."

"I'd call them world monuments, Oscar. They are so good—when they're done well—that they can't fail to please no matter where you are on the planet. In your Eataly in Paris, so they tell me, the French are stuffing themselves with tiramisu and panna cotta. The great thing about pastry making—and I think it also applies to many other crafts—is that it builds a small cultural exchange between one population and another."

I don't need to worry, says the pastry chef, with his carefully trimmed white moustache. He does indeed know both desserts well, makes them himself and often teaches others how to make them. And to him they're wonderful regardless of whether they're made in France or anywhere else. He has nothing but admiration for his colleagues across the Alps, and many of them are his good friends. "I must tell you that the greater the French pastry chefs are, the less self-important. But that's more or less the case all over the world, including in Italy." We're in agreement there, but I'm curious to know the stories behind those two cases of serendipity.

"Shall we start with the crêpes Suzette?" I suggest. But then I remember a small favor I have to ask: "The thing is, I'd like your recipe."

He smiles. He'll happily give it to me, but first he'll tell me how they came into being. For that we need to go back to the end of the nineteenth century: 1895 to be precise, to the Café de Paris in Monte Carlo. On one particular night, the kitchen was in turmoil because they were about to welcome an illustrious guest, possibly the most illustrious English person the French could host after Queen Victoria: her son the Prince of Wales, who would become King Edward VII a few years later.

Working on the dessert team was a young apprentice named Henri Charpentier, highly regarded because he'd come from the school of the renowned chef Auguste Escoffier. Each course brought compliments, but when it came to the dessert there was a disaster. Charpentier was cooking the crêpes when he accidentally poured liqueur into the pan. It caught fire and created a flambé effect. The kitchen staff weren't sure whether they should serve this unintended version of the crêpe, but in the end decided to risk it. Wouldn't you know, it was a great success. The prince asked for seconds, and everyone with him followed suit.

When the cooks were asked for the name of these exceptional crêpes they were embarrassed and didn't have an answer. Someone suggested "princess," but the Prince of Wales, who was famous for his love of women, had a better idea: Suzette! In honor of the most beautiful of the women at his table. "The story might have been whipped up a bit in over a century of telling, but as you know we pastry chefs specialize in 'whipping up,' right?"

Here is the recipe, dictated by the maestro himself.

INGREDIENTS:

Crêpes

3/4 cup flour

2 tsp sugar

2 eggs

pinch of salt

1-1/2 tbsp milk

4 tbsp melted butter

1-1/2 tsp oil

grated orange and
    lemon rinds

Orange butter

2 oranges

17 sugar cubes

3 tbsp orange juice

2 tsp lemon juice

8 tbsp butter

1 tsp Grand Marnier

thin strips of orange peel,
    to decorate

METHOD FOR THE CRÊPES:

1   Sift the flour with the sugar.

2   Mix the eggs and salt and pour onto the flour and sugar, mix in the milk and then the melted butter.

3   Add the oil, and lastly mix in the orange and lemon rinds.

4   Leave to rest for two hours.

5   Heat a nonstick pan and wipe the hot surface with butter before you pour in the crêpe batter to cook.

METHOD FOR THE ORANGE BUTTER:

1   Rub the oranges over the sugar cubes to saturate them with the essential oil until well colored, then add the sugar to the orange juice plus a little lemon juice. Bring to the boil.

2   Whisk in the butter together with the Grand Marnier.

To serve: As each crêpe is cooked, fold it in four and decorate with strips of orange peel. Glaze with the orange butter before serving.

There's a story of another dessert to savor and perhaps try making at home: the tarte tatin.

We're looking at a great classic here, and yet again we have a mistake to thank; or to be more specific, the sisters Stéphanie and Caroline Tatin, who worked in a restaurant opposite the station in Lamotte-Beuvron, a town in the Loire Valley in Central France.

Gino has been there. It must have been a Sunday early in the twentieth century, he tells me, when the Tatin sisters were making their famous apple tart. The local hunters were regular customers, and they were crazy about it. Actually it was the Tatin sisters who went crazy, trying to meet all the requests for it on weekends.

You may not know it, but in the kitchen (I'm talking mainly about professional kitchens here) it's quite common for an ingredient to be forgotten or a procedure to be left out. Sometimes you're performing several operations at once and unfortunately mistakes can occur. On this day, in fact, one of the sisters actually left out the shortcrust base for the tart. As a result, the apples caramelized directly in the sugar and butter. But this was a woman of taste and foresight. She wasn't prepared to throw it all out, so she placed the shortcrust base on top of the apples and inverted it onto an attractive serving plate. The customers were enthusiastic, and that's how one of the world's greatest treats was created.

"It's still being made in that same place today," Gino continues. "And there's a big sign on the front of the restaurant that reads: *Ici fut créée la célèbre tarte tatin.*"

"There are loads of possible variations of the tarte tatin, and the type of apples used should be specified. Now I'll give you my recipe using the rennet, which I think is the variety the Tatin sisters used because it originated in France and it's grown all over their region. I get them in Trentino, in the Val di Non. You can also use annurca, a fantastic apple from the Campania region. But if you like some other variety feel free to use that: our only problem in Italy is that we're spoiled for choice."

INGREDIENTS:

3 cups flour	1 cup sugar
4-1/2 tsp baking soda	2 lbs apples
1 tsp salt	
1-1/8 cups butter	
1/2 cup superfine sugar	

METHOD:

1 Make a shortcrust pastry by pulsing the flour, baking soda, salt, butter and superfine sugar in a food processor and then adding 2 tablespoons cold water. Form the mixture into a ball of dough, cover in plastic wrap and allow to chill for 30 minutes.

2 In a saucepan (preferably copper) heat the sugar until it caramelizes, taking care to add it gradually so it doesn't burn or go lumpy. (Start with a small amount and when that dissolves add a little more, then continue in the same manner. It's a good idea to wet the edges slightly with a moist pastry brush to prevent escaping sugar from burning.)

3 When you have obtained a good caramel, pour in enough water to make a caramel syrup of the density you want (darker or lighter according to taste).

4 Peel and core the apples, cut them into wedges (not too thick) and arrange around the base of a baking tin.

5 Add the caramel syrup, cover with a sheet of foil and bake in a conventional oven at 320°F to 350°F for about 30 minutes, or at least until the apples are soft and caramelized.

6 Flatten the apples to a thickness of 1/2 inch on a baking sheet, and place in the freezer.

7 Roll out the pastry dough 2mm thick and cut to the desired size (you don't want it too large).

8 Bake at 320°F until golden.

9 Take the frozen apples from the freezer, cut them to the same size and shape as the pastry base and place them on top. For an attractive glossy effect, brush the apples with jelly before serving.

I'm not a great fan of desserts, but if there are two things I'm a glutton for they are tarte tatin and crêpes Suzette. So thank you, France. And thank you, Gino.

17

THE *FARINATA*

Simplicity is not easy

WITH ELIO BOTTARO

I've just stepped off the derrick in the old port of Genoa. It's a beautiful sunny day and the breeze is just right, fresh and light. I've made an appointment to meet Elio Bottaro, and as I wait for him I think back to the first time we met.

Elio belongs to the Friends of the Varenna Valley club, which works to promote the products of the valley that starts in the Genoan village of Pegli and rises toward the Maritime Alps. He's a founding member of the club, responsible in particular for the *farinata*, and he never tires of celebrating this simple and very tasty flatbread. It's one of the main food products associated with Genoa, first created there many hundreds of years ago. It went on to conquer Italy and then the world, thanks to the many Genoan emigrants who've been able to replicate it according to the old recipe.

I met Elio and the other members of the club in 2013 when my friend Claudio Burlando, then president of the Region, took me to the club's headquarters. I remember the first thing I saw when we entered was a lovely antique stove, warmed up and waiting for the pans of *farinata*.

I was a bit concerned. I definitely wasn't a fan of *farinata*, and strangely that day I didn't have any bottles of the good Langhe wine with me—I say strangely because usually they're as sure to be in the trunk of my car as the spare tire. It wasn't just concern about not being able to repay a favor, but the truth is that some Ligurian light wines—how should I put it—don't guarantee great drinking. I sat down at the table, and in a flash my fears were buried under a new appreciation of simple home cooking. The *farinata*, just removed from the oven by expert hands, was sublime, and the fresh Vermentino was wonderful as well. But the thing that made me happiest was discovering that small community of "priests" of the *farinata*, so kind, so cheerful: I'd even dare to say tender in the love they showed for their roots. Elio was among them, talking on and on and never pausing for breath. Guess what about? *Farinata*, of course.

A sincere friendship was born from that convivial evening. In 2015 I invited them to the Milan Expo, where they ran a remarkably success-ful *farinata* kiosk. Elio never stops thanking me for that.

Ah, here he is. I see him approaching among the crowds strolling along the dock; we give each other a hug and decide to sit on a bench. We must have looked like two businessmen meeting to reach an agree-ment on something very important. After a good half-hour of exchanging compliments we got to the crux of the matter (and about time too!)—the origin of the *farinata*. Elio was the right person with whom to talk about it.

"I can even tell you the exact date of its first appearance because it was the festival of San Sisto, patron saint of Pisa. On August 6, 1284, the Pisan ships in the Secche della Meloria near Livorno were confronted by the Genoan fleet, captained by Oberto Doria. The clash was settled by thirty galleys hidden behind the Montenero headland, under the command of Benedetto Zaccaria. He was just twenty at the time. Genoa won easily, and more than half of the Pisan fleet was destroyed. It was nothing short of a massacre, with more than five thousand dead and ten thousand prisoners in chains.

"On the return voyage one of the galleys, weighed down by its cargo of prisoners, fell behind and ended up caught in a storm. The hold was tossed about, earthenware jars shattered and sacks were ripped open. The oil from the jars mixed with the chickpeas spilling out of the sacks, with the seawater as 'dressing.' When the good weather returned, the sailors looked at this mush and decided to serve it as a meal to the prisoners manning the oars so it wouldn't be wasted. A few refused to eat the yellow puree, but most were so hungry that they demolished it under the curious gaze of the Genoan. That night, one of the Genoan men thought they could heat it up and serve it for dinner, but at that point a new problem arose: what would they cook it in? Then there was a light bulb moment: in an earlier battle with a Saracen ship they'd salvaged a few circular copper shields they now realized could be put over the fire. That's how the first *farinata* came about, entirely by chance. The Genoans' dinner was excellent, and the heavy copper shield was the prototype of the cast-iron baking tray now known as a *testo*."

That's the name of the container they put the dough in before it goes into the oven. The *farinata* has come quite a long way since that day 738 years ago: in the following centuries it spread like wildfire throughout the Mediterranean, and later in South America as well, thanks to the mass migration of Ligurians. Elio tells me that in Montevideo they've been celebrating *El día del auténtico fainá* for over a hundred years. "A great example of how attached our fellow countrymen are to their values and traditions," he continues, "so you can see that pesto and focaccia aren't the only representatives of Ligurian cuisine around the world. The 'no-frills' farinata has an important place as well, because it's really simple to make."

"So you'll have to tell me how it's made," I say, throwing down the challenge.

"One part flour, three parts water, extra virgin olive oil and salt. Those four simple elements blend together in the heat of an oven fueled by olive wood to create something truly excellent."

In a way the *farinata* seems to be simply the tangible application of a phrase I use all the time: "It's hard to be simple."

Elio tells me the secrets to enjoying it to the max. "To begin with, it must be eaten very hot, because heat is one contributor to its success." Over time there have been various additions, a bit like what happened with the focaccia: onions, artichokes, capsicums, rosemary, stracchino or gorgonzola, sausage, mushrooms ... but my friend the Ligurian maestro screws up his nose slightly. These days everything changes quickly, people are always trying to add something extra, whereas up until less than a century ago, specialties—like many aspects of everyday life—were kept simple and unchanged, especially in rural areas. He believes that in the last fifty years globalization has changed traditions by adding touches that are sometimes absurd. He likes the *farinata* "naked": a generous portion with a good glass of white wine.

He winks. "These days that option doesn't have a lot of disciples, but believe me it takes you to heaven. Don't worry, Oscar, we're not giving up. Nearly all the restaurant owners in our valley have a wood-fired oven and know how to make it work hard. Our 'yellow gold' flows like the Varenna stream from Pegli to San Carlo di Cese. With the proceeds from the Expo we were able to make a dream we've had for years come true: we built a new meeting center in the valley."

Now the club runs a restaurant with about thirty places and a kitchen with a superb wood-fired oven. It was built by a dear friend of the club, an eighty-two-year-old whose entire working life has been spent just making ovens; he wouldn't accept payment.

They're open on Friday and Saturday nights and Elio says they're very happy with the results they've had so far. Then he adds: "We've even been able to redo the toilet in the old church that we've been looking after for years! But you must come back, Oscar. You've got to come and see it!"

There are still some lovely people in the world, people who can turn things the inattentive eye might see as insignificant into something great.

*

By now we've stood up from our bench, the sun has changed direction and it seems about to set on our meeting as well. Sure, Elio, sure I'll come and see your dream that's become a reality. He smiles, shakes my hand again and walks off. Then I hear him shout from about thirty feet away: "We'll take you to paradise with *na bella papeâ de fainâ boggîa e in te l'oexin!*"

If you're wondering what that means, it's "a lovely paper-bagful of hot *farinata* with a crunchy edge."

How good are the simple things in life?

18

FINOCCHIONA

From finocchio *to* infinocchio

WITH SERGIO FALASCHI

"Between August and September, wild fennel grows along the paths and around the edges of our Tuscan countryside. After the first rains the scent is unmistakable, and in some cases it's blended with aniseed. After the harvest, it's threshed and hung out to dry, and at that point it releases a very elegant balsamic perfume."

That's what Tuscans are like. They know how to celebrate food in a poetic manner.

You might have thought those phrases were written by the famous nineteenth-century Tuscan cookbook writer Pellegrino Artusi, but no: they're the words of a contemporary Tuscan who works as ... a butcher.

His name is Sergio Falaschi, and that's how he wants to be described, as a butcher in San Miniato, a beautiful town set on a hill in a strategic location exactly halfway between Florence and Pisa.

In reality Sergio is more than just a butcher; I'd call him a "meat gastronome." His grandfather Guido emigrated to Argentina in 1918 and worked in the government abattoir in Buenos Aires. Fortunately after a few years he decided to return to Italy, and in 1925 he opened the shop in San Miniato.

Now, almost a century later, the butcher's shop is still there in the center of town, duly modernized. In addition to the classic space for selling raw and cured meats, Sergio has come up with the idea of Retrobottega, a restaurant and a place where he conducts lessons. He's in charge of *mallegato pisano,* the black pudding of Pisa, in the Slow Food Presidium, is a member of the consortium for the protection of the Sienese domestic pig *cinta senese,* founder of the public abattoir in San Miniato, and a teacher of Tuscan cooking and meat cuts. Best of all, he makes a mouthwatering fennel salami from semi-wild gray pigs.

When I tell him about this book his immediate response is: "Ah well, the most famous story is that they used to use the *finocchiona* to make money. What else do you need to know?"

"Wait, Sergio, forgive me, but we have to take things in order. We can say there are two serendipitous things about fennel salami, the first concerning its creation and the second its use. I mean its use back in the day, obviously. I hope you don't use it these days to *infinocchiare* anyone!" Sergio laughs and assures me he doesn't.

The term *"infinocchiare,"* meaning to trick or cheat, has nothing to do with the birth of this salami. It's a word that emerged much later, when the *finocchiona* was already well known.

Sergio tells me the story of the salami.

Its origins are disputed between Campi Bisenzio and Greve in Chianti, but everyone knows (and even Sergio admits) Tuscans are good at controversy, especially between neighboring towns. In the late Middle Ages, the price of pepper increased so much that it became a rare commodity, so it could no longer be used to season cured meats. Some of the *norcini* (traveling butchers) tried using the seeds of wild fennel because it was plentiful and very cheap. It could be used to add flavor and fragrance, and to improve the preservation of meat that wasn't always the freshest. It seemed to produce a good result, and soon the inhabitants of the Chianti valleys got used to the aniseed flavor. Then it reached

Florence (Sergio tells me Machiavelli loved it), and from there it was an easy road throughout Tuscany and far beyond. Now people everywhere love the salami, christened *finocchiona* in a nod to the fennel.

For a long time, pepper was abandoned in favor of fennel. The knowledge and the culture of pepper usage in cured meats only resurfaced in the eighteenth century. Even today the guidelines for the Macchiaiola Maremmana breed of pigs don't include pepper in the production specifications for cured meats.

"Il Falaschi" (in Tuscany it's de rigueur to put the definite article in front of the surname when it's used on its own) seems to know this story very well. It's one of those handed down by the masters of the art of butchery since time immemorial, like all the old legends that help us understand where things come from, in this case a word.

"You know, Oscar, it was customary for families to go directly to the farmers to buy wine, because they quite rightly insisted on tasting it first to make sure it was good. Often wine was full of defects, especially after the end of summer, so the cunning farmer would give them a snack of *finocchiona* to eat with it, always a strong one with loads of wild fennel seeds. The potent flavor would flood the nose and mouth and tongue so it was impossible to recognize the flaws in the wine. After four or five slices of *finocchiona*, any wine seemed superb! This fake kindness was a cover for deception, and that's the origin of the term '*infinocchiare*' as it's used today, well beyond the borders of Tuscany."

A simple hoax. But at least there's a pleasant aftertaste.

Speaking of the present day, the Falaschi butchery has been handed down to the fourth generation. Sergio's children, Anna and Andrea, and his wife, Lina, are always on the job. Their interpretation of the *finocchiona* is serious, rigorous and at last it has official recognition from the IGP, the protection consortium with specific guidelines governing the quality of this splendid salami. There are two different types, Sergio explains: the classic compact, lean *finocchiona* and the crumbly *sbriciolona,* not part of the consortium because it's slightly fattier and tends to break up when you cut it. The aromas in the classic version are more restrained, but the taste is exemplary. In the second version the meat is younger and has more fat, so there's less depth of flavor; this allows the fennel to take over so the fresher and more floral aromas can come into their own.

"My work as a producer is bound up with the legacy of my grandfather Guido, my father, Vasco, and my uncle Bruno, and their experience in the butchery that's still there in our historic town center. Back then, you know, the masters of the trade didn't talk much. You had to learn from watching them at work. Without their teaching I would never have been able to invent the new production techniques I've introduced, but in doing that I never lost sight of tradition. We've built a modern laboratory out in the countryside among vineyards and olive trees, and we can use a cold chain that helps us avoid preservatives. Thanks partly to the knowledge behind the Slow Food movement, we understand that the first rule for achieving a great product is investing in animal welfare. We work with various small local breeders who are committed to natural feed for their animals and letting them live in the open with decent shelters. Along with strict temperature control during production and aging, that means we don't need to add nitrates.

"The classic *finocchiona* is made from the 'noble' parts of the pig. We grind the meat coarsely and knead it with salt and black pepper, wild fennel, garlic, and wine as an antioxidant. Then we stuff it into a natural casing for better aging. That's the traditional processing. I came into the butchery in 1968 and I still have vivid memories of watching the mastery of my father and my uncle as they worked. I hope the same happens with my children, and maybe a grandkid or two, you never know."

*

Now, as usual, I've ended up ravenous.

He chuckles. "I think I'll start with two slices of *sbriciolona* and a glass of young Chianti, what do you say? Then I'll move on to the genuine *finocchiona*, maybe one that has aged for a while. I feel like a good Brunello and a few slices of Tuscan bread to go with it—the one without salt—would that do?"

As Sergio goes off to put a nice tasting board together and to fill my glass, I remember something: "Sergio, wait!"

"What's up?"

I grin. "I forgot to say ... bring me the wine before the salami, okay? You know how it is, I wouldn't want to be *infinocchiato*!"

19

CHIANTI'S
BLACK ROOSTER

The hungry insomniac rooster of Florence

WITH MARCO PALLANTI

There he is, on every bottle of Chianti Classico: the Black Rooster, always ready to startle the world with a cock-a-doodle-doo.

I owe it to this black rooster that I met Marco Pallanti, a man I greatly respect. He and his wife, Lorenza, make Chianti Classico in one of the most beautiful places in the world (which might be one reason why it turns out to be so good).

Castello di Ama in Gaiole in Chianti is a beautifully restored hamlet, and the Pallantis help to make it lovelier still with the works of art they've installed in its courtyards, gardens, houses and even in the cellar, for their enjoyment and ours. Marco is an exceptional winemaker. He's also worked in France, and he was president of the Chianti Consortium for two terms until 2012. In other words, he's a Black Rooster aficionado.

When I sniffed serendipity in the air and wanted to know why this bird appears on the bottles of Chianti Classico, Marco took me to the city center in Florence. I wasn't prepared to get into the car though until

I was sure we'd be coming back to the castle to taste his Chianti. No way was I going to miss out on a drinking session here. He gave me his word, and we headed for the city.

The Palazzo Vecchio is a wondrous thing. Its solid Gothic architecture stands out like an impregnable fortress on Piazza della Signoria. The interior leaves you even more breathless. Marco and I head toward the Salone dei Cinquecento, but at this point, as a Florentine, he can explain it better.

"The Salone dei Cinquecento was built in just seven months in 1495, under the direction of Savonarola, the friar from Ferrara. As de facto lord of Florence, he wanted to establish a Grand Council with as many citizens as possible making the political decisions. This huge hall was supposed to hold about five hundred people so the decision-making power of the Florentine Republic would be widely shared. These days we'd call it democracy, and it's also clear which movement Savonarola would be part of today. Replace the salon with an online platform and you see how some ideas come from far away."

That was the purpose the Salone dei Cinquecento was created for, but at the time the impression would have been different because the ceiling was much lower.

"Then with the return of the Medici, this room became the duke's state room for receiving guests. Cosimo I put his visionary trusted architect, Giorgio Vasari, to work on it, and it was he who made the rooster eternal. It took seventeen years to raise the ceiling an extra twenty-three feet and transform this impressive space, 177 feet long, seventy-five feet wide and fifty-nine feet high, into the biggest hall in Italy for the management of power. Look at that ceiling! Magnificent, isn't it?"

It is indeed. The vaulted coffered ceiling is framed with gold carvings. Marco tells me Cosimo I, delirious with his omnipotence, asked Vasari to paint him bang in the center of its forty-two squares. "Now, Oscar, look at the space around Cosimo. See? There are different allegories of the mighty Medici family, like the scenes of the subjugation of the dominions and the wars with Pisa and Siena, and various portraits as well."

It's impressive. My guide points out one portrait in particular. One of the squares in the coffered ceiling shows the allegory of Chianti, and next to Bacchus there's an armed youth carrying a large shield with a black rooster on a yellow background. It's the symbol of the ancient League of Chianti. In the background you can see the outlines of Castellina, Radda and Brolio, Florentine fortifications representing the controlling power of the Medici Grand Duchy. At the time of Vasari, the Chianti League was already active on the military and legislative fronts and was strengthened after 1260 following the resounding defeat at Montaperti, a trouncing at the hands of the Sienese that the Florentines never came to terms with.

So one thing is certain: the rooster was already an emblem of Chianti in the sixteenth century. And in the fifteenth and the fourteenth; in fact, for this story we have to go back to 1208. After many years of conflict, the border between the republics of Florence and Siena was decided by an encounter between two knights, one Sienese and the other Florentine, who had left their respective cities when the cock crowed. Each city chose its bravest knight, its best horse, and even the rooster that would set the contest in motion. All attested to by the notaries of the rival cities.

The Sienese selected a handsome white rooster, which they looked after, fed and lavished with care and attention the night before the contest. But the Florentines were cunning. They chose a black rooster, not too imposing, and that evening they shut it away in the dark early, without even feeding it. That black rooster started crowing long before dawn.

The Sienese notaries couldn't deny that the Florentine knight had in fact set out when the cock crowed, but that was a lot earlier than the crowing of their own lazier bird, unfortunately for them. So the knights met in Fonterutoli, a few kilometers from Siena, and that's how Chianti came under the power of Florence.

How much truth is there in this story? Even Marco can't tell me with certainty, but he always enjoys telling it. The fact that the rooster is the emblem of the territory makes him proud.

The production area for Gallo Nero Chianti was defined much later, in 1716, when Grand Duke Cosimo III proclaimed the boundaries. They were the first set borders for a wine territory in the world.

The first consortium for the protection of Chianti's wine was founded in 1924, and the Consortium for Chianti Classico in 1932. The Black Rooster that had secured the supremacy of Florence centuries earlier and was later taken up by Vasari became its distinctive emblem. "The Consortium is a prestigious body," Marco explains. "It has over six hundred associates, making it Italy's largest, and it covers about seventy-two thousand hectares planted with vines. I was president from 2006 to 2012 and in that time, thanks to a brilliant and dynamic council, we were successful in creating a new category of Chianti Classico. It's called Gran Selezione because it's closely linked to the original vineyard, and that's a zoning obtained from the producers' own descriptions."

You can see this man is in love with his land. He seems like one of those people who understand they're very lucky to have been born in a lovely place, so they work long and hard as if they must make up for such blatant good fortune.

"When I graduated, it was clear to me straight away that my future would be in the world of wine. I've always loved drinking it, but above all I love the values it brings with it, the history and culture and traditions. Wine for me is a part of civilization. I love the conviviality, the sacred sharing of a good bottle. Drinking a great wine alone I find really sad—a bit like going to the cinema on your own, which is something I can't do. Florence is my native city, and Chianti was the only possible place I could go to fulfil my dream. In the early 1980s, Castello di Ama offered me the chance to work toward that. At the time, Chianti's image in the world had been almost totally wiped out after decades of faded, acidic and sometimes defective wines, like the ones in those horrible flasks with the plastic cover. Another reason for the decline was people confusing Chianti and Chianti Classico, because historically and geographically there's only one Chianti. Unfortunately there's still a bit of that around. Beware, though, not all Chianti is the same, and again what makes the difference is the Black Rooster, the exclusive emblem of the Classico."

A lot of water has passed under the bridges that span the Arno river, and today Marco feels he really is living the dream, with the possibility that Chianti Classico has risen to rank among the best wines in the world. It has taken the commitment of many good entrepreneurs, including some from outside the region, who were initially attracted by the beauty of the landscape and the houses, and later came to love this wine as well.

It stands to reason. Tuscany has always been a tourist attraction for its art and its landscapes. Florence and Siena have endless masterpieces in their city centers, but there's no doubt their rural areas are powerful draws too. On the way back to the castle, driving among vineyards, olive trees and cypresses, Marco tells me the harmony that reigns supreme in the Tuscan landscape has its roots in the Renaissance, and it can't be explained only by the agricultural technique that has always been used in the region. He turns to literature to illustrate his point. Emilio Sereni tried to explain it in his history of Italy's agricultural landscape as the special union of intention between the peasant's taste for the "beautiful agricultural landscape" and Boccaccio's taste for the "beautiful poetic landscape." That's how a shared aesthetic first emerged in Tuscany.

Now Chianti Classico is something else. The sangiovese grapes take charge and the wine has longevity, but still with an elegance worthy of the world's best wines.

Marco is confident: "Little by little it has earned the appreciation of consumers around the world, and now we must protect its name because the imitations are starting to come thick and fast. And who have we decided to trust with protecting its origin? Again, it's that blessed Black Rooster, the historical symbol of the League of Chianti. Double serendipity, don't you think?"

We head back to Castello di Ama for a vertical tasting (the same wine from different years, from the same producer) of Chianti Classico, the one with the Black Rooster. Fantastic. I'm lost for words.

20

CHOCOLATE GANACHE

Numbskull! What have you done?

WITH GIOVANNI BATTISTA MANTELLI

"Dear GB, is it true that chocolate ganache was created by mistake?"

"That's right, Oscar, one of the most delicious bungles to result from carelessness. But the same has happened to me much more recently. I accidentally invented a recipe or two when I was trying to help my grandfather in his lab."

Giovanni Battista Mantelli, known as GB, is the greatest connoisseur of chocolate I've ever met, and he might just have a touch of chocolate in his blood. His grandfather Pietro was the founder of Cuba, master chocolatiers and suppliers to Venchi, the historic chocolate-makers established in 1878 in Via degli Artisti in Turin.

But after a century of glorious history, Venchi went bankrupt in the 1980s, and Pietro's payout was the trademark, by then out of use. Whether it was foresight or just because that was the best he could get, he accepted it, and in 2000 he and some other investors relaunched the brand. Now it's riding high with sales all over the world.

GB was close to his grandfather from early childhood and would watch admiringly as Pietro invented new recipes with chocolate; in the process he developed an unconditional love for it. Following Venchi's renaissance, he rediscovered the role of the chocolatier (chocolatier, take note, not *cioccolataio*, because being a *ciculaté*, as it's called in Piedmontese dialect, is a bit different) by inventing—or reinventing—delicious specialties using cocoa. He knows all there is to know about that raw material and the art of transforming it. "It does seem absurd that one of the greatest specialties of the chocolatier tradition has a name meaning 'numbskull' in French."

One day, about halfway through the nineteenth century, in a well-known Paris chocolate laboratory, an insult pierced the air: *"Ganache!"* A famous confectioner was shouting at a naive apprentice who had absent-mindedly poured boiling milk into a container of chocolate squares. The resulting soupy mess would normally have had to be thrown out, but in those times of crisis nothing was wasted, so the confectioner tried to remedy the situation by rapidly stirring the mixture. To everyone's surprise, what emerged was a sublime chocolate cream that could be used as a filling. All it needed was a name, and what better than the insult directed at the careless apprentice? *Ganache*!

GB confirms that these days the chocolate with ganache filling is one of the most common varieties made in Europe, partly due to the large quantity of milk available in northern parts and the cold climate that makes everyone want to eat something rich. From that fateful day in nineteenth-century Paris, ganache, or rather ganaches, given the many different types available, have constantly improved. You can find them made with cream and sugar syrup, with butter and cream in northern Europe, and with caramelized sugars and other fats in English-style fudge.

GB explains, "According to the traditional recipe, true ganache is made by immersing flakes of good-quality chocolate in warm boiled cream, with inverted sugar syrup for balance. You allow the chocolate to melt slowly and then amalgamate it with a spatula using a circular motion from the surface to the bottom, until the mixture is silky and elastic. The temperature must always be hotter than your lip (a substitute for a thermometer, more or less): between 35 and 40 degrees

Celsius [95 and 104 degrees Fahrenheit]. The most important thing, if you want to try making it, is to keep the balance between the natural fats in chocolate and the fats in cream. As a guide, the correct ratio is 1:2, or five hundred grams of chocolate to a liter of fresh cream. To make it the northern European way using butter, remember the butter must be added after you've created the first cream mixture. This method ensures the filling will be thick and ready for cutting into squares and coating with melted chocolate."

"You've done a Piedmontese interpretation of your ganache too, is that right?"

"Here in Piedmont there's no shortage of good milk, and I've invented a few recipes using the milk, cream and butter from our magnificent mountain pastures. With those first-class ingredients I was able to create balls filled with chocolate mousse, for example. Then I tried adding a few drops of Gin Occitan (a gin made with juniper berries from the valleys of Piedmont) to a white chocolate ganache. The result was fantastic gin-flavored chocolate pralines."

However, in the face of such an abundance of milk, GB has introduced a new, very "Mediterranean" variation of his chocolate creams, trying a different slant with extra virgin olive oil.

In some recipes he's reinterpreted ganache by replacing cream with other ingredients that harmonize perfectly with the philosophy of the Mediterranean diet: in addition to the oil there are nuts, in particular the Piedmontese PGI (Protected Geographical Indication) hazelnuts, but also Sicilian pistachios and almonds. He believes these ingredients put the best possible Italian stamp on the chocolate.

"But be careful," he adds, "it would all be pointless without painstaking care in the selection of your cocoa. And it's always been extra virgin olive oil that envelops and binds our Piedmont hazelnut cream."

There's a philosophy behind all of this, and GB describes it as making specialties for the sweet-toothed without any of the guilt involved. In order not to feel guilty, judgments must be made on several fronts. Choosing the best ingredients, treating the farmers and suppliers well, creating recipes with smaller amounts of unhealthy ingredients like sugar.

Before I let him return to his work, I ask him to satisfy my curiosity: "From one Piedmontese to another, and since you're a consummate chocolatier, tell me why in Italy there is a common saying that someone who's foolish, or rather mean, 'looks like a chocolatier.' What have you chocolate-makers done?"

It started in the mid-1900s when Turin became Italy's chocolate capital. Orders streamed in from all over the country and from many European capitals as well. The artisan chocolate laboratories expanded rapidly, and within a few years some of Turin's chocolatiers grew very rich. A few became arrogant and rode around in carriages like the ones used by aristocrats in the old days. But their behavior exposed the slightly boorish style of people who had got rich quickly, and they became a laughing stock around the city.

So when one of these nouveau riche alighted from his elaborate carriage, people would be murmuring, or even shouting: "*Tensiun cu pasa un ciculaté*," "Look out, there's a chocolatier going by."

It didn't take long for the expression to be applied to anyone who behaved like that—something of a poser and a bit tacky.

But GB reassures me: "Never fear, Oscar, these days we don't get rich so fast."

21

THE ICY POLE ...
AND THE PENGUIN

Freedom to eat on the move

WITH ALBERTO MANGIANTINI

Alberto Mangiantini is the administrator and a partner at Pepino Gelati in Turin, a company that's been around for a century and a half. Pepino invented the *Pinguino*: vanilla ice cream coated in a thin layer of dark chocolate, presented on a wooden stick.

I thought whoever invented the Pinguino must surely have been inspired by the icy pole, so I sought out Alberto to tell me the story.

Alberto tells me about an eleven-year-old boy named Frank Epperson who lived in Oakland, California, where the climate was freezing. It was winter 1905, and Frank was mixing water and soda in a glass with a small stick. He got distracted and left the drink on the windowsill, and in the sub-zero temperatures it froze in no time. The next day, with a lot of effort and some hot water, he managed to extract the block of ice from the glass. There he was, holding the first icy pole in history, and he instinctively took a lick.

"But we can't just talk about chance," Alberto continues, "because clearly if Frank had been less curious and alert, he'd have taken the glass inside and put it in the sink. Or it would have stayed on the windowsill until spring and by then the contents would be unusable, and perhaps the history of the icy pole would have been for another time, started in another place."

So it was by chance, then, but also due to attention and curiosity. What my friend stresses here is that intuition and change are reflected not in the frozen mixture but in the stick. It was a simple thing that radically changed eating habits: the custom of adding syrup of various kinds to crushed ice already existed, but eating it required crockery and cutlery.

"The stick gave us the freedom to eat on the move because it only required the use of one hand, and that was a genuine revolution, as confirmed by the fact that the icy pole has never gone out of fashion."

"Maybe it's one of those sweet treats that awaken people's childhood memories," I suggest. "In my early teens, for example, I ate lots of them. In my hometown of Alba we used the English term 'sticks.'"

Alberto nods. "That's what we called them in Turin too. The word 'stick' comes from *stecco*, and like all good Piedmontese we placed great importance on infrastructure. Without the little stick the icy pole would have no reason to exist."

But let's get back to the story. The icy pole was patented in 1923 by ... can you guess? The lad who'd invented it by mistake in 1905. In the meantime young Frank had become an entrepreneur, and clearly he'd managed the difficult task of keeping the secret for eighteen years. When he was ready, he launched his invention on the market and called it Popsicle. The rest is history: the Popsicle arrived in Italy after the war in the wake of the American troops, along with American chewing gum and canned meat.

Now, to return to the Pinguino, the first gelato on a stick covered with a fine layer of dark chocolate. Here we're talking about an even more ingenious idea that came out of Turin in 1938, covered by patent no. 58033.

This was a truly revolutionary product: before the Pinguino, gelato was served and eaten in either a cone or a tub. But there's a significant difference to underline here: in contrast to the icy pole, the birth of this fantastic gelato was anything but accidental.

Alberto tells me that confectionery manufacturer Giuseppe Feletti and his son-in-law Giuseppe Cavagnino acquired the Pepino gelateria on June 17, 1916 for 10,000 liras, but only managed to make the Pinguino a commercial reality after years of research and endless experiments.

"Combining the soft, cold ice cream and the hot layer of chocolate wasn't easy. Obviously if it weren't for that cold winter night in Oakland the Pinguino probably wouldn't exist either, at least not on a stick. But they had plenty of problems to solve in relation to the stick because they had a very precise goal: an ice cream that was easy to carry and wouldn't collapse and stain people's clothes—but it also had to give the same sensation on the palate as the ice cream in a cone or a tub. In Italy, eating ice cream was associated with relaxation and going for a stroll with family around the old town center or in the park."

After much testing, the new ice cream came onto the market at a cost of one lira, the same price as a movie ticket, and you could choose between vanilla, *gianduia*, hazelnut, mint and violet. Popcorn was yet to make its appearance at the movie theater, but for just two liras you could enjoy the film and a luscious Pinguino. The citizens of Turin, and soon the rest of the nation, were enthusiastic about it, and the Pinguino earned its place in the history of the city.

Its success has been incredible and consistent; the recipe is still the same and so is the care and attention and the selection of ingredients that go into it. It's a source of pride for Mangiantini and all his coworkers that they can say the Pinguino has traveled all around the world as the ambassador not just of a terrific story, but also of ingenuity and the pursuit of quality typical of the best Italian traditions.

I agree with him, and as a Piedmontese I too am proud of the Pinguino.

22

GIANDUIOTTO

The perfume of life

WITH GUIDO GOBINO

I've chosen Guido Gobino to tell us the story of *gianduiotto*, a distinctive Piedmontese hazelnut chocolate. In 1995, Guido came up with the idea of reducing the size of his *gianduiotto* to make it more elegant and easier to manage, and that turned out to be a masterstroke. In the twenty-seven years since, his commitment to perfecting it has never wavered, and he now exports it all over the world.

I asked Guido to talk to me about this chocolate—the icon of Turin's chocolate-making industry. It appears to have been created to get around one of Napoleon's edicts way back in 1806.

And that's where our story starts. Napoleon had just declared a continent-wide embargo on English ships, the main carriers of spices and products from Central America. Chocolate and cane sugar were therefore automatically blocked. Guido reminds me that just before this, in 1747, a German chemist named Andreas Sigismund Marggraf had discovered the similarity between beet crystals and the crystals from sugar cane, but it was only after Napoleon's sanctions that organized and extensive cultivation of beet began.

"This embargo caused a substantial price hike for end users like the chocolatiers in Turin and led to a hunt for alternative base ingredients," Gobino goes on to explain. "Luckily our Piedmontese soil produces excellent crops, not least the Tonda Gentile Trilobata hazelnut, and its potential was recognized immediately. They soon began using it in the chocolate factories, and I suppose it was during this period that *gianduia* chocolate was created. Then in 1865, thanks to the genius of a master artisan chocolatier in Turin named Michele Prochet, *gianduiotto* arrived. And one day, apparently, an apprentice of his suggested making a smaller size that people could eat in one bit."

Guido sighs. "Great idea, that! And he had it before I did, dammit!" Then he has another thought: "Well, we can say I managed to make it even smaller, can't we?"

Thinking again about hazelnuts and the fact that this hunch was a preliminary step toward the creation of Nutella, it seems to me a genuine revolution.

But it wasn't so easy to produce the *gianduiotto* in significant quantities suitable for distribution all over Italy. It was unusually rich in fats, essential oil from Piedmont hazelnuts and cocoa butter, and the fats would deteriorate and oxidize quite quickly. This explains why the *gianduiotto* had to be protected from the air ASAP and also explains its unique wrapping—a light layer of foil, usually gold, which makes it stand out among all the other chocolates. It was actually the world's first wrapped chocolate.

"How was it made, and why the unusual shape?" I ask Guido.

"You know, there were (and still are in a few companies like mine) women who were exceptionally good at tempering *gianduia* chocolate and cutting it with a special large knife called a *coltella*. With their unique skill and dexterity, these women ensured the *gianduia* paste was at the right temperature, then they shaped the chocolates with the knives into their typical triangular shape and wrapped them in gold foil."

Today the formula is largely the same as it was then.

Guido explains that a fundamental requirement for the *gianduia* paste needed for the *gianduiotto* is a perfect thermodynamic balance between the low temperatures and the crystallization of fats, cocoa butter and hazelnut oil. The external temperature and humidity are absolutely critical too.

You'd have to admit that good as it is, the mixture of cocoa, hazelnuts and sugar is extremely climate-sensitive! This is where the knowledge and skill of the chocolatier come in.

"Only patient crafting can give the chocolate that special shape without the aid of the classic molds used for the other chocolates. Currently the typical *gianduiotto* is made with a high percentage of Piedmont hazelnut, using special machines called extruders. They allow us to produce more chocolates without altering the shape and quality of the traditional formula. Imagine those chocolate-makers in the nineteenth century mass-producing hand-cut *gianduiotti*; in the larger laboratories they had *anlupoire* as well, the women who wrapped each chocolate by hand. These days, in order to obtain larger quantities, we have to rely on machines that can replicate those actions, but much faster. They're very challenging to build, and the imperfection that's a mark of artisan production is missing. The true *gianduiotto* formula has only cane or beet sugar, PGI Piedmont hazelnuts, cocoa and cocoa butter."

Today, this little chocolate is a big hit all over the world. When I was in New York recently, Eataly had an entire shelf devoted to it. They told me it has become fashionable. When many discerning Americans are now invited to dinner, it's not brownies they take as a gift, but *gianduiotti*.

Guido isn't surprised. "Because they're good—really good! And good things transcend borders."

The *gianduiotto* caught on early in the twentieth century and big corporations joined the artisan chocolate-makers in the market. That's where the problem started: the use of metal molds, and later polycarbonate ones, distorted the classic irregular shape. It made production more efficient and cheaper, but decidedly less artisanal. Distribution went global and these days, along with the original products found all over the world, there are plenty of low-quality ones.

To some extent this is Guido's battle. "Behind any great food product there are always great raw materials, and behind great raw materials lie the knowledge and professional ethics of good people. You need to go beyond the economics, and in order to guarantee a future for the supply of first-class ingredients it's absolutely necessary to pay the growers a fair and profitable price."

For this reason, fifteen years ago Gobino set up a collaboration with seven agricultural companies in the Langhe region of Italy that guarantee the supply of nuts to cover his production needs. His Langhe origins, the hours spent with his grandfather in the summer holidays gathering nuts, the smell of the dried hazelnuts in bags crammed into the hayloft—these memories help to keep him on track.

As we talked about his roots and where he is today, I learned that in Cortemilia, home of the world's best hazelnut, Guido has been named ambassador of the Langhe Tonda Gentile hazelnut.

And what of the future?

"The future will probably be in the hands of my son, Pietro," says Guido. "He's finishing his studies in food technology and he seems to have the desire and the ability, as well as the necessary imagination and enthusiasm."

As for the master of the *gianduiotto* himself, Guido believes he'll always be the same: a stubborn artisan chocolatier fanatical about quality. It's a profession he can only be grateful for. It's meant he has come to know and appreciate the *Langhetti*, the people of the Langhe hills—rough, he admits, but dedicated to work and sacrifice, and in love with their terrain and traditions, just as his father, Beppe, and his grandfather Pietro were.

When all is said and done he's a romantic (perhaps it couldn't be otherwise for a man who makes chocolate), and lives for the taste and aroma of cocoa and hazelnuts. He seems like a truly happy man.

23

GORGONZOLA
Churchill's cheese

WITH RENATO INVERNIZZI

Traveling around the globe selling quality Italian food is my job, and I can tell you the name "gorgonzola" has incredible potency all over the world. People like the word, the taste and the way it pairs with other foods.

Not many people know that the cheese is named after a town. Maybe it's better that way, because if they went to Gorgonzola today they wouldn't find a single cheesemaker.

People like gorgonzola because if it's well made it's really very good—even the most modern version, the sweet, creamy one that currently dominates the market. In fact, today gorgonzola is made by a different method from the one used in the past. These days, the milk is pasteurized, the mold responsible for the blue veins—Penicillium roqueforti—is injected, and the cheeses are pierced with needles so the oxygen can penetrate and cause contamination. But there was a time when the cheesemakers didn't want blue veins in the cheese.

What led to the creation of one of the world's most famous cheeses is a story of serendipity.

To find out more I went to see Renato Invernizzi. Not only does he lead a company that can still claim to be artisanal, SI Invernizzi, but he's also been president of the Gorgonzola Consortium for many years. Renato represents this cheese like no one else. When I called him, he didn't invite me to his cheese factory in Trecate, Novara, in Piedmont. He asked if we could meet a long distance away in Valsassina, where gorgonzola was born a long time ago.

Valsassina is in the Alpine foothills in the province of Lecco, east of Monte Grigna—the valley parallel to "that branch of the Lake of Como" to use Alessandro Manzoni's much-quoted phrase from his masterpiece, *The Betrothed*. The valley begins at Ballabio and ends at Bellano. Some say the Brown Alpine cattle that grazed in the Po Valley, along the Adda and Ticino rivers on the alpine slopes, were first herded here in the eleventh century, although we only have reliable reports starting in the fifteenth century. The herds had to spend winter in the valley for obvious climatic reasons, guaranteeing more forage, but in summer their herdsman or *bergamino* led them on the long and difficult journey to pastures in Valsassina. In the cold months the cows enjoyed the water meadows, a common feature of Lombardy where the surface was continually irrigated, so the grass could grow even when it was freezing; but for the whole of summer they were in the mountain pastures where the grass was fragrant and the air cool.

Renato tells me that a cow would always be milked immediately after she gave birth. In those times male calves were sacrificed as soon as they were born and the rennet in their stomach was used to coagulate the milk.

"So in the summer they made the cheese in the mountains?" I ask.

"Sure. As soon as the cow was milked, they poured the milk into a caldera along with the rennet to start the coagulation. This happened twice a day, in the evening and early morning. Normally the cheese from the evening milking was left in the cabin, which was also the *bergamino*'s shelter, until dawn. Then it would be added to the morning's coagulation. So what you got was a double-paste gorgonzola, an uneven mixture with cavities and breaks in it."

The caldera takes its name from the depression in a volcano, a funnel-shaped hole alongside the crater. In the case of cheese, the caldera was an iron or copper cauldron they suspended over the fire after pouring the milk into it. The caldera was essential for cooked-paste cheeses like fontina DOP that needed to reach a temperature of about 104 degrees Fahrenheit.

SI Invernizzi can consider itself an artisan gorgonzola company in part because it has kept the calderas rather than relying on large modern machines. Those "buckets" or cauldrons are bigger these days, made of stainless steel and no longer set over the fire because the uncooked paste curdles at about 86 degrees Fahrenheit.

Back in Valsassina, the *bergamino* (but now we'll call him a *casaro*, a cheesemaker) had nowhere to shelter the cheese and protect it from the sun and the flies, so he would take it to one of the natural caves known as *casere*. They were cooler and more protected than the huts and they had a special feature: their "sky" was naturally covered with a mold called Penicillium roqueforti. When its spores fell they contaminated the cheeses and apparently ruined them. The intention was to preserve the cheese, but when the *casari* went to check the result they found contamination. Luckily in those days people didn't throw anything away and pretty much everything edible was eaten. Sometime after that, the cheesemakers noticed that the moldy cheese had better organoleptic and preservation properties than other cheeses.

Renato tells me that the herdsman would make his cheeses and stay in the alpine pastures from May to September, more or less. For the return journey he would load the cheeses onto donkeys and cows, and once back in the valley the herdsman-cheesemaker would set up house in the barn and support himself by selling his products.

"Do you know what that cheese was called?" he asks.

It was called stracchino. In the Lombardy dialect *stracchi* means tired, and the cheese acquired that name because it came from exhausted cows that had to walk tens of kilometers. There were two stracchini in Lombardy: the Milanese one, which was and is the cheese we also know as *crescenza*, and the gorgonzola stracchino, a blue cheese similar to today's gorgonzola. Then, over time, the word stracchino gradually disappeared and only gorgonzola remained. There are no cheesemakers in Gorgonzola now, but up to the early years of the twentieth century there were plenty. The two most important families in the area of migratory herding were the Galbanis and the Invernizzis, both major cheese producers to this day.

So it's thanks to those grottoes full of mold that gorgonzola exists.

"But from the *casari* and their local buyers to discovery by the rest of the world: how did that happen?" I ask.

It happened in the period between the two world wars, Renato tells me, when a flourishing trade developed between Italy and England. There was no cold chain in those days and in order to preserve the gorgonzola it was sprinkled with baryte, a mineral extracted from the Valsassina quarries. The white clay-like paste served as protection from dirt and also prevented the cheese from drying out. The cheeses were packed in wicker baskets with straw, and the freight cars set out from Novara in large numbers, headed for London.

Winston Churchill was a great admirer of gorgonzola. Apparently when plans were being made for the Allied planes to bomb Milan, he drew a circle on the map around the town of Gorgonzola and requested that it be saved so as to protect his beloved cheese.

After the war ended in 1945, the food processing industry emerged. Migratory herding was gradually abandoned, and the animals began living a sedentary life on the plains and in their stalls. There was a focus on food security as the national health system worked to fight tuberculosis and other infectious diseases.

And perhaps this is where everything changes, because Gorgonzola Piccante was made with unpasteurized milk. Consequently, around 1950, the pasteurization technique was introduced to ensure safe cheeses without pathogenic agents; the bacterial microflora naturally present in milk had to be replicated and added later, with lactic bacteria selected and standardized for each different cheese.

I have to say that today there are cheeses labeled "raw milk" that are completely safe, but I'm curious about the fact that the most successful type of gorgonzola is the sweet, creamy one. This version horrifies some gastronomes, but I must confess that I love it. It wasn't born by chance this time, but in response to a market need.

"They had to satisfy consumers' taste for a gorgonzola that was softer and not so strong. So they invented and marketed one with a sweeter taste, lighter in color and creamier than the original. Today the creamy version makes up 90 percent of total production. The fresh whole cow's milk is the same, but the recipes, ingredients and aging are different. In the 1970s a multitude of cheese factories—a hundred or so—joined together in a voluntary consortium, and in 1996 the European Community officially granted gorgonzola the important designation DOP (Protected Designation of Origin). That's how the consortium for the protection of gorgonzola cheese originated."

Renato Invernizzi says he feels very honored that he was elected president of the Consortium in 2008 and is currently serving his fourth term. It's certainly not an easy task, but the producers are a close-knit group, focused on sharing a great future. Today gorgonzola is the only blue-veined cheese in the world with a sweet and creamy taste, in contrast to other European and American blue cheeses such as Stilton, Roquefort, Bergader, Danish blue, niva or queso azul. But it's Italy's gorgonzola that's most imitated all over the world in terms of its name and technology.

Renato bemoans this fact. I console him by reminding him of what Aeschylus wrote more than two thousand years ago: a man whom nobody envies or imitates is not happy. Better to be imitated than to imitate.

24

BURNT FLOUR

Dignity rediscovered

WITH PEPPE ZULLO

Today *grano arso* (burnt flour) is specially made, following a specific procedure for toasting the grains and taking care not to burn them; but in the beginning things were very different.

The story of *grano arso* is one of great poverty, interwoven since the time of Italian unification with the history of Apulia and in particular an area in the province of Foggia called Capitanata.

There was a time when the poor people of that area would go into the fields after the harvest to glean the burnt wheat, scraping up a few grains to grind for making bread: it was the custom for rich landowners to clean up their land by setting fire to the fields where the wheat had been growing.

Grano arso was the wheat from the ears gathered in the fields of burnt stubble. The grains were then ground in stone mills or by hand in mortars and added to a quantity of white flour. This way the peasants could get a reasonable amount of the flour they needed for cooking.

It was the food of the poor who couldn't afford to use white flour alone.

Living among them were a few Foggia citizens very familiar with harvests and the use of the burnt flour: the so-called *terrazzani*, somewhere between city and country dwellers. These people adapted to gathering natural grasses, fishing out and gleaning wheat of any kind, including from the burnt fields.

The man telling me this story is Peppe Zullo, an amazing cook from Orsara di Puglia, a town in the Foggia province. We are in the southern Daunian Mountains community, where nature offers enchanting glimpses of a terrain that's perfect for good produce. Peppe calls himself a "farmer cook," because his restaurant is in the middle of a large property where he has created a huge garden covering two hectares. He grows all manner of things there and looks after them himself. Another three hectares are given over to the vineyard and a delightful wood that's useful for gathering herbs for medicinal preparations, as well as mushrooms and wild fruit and nuts. There's another space reserved for breeding animals native to the area and for making cheeses and cured meats. All strictly organic. In a way Peppe invented the agri-food theme park well before I established FICO (Fabbrica Italiana Contadina, the Italian Farmers' Production Center).

But before turning to all this, Peppe traveled the world including much of America. In 1978 he decided to stop moving and opened a highly successful restaurant in Boston. But in the late '80s the call of his native land brought him back to Italy, and I must say that was a stroke of luck for the patrons of his country restaurant.

One day I was at the Milan Expo where he was representing Apulia, and I heard him telling the *grano arso* story to a lady who couldn't make up her mind what to order.

So who better to explain it for this book?

"Peppe, *grano arso* is considered a delicacy these days, a favorite of food-lovers and the well-to-do. But it was born by accident from the needs of the poor. How was that possible?"

"When the era of large landowners was over and the economic boom meant the end of the hunger we endured during the world wars, *grano arso* disappeared from Apulia's tables because it was seen as poor people's food. It returned very recently, and that's due to local restaurateurs and producers. Together they rediscovered the use of burnt wheat in cooking. Daunia in Foggia was the first area to rediscover *grano arso* and revisit it in a contemporary context."

But it's not only the restaurateurs we have to thank. Peppe tells me, for example, that post-World War II, the story of burnt wheat was picked up and brought back into vogue by local singer-songwriter Matteo Salvatore, who wrote a song about it called "*Pasta Nera*" black pasta. He sang about the pain of the poor, who were forced by hunger to eat the burnt wheat. Other artists after Salvatore delved into the question too, including film director Alessandro Piva with his documentary *Pasta Nera*.

Today, Peppe explains, the law forbids using burnt seeds in cooking because they contain toxic elements.

"So the wheat grains are toasted in a safe way before grinding. There are lots of companies making burnt wheat flour and burnt wheat pasta these days, and you'll find it in Italy and abroad. Lots of people love this kind of toasting. It gives the flour, and consequently the pasta, an attractive amber color and aromas of almond and hazelnut and roasted coffee. Now people even pay more for it than they do for white flour!"

He's as proud of this product as a new father.

Peppe has been doing research on *grano arso* for over twenty-five years. In the beginning it wasn't easy to find fans of the lightly toasted flour; in fact, when he offered burnt-flour orecchiette on his menu (paired with other specialties of the Apulia region such as wild asparagus) people looked at him strangely. But the trick is never to give up.

He tells me the wheat produces a flavorful pasta with a taste that integrates perfectly with pulses, greens and other vegetables, and fresh herbs. Currently, in addition to the various fresh pastas, he makes *taralli* (a pretzel-like snack) and many types of dessert. Often the burnt wheat flour is mixed with white flours, but it can also be used on its own. Sometimes a proportion of 10 or 15 percent of the whole is all it takes to add character to focaccia, bread or pasta made at home.

The *grano arso* story is the story of a specialty given back the dignity it deserves by the work of people like Peppe Zullo and the local producers and managers of the mills.

Finally, my Apulian friend tells me with pride: "I always say that with this product we've moved from storytelling to 'storydoing.' In other words, by explaining it we've created a masterpiece, because we've changed a sad but true story into a positive gastronomic rediscovery."

25

THE GRISSINO

The "little sticks of Turin"

WITH MARIO AND GIOVANNI FONGO

People have been making bread for thousands of years, but it's hard to put an exact date on its invention. Our ancestors were crushing the seeds of wild wheat, mixing it with water and cooking it over fire long before agriculture emerged. Obviously this produced some very strange shapes because—depending on climate and temperature among other things—the way the dough swelled naturally would always be different.

For the grissino, on the other hand, we have an exact year of birth—1679. We also have a precise location: the city of Turin, and more specifically Venaria Reale. And the exact name of the inventor, Antonio Brunero.

Four centuries ago, in the absence of the medicine we have today, people relied a lot on nutrition. It was more or less what we now call nutritional medicine, treating people by prescribing foods to avoid and others to favor. If the patient was someone of importance, the best doctors would be called, and they were well versed in the effects of different foods on human health. In Piedmont there was nobody more important than the Duke of Savoy, who lived in the vast Venaria castle and acted as (quasi-) king.

In 1679 the Savoy duchy was vacant: Carlo Emanuele II had died four years earlier and his son, Vittorio Amedeo II, was only thirteen. The little boy grew up in the care of his mother, Maria Giovanna Battista of Savoy-Nemours, a brilliant Frenchwoman who acted as regent until her son was of an age to ascend the throne. But there was a major difficulty: Vittorio Amedeo was unwell, with significant digestive problems manifesting as excruciating stomach pains. It didn't take long for the excellent court physician, Teobaldo Pecchio, to realize that the little prince's problem was bread: Vittorio Amedeo was not digesting leavened bread.

At the time it wasn't a rare phenomenon; bread in general was not well cooked and the wretched yeast would continue fermenting in the stomach, especially in children, causing cramps and problems right through the digestive system.

Dr. Pecchio first tried giving him just the crust of the bread and found he was perfectly fine with it.

At that point he brought in the court baker, a first-rate breadmaker and pastry cook named Antonio Brunero. The challenge put to him was simple to explain but difficult to meet: the doctor wanted a *ghersa* (the Piedmontese name at that time for a loaf of bread) with lots of crust and little or no soft center. Antonio went back to his kitchen and started experimenting. The future of the realm was at stake: he absolutely had to find a solution. So you see how the grissino was invented. Pure breadmaking art and plenty of imagination and manual skill, for a cause that had nothing to do with good food, but with healing. Coming up with a name wasn't hard: *ghersin* is the diminutive of *ghersa*, and it's what grissini are called in Piedmontese dialect to this day.

The grissino turned out to be the right medicine for the future King Vittorio Amedeo II and he quickly recovered. Surprisingly, the rest of the diners at court also liked the well-cooked breadsticks with no soft center. Within a short time everyone wanted them on the table and Antonio Brunero had to keep turning out more and more of them.

The grissino's popularity spread first among the nobility, and then gradually to middle-class families as well. Other bakers in Turin and throughout Piedmont started making them, copying the technique the court baker had developed as he invented them: rolling the dough between his hands until it became a thin stick about forty centimeters long.

The Piedmontese called them *robatà* (which means "fallen" in their dialect, but also "rolled"), because of the technique of rolling them between the hands. This also gave them their distinctive knotty appearance. Soon they were popular throughout Piedmont, and a town near Turin called Chieri became so specialized in the art of making them that the *ghersin robatà* became the food symbol of that community, and still is.

But soon another technique was perfected, known as *stiratura* or stretching. Instead of rolling, the dough would be lengthened by stretching the edges and opening out the arms. The result was even more brittle and was a great success.

Stories and legends about the deliciousness of grissini have helped turn them into an icon. King Carlo Felice was crazy about them and would apparently munch and crunch so noisily through entire performances at the Teatro Reggio that it disrupted the show. Napoleon Bonaparte insisted on a weekly transport service between Turin and Paris so he would always have fresh grissini, which he called "the little sticks of Turin." The city's major bakeries were baking them continually, in ever-increasing quantity. It got to the point where they had to get organized, and they created four categories of staff: the *stiror*, the *taior,* the *coureur* and the *gavor*. In this simple assembly line, the first one stretched the dough, the second cut it, the third put the grissini on trays and into the oven, and the fourth took them out when they were ready.

*

I went to Rocchetta Tanaro, a magnificent town in Monferrato of Asti, to talk about grissini with Mario Fongo and his son Giovanni. The Fongos are masters of the grissino. Mario started off as a simple baker and now manages a factory with eighty highly specialized artisan bakers. Grissini, mother-in-law's tongues (a flat biscuit) and various other specialty bread substitutes are made strictly by hand, and the Fongos export them to half the world.

They've been able to make large numbers and at the same time maintain the high quality and respect for the history and tradition of Piedmont, of which the grissino is the most important product. Giovanni is very proud of his father, who has introduced his own interpretation with grissini stretched, hand-processed and in many delicious varieties: classic, corn, whole wheat, without lard, and other specialties. Mario had been one of those kids who know what they want to do from an early age, and he knew he wanted to be a baker. These days the eighty workers, divided between three shifts, produce ten different kinds of grissini to please the palates of the new "Napoleons" of the world.

Their products are artisanal and they are firmly committed to improving packaging and transportation. But the brittleness—in this case an indication of goodness—sometimes means they don't reach their destination in one piece; some will break along the way, but the taste of the artisanal Turin *ghersin* remains the same. Giovanni reveals that it's the hands that make the difference. "For the hand stretching, Oscar, the bakers pull the edges of the dough out to the length of their arms, and this gives the grissini a fragrance and brittleness you can't get with mass processing. Hand-stretched grissini are instantly recognizable ... and they have crunch, taste and a smell that you recognize straight away as authentic."

The list of ingredients the Fongos use is short: flour, water, Italian organic extra virgin olive oil, salt, yeast, and for some varieties lard as well. No preservatives or other additives. The combination of different flours selected in collaboration with trusted millers, whether the type is 0 or 00, whole wheat or cornstarch, gives them a unique taste depending on the mix. The recipe is simple, but the secret is in the preparation. I ask Mario, the man responsible for all this, what that secret is. I'd really love to know how it's done.

"Oscar, you know I'm not good with words, not like my son Giovanni. I'd rather use my hands. You want the recipe for my grissini? I'll give it to you, but don't tell everyone: first the hands, second the hands, third the hands."

Then he says with a chuckle: "Oh, I forgot! You also need a lot of passion for this craft; it's a job that ignores the holidays marked on the calendar!"

And the lovely thing is, you can tell that even after so many years he wouldn't have it any other way.

26

GUINNESS

That fortuitous fire

WITH TEO MUSSO

Teo Musso was the first person in Italy to make unpasteurized artisan beer and sell it all over the country through restaurants and wine bars.

He started twenty-five years ago and found remarkable success pretty much straight away. The business has expanded, and his new Birrificio Agricolo Independente is a gem, providing good production capacity while maintaining the features of the original artisan brewery. These days he sells his beer almost everywhere in the world.

His business, Le Baladin, is actually a farm. He grows his own barley and Italian hops, so his bottles come out of a supply chain that's totally within his control. Teo has devoted his life to this beverage, whether golden, amber, red or dark ale. He's traveled a lot in the countries where beer-drinking is an integral part of their custom and tradition, including Belgium, Germany, the Netherlands and Ireland. For the Guinness story I instinctively took the road to Piozzo, a lovely little town on the border between the two Langhe regions of Barolo and Mondov to talk with Teo.

*

Teo is a highly intelligent person and it's always a pleasure to sit down with him for a chat—even better if we're talking about beer with a glass of it in front of us.

I get straight to the point because I'm eager to hear about the history of Guinness. Guinness is synonymous with Ireland. It's a dark beer, almost black, with a light creamy foam and an intense flavor. A beer not everyone finds palatable, but the world has fallen in love with it partly thanks to effective marketing through the images and slogans on its iconic posters.

Teo explains that the origin of the dark beer goes back to 1759, when its founder and master brewer, Arthur Guinness, opened his brewery in St James's Gate, Dublin. The building was rented for forty-five pounds a month, an amount that wasn't exactly peanuts in those days, but the incredible thing is that the contract was for nine thousand years. You read that right: ninety centuries. Initially they focused on the bitter styles of beer most popular at the time, and moved on later to making black stouts.

Some say it was serendipitous, whereas others think our master brewer was simply inspired by the existing English (or more specifically London) beers known as porters, which had more hops and a higher percentage of alcohol and were dry and—obviously—dark.

The name "porter" came from the London street and river porters; "stout" is a term that implies tenacity and robustness, but also pride; so porter stout meant a beer that was popular but strong, with an even higher alcohol content than other stouts.

Knowing Musso I can say he's the kind of rational person who tends to steer clear of legends. But the fact is that even in the stories handed down over centuries, and no doubt adapted and revised over time, there's always a grain of truth. When it comes to Guinness, the likelihood that there's some truth behind the story is increased because it involves not one but two cases of serendipity.

"If you visit the St. James's Gate company in Dublin, where Guinness was created and will most likely remain, given the expiry date of the lease, and if you go to the museum there, you'll hear the fascinating story of Arthur Guinness. On the other hand, if you go to London and visit any porter brewery they'll tell you a different one. Naturally the first is more famous, partly because it's the one chosen by the company, which as I said has been strong on storytelling right from the start."

Briefly, it goes like this: a fire in one of Arthur Guinness's warehouses burnt some of the malt that was stored there. He wasn't a fan of waste and certainly wasn't going to throw out his precious barley shoots, so he improvised a batch of beer using the unintentionally roasted malt. The result was so interesting, and so popular with his customers, that he decided the company would specialize in making beers with roasted malt.

That's serendipitous version number one.

Musso is even briefer with story number two: "If you go to London, though, they'll tell you the credit belongs to King Charles II of England, who ordered the brewery to use malt that had been burnt in a fire in the London stores. The beer was to be given free to the port workers, hence the name porter: the river porters' beer."

In 1831 the Guinness brewery became Ireland's largest, and by 1914 it was the biggest in the world. If its record has been overtaken by other producers today it's because the company has decided over the years to stick to its original style of beer and limit its explorations into the "easier" product segments.

Today it sells around two billion pints a year, but the most interesting figure is the number of pints of Guinness consumed in Dublin in a weekend: apparently it can get to ten thousand. I have an image of young and old gathering in the pub on a Friday night, carefree and happy, their glasses always half full and live music echoing around the tables.

The version more familiar to us in Italy has a lower alcohol content of 4.3 percent, but the biggest export is the "strong" version, Foreign Extra, with an alcohol content of 7.5 percent. Currently the group has about fifty factories, and the second market in the world for this beer is

Nigeria, a former British colony and home to the first production site outside of Great Britain.

Teo Musso started serving Guinness in his restaurant, Le Baladin, in the late 1980s. "I still remember the bewildered reaction from my customers (mostly country folk from around Piozzo) when they first tried it. They were curious to sample a "black" beer, but they weren't expecting to taste something so extreme, with notes of roasted coffee and chocolate and at the same time the slightly bitter taste of the hops. On the first sip the uniqueness of the beer overshadowed any unpleasantness, on the second it became seductive, and after that they couldn't do without it.

"This phenomenon has always fascinated and surprised me, and I've thought a lot about it."

And so, when Musso started producing beers himself, he created his Brune stout.

It wasn't easy. "Working on roasted malt and trying to make a great beer out of it without sacrificing our artisan values kept me awake for many a night ... and the number of batches I had to throw out! But while I wanted to meet the needs of my customers, on the other hand I was totally committed to honoring the legend that had fascinated me, or I should say tormented me, for so many years."

The first Baladin stout, the Brune, finally appeared in 1997 and has never been out of production since. It was only served in the pubs in Piozzo to begin with, then later it was introduced into all his restaurants in Italy—on tap, of course.

And that's the point: Brune doesn't come in bottles.

Musso confirms that it can only be served pumped by hand. "It's a mechanical action that avoids the use of gas 'thrust' and it keeps the beer true to its original fresh taste with no added fizz. Sometimes pumping is done with a mixture of nitrogen and carbon dioxide, and that practice is often used in serving Guinness because it adds a minimal amount of gas to the original product and enhances the creaminess and the ease of drinking."

You've got to envy this man for his textbook learning and precision.

I feel I should thank him for marking out a path for so many other Italian breweries.

In the end it matters little to him whether Guinness stout came out of a fire in Dublin, was invented in London, or is simply the result of a commercial decision. "What counts is that thanks to the success of Guinness this style of beer has become popular all over the world. And that it's made so many drinkers happy, who were dumbfounded at the first sip, started licking their mustaches after the second, and on the third sip decided this would always be the beer for them."

27

ICE WINE/EISWEIN

The frosts of the old days

WITH OTTO GEISEL

I'm at Eataly in Munich, nearing the end of one of my frequent fantastic dinners with Otto Geisel.

Otto is considered one of the most knowledgeable wine connoisseurs in Germany, but in reality he knows the wines of the whole world. Apart from family, wine is Otto Geisel's reason for living.

I met him fifteen years ago on a food and wine tour around Spain, and on that trip he helped me get a better understanding of Spanish wine, explaining the differences between an Albariño from Galicia and one from Cantabria, between the various verdejos produced in Valladolid and between the dozens of interpretations of tempranillo in Rioja.

"Smell this wine—it has a whiff of rubber because it's been damaged by the heat. In this part of Rioja if the tempranillo is single-variety it has an aroma of black currants, do you smell that?"

We've never lost contact since that summer, and often we meet in Bavaria or in the Langhe, which he loves. He's third generation in a family of Michelin-starred Bavarian pub owners, and for several years he managed a restaurant. But in the end he decided to sell the business and concentrate on wine journalism and consulting.

Back to that dinner in Munich.

He'd turned up with a mind-blowing supply of wines from his bountiful cellar at home. I can't tell you how many we tasted, but I clearly remember the sublime quality of a few bottles of silvaner, riesling and pinot noir.

We were almost finished when Otto brought out a bottle for a blind tasting. It was completely wrapped in foil so it was impossible to tell the provenance.

"Now tell me what you think of this," he said as he poured me a glass. "Do you like it? Do you know what it is?"

It was marvelous. A very sweet white, but not at all cloying; in fact there was an acidity you never taste in Italian *passiti* or the French *muffati* dessert wines. Simultaneous sweetness and acidity: pure enjoyment. Usually with sweet wines I only drink a drop or two, but I had at least two glasses of this one and would have drunk it during the meal as well.

So what was it?

Otto was clearly proud, and had the answer ready.

"You're drinking Germany's best Eiswein. It's called ice wine because these days Canada is the main producer, but it was made here in Franconia and it should be called by its real name, Eiswein."

The famous ice wine. Actually this wasn't the first time I'd drunk it, but it had never excited me so much, either because previously Otto hadn't been there to explain it or because the producers weren't up to the standard of Horst Sauer, who's been awarded 100/100 in Gault and Millau's wine guide.

I wanted to know more about it.

*

The year in question was 1794 and the town was Würtzburg, the main town in Lower Franconia, 155 miles north of Munich. A splendid area for riesling, silvaner and pinot blanc.

However, in that particular year the frosts had started as early as September and continued through to November. The despairing wine-growers decided to harvest the frozen grape clusters anyway. They had zero hope of making wine from the frozen grapes, but even a little would be better than nothing and so they had a go. The result was indeed meager in quantity, but in terms of quality they discovered an amazing new world. What emerged was a genuine nectar, really sweet, and their customers loved it.

From that year on they waited for the frosts before harvesting.

So ice wine was born, the result of an unforeseeable natural event and the stubbornness of the German farmers.

That's the story handed down from generation to generation, but it's not the only one. There's another small village that claims to be the birth-place of Eiswein: Dromersheim in the Rheinhessen wine region. It's even further north, more than 250 miles from Munich, and in those parts they claim to have made the first ice wine in the winter of 1829–30.

Is one of these stories true? Have they both been exaggerated from one generation to another? We don't know, but the fact remains these pioneers were the trailblazers for ice wine as we drink it today.

Dr. Hans Georg Ambrosi perfected the technique for making it, Otto explains, and today he's known as "the father of Eiswein."

"Hans was the distinguished head of the famous Kloster Eberbach in Rhineland; he started producing this wine and it got better with each 'lucky' harvest, and by lucky I mean frozen. Soon lots of other German winemakers were copying it."

Germany, then, is the legitimate mother of Eiswein, but climate change means it can no longer be made every year. Canada entered the market in the '70s, and there the frosts are guaranteed. Now Canada is the world's main producer of ice wine.

And although Otto prefers the German product, he recognizes that it's no longer possible to make it from every harvest. Suitable climate conditions, short timelines, a complex grape-stomping technique ... this probably explains why Eiswein—the good stuff—is so expensive.

I ask Otto to tell me how it's made.

"Beware, there's an artificial version out there as well where the grape clusters are frozen in the winery with blast chillers, but it's no good—you recognize it at the first sip, as well as from the much lower price. Here in Franconia there are serious producers making so much money you wouldn't believe it! In the meantime they prepare the vineyards with intense pruning so the remaining grapes will stay healthy for as long as possible. Silvaner and riesling varieties are suited to this type of wine because they have a strong and resistant structure. And the grape has to be protected from birds and wild animals as well. From the beginning of October it's important that there aren't any dead or dangling leaves on the grapes, and from mid-November, when there's no more absorption, the last leaves are removed by hand. At that point all they can do is hope the grapes will still be 100 percent healthy at the end of the month. Then they wait for the frost. It takes luck, luck and more luck. You might think the price is high, but in the end it never fully compensates for the effort and the many misfortunes involved in making this wine."

In general all agriculture depends on the vagaries of the weather, but that's especially so with Eiswein.

Otto tells me that in the '80s and '90s the first frosts would arrive between mid-November and late December; now they have to wait until January. They work hard to get to a certain point and then everything depends on the cold. It's a real climate challenge. If all goes well, they have to pick the right night to harvest the grapes: they need one or more starry nights with no clouds. Everything has to be done at speed: picking the grapes, transporting them to the cellar and starting the pressing, and at the same time the grape clusters must be handled with care. They harvest right through until morning, with temperatures around 10 degrees below zero Celsius, about 14 degrees Fahrenheit.

Geisel has testimony from another expert too—Horst Sauer, the greatest German Eiswein oenologist in the business, maker of the wine I'd just blind-tasted, who's had all kinds of adventures with ice wine in his thirty harvests. "My friend Horst told me that in some years they had to stop picking at five o'clock in the morning and go back at eight, when the temperature dropped back to minus 9 degrees [Celsius, 15 degrees Fahrenheit]. Other times they had to call off the harvest at 7 a.m. because the temperature had gone up 4 degrees and they were forced to wait for the next night. Not to mention a few years when there just wasn't any ice at all! Juicing the grapes for this wine requires a lot of patience; the water is trapped in the ice and they only use the concentrated juice in the center of the grape cluster."

I take a last sip of ice wine and instantly feel in my mouth the wonder of this "superb material nature has given us." But nature is not enough: it also takes a lot of hard work in the vineyard, harvesting with your heart pounding and a thermometer in your hand, and pressing with surgical precision, armed with patience and an acute sense of touch. So much "stuff" to get a small amount of wine. But it's a sublime wine. Or perhaps unbelievable is a better description, and that's the word Otto uses.

I'll never again be tempted to say true Eiswein is expensive. True Eiswein is simply a wonder, and worthy of its price tag.

28

RUSSIAN SALAD

Sometimes things return

WITH CARLO CRACCO

The mystery, or rather mysteries, surrounding the origin of Russian salad are among the most evocative serendipitous stories connected with food. There are at least four different stories about how this recipe was conceived.

One does actually start in Russia, another in Italy (Piedmont, to be exact), then there's a French one entwined with the story of Catherine de' Medici (who was Italian), and finally a Polish version. There's a whiff of Italy about this last one as well, though, because apparently the woman behind it was Bona Sforza, daughter of the Duke of Milan, who married the Polish King Sigismund I.

Here I'm going to recount the first two. To me they're the most credible, and they might even overlap.

*

If you go to Moscow or St. Petersburg and ask for a Russian salad they'll look at you strangely, because they have no idea what it is. What you need to order if you want something like it is an Olivier salad.

In 1860 the executive chef at the Grand Hotel Hermitage in Moscow, a Frenchman named Lucien Olivier, devised a salad of cold cooked vegetables and mayonnaise. But they were ostentatious times in the empire of the czars, and he presented it dressed up with partridges, river prawns and truffles. It was met with instant approval and became a huge success. But during the revolution of 1917 the Hermitage was occupied, and when the hotel restaurant came back into operation it offered an impoverished Olivier's salad, in keeping with the new standards. In place of the sumptuous ingredients there was an even bigger proportion of potatoes and carrots, both widely available in Russia. And that's the Olivier salad still served today in many of Moscow's restaurants.

Curiously, a few years earlier in Piedmont, an important Russian delegation, apparently including the czar himself, visited the Savoys and they put on a luxurious banquet in the Royal Castle of Racconigi.

At the time a salad known as *insalata rusa* or red salad (because of the beet in it) was quite popular. Some people say cream was used to bind the cooked vegetables, but most believe it was French-style mayonnaise. In any case *insalata rusa* was on the menu for the gala dinner. At the last minute the head chef at Racconigi decided to personalize it for the illustrious guests by replacing the beet with the vegetables most common in Russia—potatoes, carrots and peas. When it came to naming the new dish, he simply added another "s" to the original name so it became *insalata russa*, Russian salad. The story goes that the czar was so enthusiastic about it that he asked for the recipe to take home. I wonder if it got back to Lucien Olivier.

I had a conversation about it with Carlo Cracco, a man who's had a special relationship with this dish. He tends to go for the Piedmontese legend, but as we've said before the history of any dish includes multiple versions and there might be a bit of truth in every one of them.

"The fact is that as the stories pass from one generation to the next they carry new bits with them, and in the end they become legend. But here we do have substantial proof. Pellegrino Artusi devoted an entire chapter to the Russian salad in his 1891 tome *La scienza in cucina e l'arte di mangiar bene (Science in the Kitchen and the Art of Eating Well)*, where he described it as being very Italian. And in his recipe he added anchovies as well."

Cracco's restaurant in the Galleria Vittorio Emanuele II in Milan is a wonderful place. His cooking is rigorous but innovative, and I love it. Exactly what was needed in Italy's most international city. I also respect Carlo: he has courage and he puts in the effort. And he's put a lot of effort in for this salad, which is both cursed and blessed.

"My history with this dish started as soon as I began cooking, I mean when I went to catering school as a boy and did my work experience in a restaurant. I was catapulted into a world where the food was a far cry from what we cooked at home and everything I was used to. This was in the late '70s, early '80s, the golden years for capricciosa salad and champagne risotto, penne with vodka and salmon or prosciutto and cream and peas, and lots of other rich, high-calorie dishes. Russian salad was possibly one of the most significant dishes in that time of prosperity and sumptuous dining: a cold antipasto of mixed vegetables and mayonnaise more focused on filling the mouth than sharpening the senses. I think my relationship with it has always alternated between highs and lows."

The Russian salad had been a passion of Carlo's, a treat he couldn't resist, since he was a small boy. But with his work in the restaurant, things got complicated. Russian salad was in high demand, so they made it in large quantities to ensure it was always ready to be served. One of the first tasks assigned to him was preparing the vegetables, which had to be washed, cut, cooked to the highest standard and then cooled.

Carlo tells me he still remembers those exhausting afternoons side by side with his workmates, coming to grips with the preparations for Russian salad. "The hours were never-ending. For me it was a penitence; the responsibility was stressful because every time you had to do kilos and kilos of ingredients—potatoes, carrots, beans and peas. And if something didn't go right, say for instance the cooking went on a bit too long, I had to throw it all out and start again from scratch. Then it was panic stations. Apart from anything else it was a paradoxical situation, because the more I slaved away at the Russian salad, the more we had available for table service, but the more we had, the better the waiters had to be at selling it because after a few days it wouldn't be any good. I was so relieved when I didn't have to do it anymore that work almost felt like a holiday!"

For quite a while the salad virtually disappeared from his life. He went to work with Gualtiero Marchesi and found it was not on the menu. At first that surprised him, but it wasn't long before he realized that the innovative Marchesi had given Russian salad a red card. So goodbye mayonnaise, potatoes and cooked greens.

But sometimes things come back. In the early 2000s, Russian salad came back into Carlo's life in an unexpected manner. "You see, Oscar, the truth is it never disappeared. People went on happily buying it, and in fact at the Peck deli, the most important food store in Milan, they made huge quantities of it every week. Partly as a joke and partly from the temptation to bet on what seemed to be an indestructible dish, Mario Stoppani threw us a challenge. He was the owner of Peck's and my partner in the restaurant I'd just opened. 'You're such a clever bunch,' he said, 'can you make a Russian salad as good as ours?'"

Carlo and his right-hand man at the time, Matteo Baronetto, got to work. He tells me their chief dilemma was how to reinterpret the dish. Clearly it wouldn't be enough to simply change the ingredients or make the salad lighter. Cracco felt they needed to be daring and push further. He had to create a Russian salad in keeping with his idea of cooking, but where would it fit? And how could he serve it?

At the time, in the wake of the food revolution driven by Ferran Adrià, the spotlight in cooking was on research combined with ingredients and textures. Enlightenment came in the form of one ingredient: an interesting product called isomalt, used in the confectionery industry as a sweetener for hard candy.

"It took about six months to find the right fit," Carlo tells me, "but our starting point was the sweetness of isomalt. It was the trampoline we needed to give our recipe a twist and present it as a gourmet response to Peck's challenge."

So the caramelized Russian salad saw the light of day in 2004, presented as one serve of the salad sealed between two thin isomalt wafers heated with the chef's torch to create a solid but light envelope that would break when you sank your teeth into it.

This gives a good result on two levels, Cracco explains, and the first is flavor. The sugar content of the exterior balances the buttery mouthfeel and tanginess of the interior, but it also works from a tactile perspective, with the crunchiness of the isomalt seal acting as a counterbalance to the softness of the sauce and vegetables.

You'll be wondering how the bet ended up. According to the incontestable judgment of someone who has eaten both, the challenge was met.

Carlo smiles. "Obviously I'm biased, but at the end of this journey we did in fact manage to create a Russian salad as good as Peck's. And Mario Stoppani's answer was: "You've done so well, now you'll have to go on making Russian salad!' So we've come full circle."

Carlo went back to what he was doing at the beginning of his career. But in between there were years of studying, experience and experimenting that make "his" Russian salad a great dish, a signature dish that appeared on his menu fifteen years ago and has stayed there.

"It's still Russian salad, but it's different. It's just the dish that's been with me for a good part of my history, and it has managed to unite past and present by reappearing as a classic while also looking to the future."

29

MARSALA

A marvelous victim

WITH RENATO DE BARTOLI

Marsala is an extraordinary wine that doesn't get the recognition it deserves. Have a look at the menus in good restaurants and you'll find port and Madeira and *passito* wines, but often no trace of Marsala.

Even the producers of Marsala over the years (though certainly not all of them) have mistreated it with different variations and flavorings, and often misrepresented it by focusing on a marketing strategy aiming for the highest price.

And yet there are a few sensational Marsalas, every bit as good as certain high-end international fortified wines. One is Marco De Bartoli's, so when I needed to talk about Marsala I remembered my chats with his son Renato. He's a true Sicilian and loves his native land but, as he says, the English fell in love with it before he did.

"Sunburnt country, white-sand dunes, crystal-clear sea with glints of emerald, a Moorish look about it, and massive city walls"—this is how the British described Marsala in the late eighteenth century. It's said that the English merchant John Woodhouse landed at Marsala by chance after a storm, took refuge in a tavern and drank a local wine he found very similar to the already well-known Spanish wines, Madeira, sherry and port.

So began a case of serendipity due to a storm in 1773. But Renato says I should be wary of the romantic legend because the English, who were skilled traders, had already had interests in western Sicily for some time. They were involved with soda ash or barilla and with sumac, a shrub grown over an area of about eighteen thousand hectares at the time and used as a citrussy spice and for tanning leathers. "And let's not forget their big trade in sulfur extracted from the mines in Sicily. Trust me, the people who started one of last century's most flourishing wine industries weren't exactly inexperienced, and they were quick to see the possibilities of the land around Marsala. There was a clear similarity with the Cadiz, Madeira and Jerez areas, all at the same north latitude on the 'sunshine strip.' What's more, the English noticed that the sandy limestone soil, the climate and the nature of the grape varieties, all taken together, would generate markedly alcoholic wines almost like liqueurs, as they still do."

And Renato is very familiar with the story of the trade coming out of that.

"Woodhouse knew how to profit from all these circumstances and began exporting the wines as Madeira imitations in 1773, when the first shipment set off for Liverpool. In 1796 he moved permanently to Marsala and transformed the tuna fishery just outside the town walls into a fortified courtyard, or bailey, for the making of this much-celebrated wine. To help it withstand the long voyage it was immediately fortified with an additional 2 percent of alcohol; that's exactly two gallons for each pipa, the typical cask for transporting 412 liters of Marsala.

"Then in 1800 a great boost to Woodhouse's business came from Admiral Lord Nelson, duke of Bronte. He wanted five hundred casks of a variety of the wine that he had personally chosen for His Majesty's fleet, which he christened Bronte Madeira. As time went on all the white wine made in Marsala was identified as Sicily Madeira, or simply Sicily. Meanwhile, in 1806 another Englishman had come to Marsala from

Yorkshire, attracted by the new wine growing frontier. This was Benjamin Ingham, and in 1812 he created a second bailey about a mile from
Woodhouse's on the same coastline."

But as De Bartoli explains, the two Brits had very different approaches.

Woodhouse is credited with identifying a need to remedy the
shortage of wines from the Iberian Peninsula, while Ingham is recognized as the first innovator of a production system focusing on quality;
he produced a book of guidelines, and that generated a big boost for
related businesses as well. In fact, he created the first business network
in the history of wine, introducing the idea of commissioning agents
and distributors initially in the United States, starting with Boston,
and expanding later to other large cities. While Woodhouse concentrated mainly on the European market of the Austro-Hungarian
Empire and the United Kingdom, Ingham looked to the other side of
the Atlantic.

There's an obvious question at this point.

"When do you Sicilians come onto the scene, then?"

"In the mid-1800s. The first major step toward liberation from the
Iberian wines came when a Calabrian named Vincenzo Florio arrived in
Marsala and started a new bailey right between the two English giants."

The Florios came from very different areas of activity but were all
highly successful: they owned the Favignana tuna fishery, where canned
tuna was actually invented, and were also involved in trading spices and
sulfur courtesy of a fleet of ninety-nine ships connecting the whole of
the Kingdom of Italy.

"So why not be content with that?"

"Because Vincenzo liked Marsala, in fact he loved it," Renato continues, "and in less than twenty years he established himself as a winemaker
as well. He was probably the first to call the wine Marsala. In the second
half of the nineteenth century the Marsala locals started stepping up
as well, creating what was for the time a huge wine-producing region:
about 250 companies spread over the entire Marsala countryside were
producing wine or grapes to contribute. At least sixty of them specialized

in Marsala, and all the activity around that spawned a substantial number of allied industries."

But the rationale of the market is merciless, and like every medallion this one had its flipside. Instead of presenting a common front to safeguard prices and quality, the local producers started a fierce rivalry among themselves. As a consequence the lowering of prices, which was intended to boost sales, instead dragged the entire Marsala industry into crisis by the beginning of the twentieth century. It proved irreversible in the following decades, and within a century the system had collapsed.

De Bartoli spells out the details: "Marsala reached its peak in 1898 with a million and a half hectoliters, an enormous number for the production facilities of the time. Marsala and its neighboring regions couldn't satisfy the demand, and so other towns were drawn in: Partinico, Castelvetrano, Campobello di Mazara, stretching as far as Alcamo and even a few areas around Etna. That record was followed by a slow but inexorable decline, and by the 1950s production was down to 700–800 thousand hectoliters. But the downhill slide hadn't yet done significant damage and Marsala was still a region with a strong economy. These days there are fewer than ten companies in total, producing a maximum of seventy thousand hectoliters."

I nod to show I know what he's talking about. "The figures aren't all that bad, but the problem is the way it's made, don't you think?"

"For me, the most tragic thing is that about 90 percent is ersatz Marsala, used in cooking to add flavor to chicken and red meats, or in the food canning industry. A Marsala like that doesn't have the identity and organoleptic characteristics that represent the winemaking values of the area. Most importantly, this ersatz version generates spin-offs that can't feed the generational turnover and investments in aging that represent the true wealth of Marsala."

I ask him to explain further which grape varieties can be used, and he says there are several. Catarratto and inzolia grapes are documented as far back as the late eighteenth century, but in reality there were other varieties that have since disappeared, including the white grapes guarnaccia, greco, malvasia and damaschino.

Some red grapes were used as well, such as the pignatello, nerello and calabrese still used today for Ruby Marsala.

Early in the twentieth century the grillo grape came onto the scene. It emerged in the post-phylloxera period from a cross between catarratto and zibibbo grapes, and was designed specifically to improve Marsala. Renato reveals that the Vecchio Samperi that I like so much (a nonfortified wine aged by the perpetuum method) is made with 100 percent grillo grapes. These ideal and very versatile grapes are picked at a level of ripeness to generate wines ranging from straw-colored to amber. They're naturally high in alcohol (around 15 to 17 percent), particularly tangy, dry, and have great structure. But the specifications cover many variations, including fortification with added alcohol. That's one reason why, over time, there's been so much confusion.

Anyone tasting a Vecchio Samperi would realize at the first sip that a Marsala that's made well, naturally, and aged at length is not to be turned down. However, even a producer like De Bartoli has to criticize the way much of the Marsala is made today.

"I think over time there's been a lot of confusion created around both production and identity. From the very beginning, the English started making Marsala with the deliberate intention of imitating Madeira on the cheap. After that the natives of Marsala copied the English, not knowing they were making a substitute where the only difference is the fortification. In the '70s my father, whose grandfathers were both industrialists in Marsala, realized it was time to end the unscrupulous cheap production and started his own business. He established Marco De Bartoli in 1978 and put in place what we might call a 'French' model that recognizes the importance of the vineyard (in the sense of cru or terroir) and the grape variety. He set about promoting the value of the wines from the traditional districts. Perpetuo, for example, is naturally alcoholic and therefore not fortified (and so can't claim to be Marsala DOC), and he named it Vecchio Samperi, the name of the district; it was the only Marsala wine before the English invasion, and proof that this was the ideal terrain.

"In my view, this is the only possible path to finally breaking free of being 'children of a lesser god,'" Renato concludes. "We need to redeem the values of our land. Let me end on an optimistic note: it will take a while yet, but you'll see that the young people of Marsala will eventually get there."

30

NEGRONI SBAGLIATO
Liquid anthropology

WITH DAVIDE PINTO

In many cocktail bars, the *negroni sbagliato* is ordered more often than the original negroni. It's simply a negroni with the gin replaced by sparkling wine—Metodo Classico if possible. It wasn't an invention, but rather the result of a huge mistake.

I've chosen Turin's "Cocktail Man" Davide Pinto, to talk about it. He owns two bars: the main one, Affini, is in the San Salvario neighborhood, and it's become a reference point in Piedmont for the art of mixing cocktails, although his preferred description is "a cultural stronghold of distilling."

Davide is likable, cultivated and eccentric, exactly what we'd call in Piedmontese a *gabilò*—an intelligent and enterprising madman.

To introduce the *negroni sbagliato* he starts in Turin, and you'll see why.

"It's 1861 and we're in Turin, the first capital of Italy. Vermouth is the basic component of the classic Turin aperitif in general, and at the royal household in particular. In 1865 the capital is moved to Florence, so vermouth spreads outside Piedmont and becomes the basic ingredient for the first mixed drinks. Its cultural context is mind-blowing: it would change the spirit of the twentieth century and set the criteria for the new figure of the consumer in the second half of the century—someone more prepared to accept a change that makes each individual experience unique." That's how Davide is—he sees the origins of history in cocktail-mixing. It's all down to a few moments in time, which he summarizes for me in four points.

First, the early 1900s: Captain Federico Caprilli was just out of the Pinerolo Cavalry Academy when he changed the way of mounting a horse. He thus modernized Italy's cavalry and made it one of the most important in the world.

Second, 1917–1920: Count Negroni and a barman named Fosco Scarselli at the Caffé Casoni in Florence are responsible for a major revolution, sparked by "the common tendency of experimenters to make mistakes." The Count wanted to come up with an exclusive drink, so he asked his trusted barman to strengthen his Americano by adding something he had gleaned from his travels. What did Scarselli add? Gin—unsweetened gin to be exact. And the negroni was born.

Third, 1930: Harry's Bar opens at the Cipriani in Venice, and here for the first time we meet the characters involved in the fateful error. Among the staff starting work at Harry's are two fellows named Mirko Stocchetto and Renato Hausammann, both keen to dive in and try something new.

Fourth, 1956. The Winter Olympics in Cortina d'Ampezzo represent a moment of cultural change that would leave its mark on future generations. The main characters in our story, Stocchetto and Hausammann, found themselves working together again in Cortina's famous Hotel de la Poste and made the most of the international atmosphere to further enrich their experience. Stocchetto, in particular, showed great foresight with his decision to take his new profession in the art of mixing to Milan, where this special alchemy was not yet known.

Davide is ready to cut to the chase.

"It's an ordinary evening in the roaring Milan of the '60s—1967 to be precise—at Bar Basso in Via Plinio. At the bar there's a speedy turnover of both orders and customers. We can imagine Stocchetto and his staff managing *la botta* (that's jargon for a spike in orders to be dispatched). The place is packed, as it is every night. Stocchetto knows very well what's needed to run a bar in Milan: quality ingredients and international flair. It wasn't uncommon to bump into someone like Frank Sinatra, Liz Taylor, Ava Gardner, Ernest Hemingway or Sandro Pertini at the bar. There's a famous photo of Pertini leaving the bar in 1981, when he was president of the Italian Republic. On the night in question, one of the bar staff reached for a bottle of gin to finish a negroni but in the chaos and confusion grabbed a sparkling wine instead. Thus the gin in the cocktail was replaced by bubbles. Not just any bubbles, mind you: this was one of the best sparkling wines in Italy, the Ferrari Brut Metodo Classico. It's easy to imagine the customer's surprise at what he found in his glass after he'd ordered a classic negroni. He took a sip but didn't complain, perhaps because what he had in the glass was a perfectly balanced drink with a striking taste.

"In any event that was the accidental birth of a cool, refreshing drink with a more restrained alcoholic content and a persistence in the mouth due to the wine. Stocchetto, who as we know was a man with a fantastic nose for business, quickly decided to add the 'wrong' version of the negroni to the cocktails list. For many years it remained just a local drink, typical of the Basso where it was—and still is—served without jiggers or measures, with a few ice cubes and a slice of orange. The worldwide success of the *negroni sbagliato* came years later, directly linked to the growing popularity of cocktails. Today, you'll find the 'wrong' version, as well as the classic negroni, in bars all over the world."

But Davide goes well beyond reflecting on a single drink. "Maybe without the Stocchetto mistake we wouldn't have the courage to make the more modern mistakes (in this case deliberate) that we call 'twists.'"

He tells me about another lucky mistake made at his bar, Affini. "After years of mixing the negroni without wine, my head barman, Michele, and I thought we'd replace the bubbles Mirko Stocchetto used with a white wine from the countryside around Turin. One night our second barman, Loris, made a mistake and used the Freisa di Chieri sparkling red instead of white wine and got a burst of color and bubbles he wasn't expecting. We decided to include this version on the menu, and the house Americano *sbagliato* is still one of our signature drinks. And it's not only popular in Turin; it has found its way to the Manzo restaurant in New York as well."

There's a reason why Davide is talking to me about history, mixing and causal relationships. He has a degree in social anthropology and his thesis was about migration flows. He gave a talk in New York titled "More than a drink. A course in liquid anthropology." So I throw him a challenge: "You've got ninety seconds to explain to me what cocktails have to do with anthropology."

"I like to call myself an anthropologist on loan to mixology. My studies at university led me to approach mixology and the market from a cultural and social perspective. When I'm telling the story of Italian liquors I present it as an example of liquid anthropology, in the sense that human history and evolution are always the result of contaminations, contact and inclusion. Take vermouth, for example. It's a product of Turin with a German name, using local and international botanicals, and it has ended up in the hands of American bartenders who are prepared to accept its differences and use them to create new things. Modern mixology grew out of the meeting of Turin vermouth and American malts, in an environment that generated many of the world's greatest drinks, including the Manhattan and the Martinez. The good things in life always come from inclusion and respect for differences, but you know that of course. Now, as I've got thirty seconds left I'll give you Mirko Stocchetto's original *negroni sbagliato* recipe."

INGREDIENTS:

1 part Brut Metodo
    Classico spumante
1 part Turin red vermouth

1 part Campari bitter
orange slice for serving

METHOD:

1   Place the ingredients in a cocktail glass or short tumbler
    filled with ice.

2   Mix well with a bar spoon and garnish with the orange slice.

Hallelujah for liquid anthropology!

31

NUTELLA

An optimistic product

WITH GIOVANNI FERRERO

Giovanni Ferrero runs what might be the finest confectionery business in the world, the Ferrero Group, makers of Nutella, Tic Tac, Kinder and Ferrero Rocher. He lost his brother, Pietro, in 2011 from a heart attack, and four years later his father, the great Michele, died at the age of eighty-nine. Now it's up to Giovanni to decide Ferrero's future strategy, and judging by the figures he's doing very well. He's surrounded by excellent directors and assisted by tens of thousands of workers who revere the Ferrero family, and with good reason. I go straight to him to find out how Nutella came about.

"If we really want to ask ourselves that question we realize that history requires us to go a lot further back than April 1964, the date it was invented. Thanks to serendipity, Nutella's roots lie in a Napoleonic edict of 1800."

He briefly outlines what happened: once Napoleon had conquered Europe he banned ships flying non-French flags (they were mainly English) from carrying foodstuffs to Mediterranean ports. Cocoa had a tax slapped on it and there was no more to be found, just when people were discovering—especially in aristocratic and middle-class salons— that it made a very pleasant drink. Then in the post-war hunger years, the master pastry cooks in the poor Piedmont region started looking for a recipe that would be just as delicious, with a thin film of chocolate, but most importantly something else that could substitute for the chocolate.

"It's ironic," Giovanni remarks, "that now the French consume Nutella as if it were going out of fashion, when back then it was their General who wouldn't let chocolate into the country."

"The Piedmontese concentrated their efforts on the hazelnut, right?" I ask.

Perhaps if Napoleon hadn't issued that edict, the hazelnut would not have been so popular. Until that time the Langhe, the Italian region known forever for its excellent grapevines and truffles, had kept the huge potential of the hazelnut under wraps. Top-quality fragrant and tasty hazelnuts were growing there in substantial quantities, but nobody imagined they could generate a story that still has relevance today—the story of Ferrero.

Giovanni proceeds to tell it.

"My grandfather Pietro was an entrepreneur from Alba with the eye and the acumen of a visionary. In 1946 he saw that the hazelnut might be the key to creating 'cheap' new chocolate products. I can still see myself at Via Rattazzi no. 8 in that laboratory filled with positive energy and magic, intent on watching my grandfather trying out new creations, focused and meticulous in his white chemist's coat. His genius was in sowing the shoots of trees that were destined to last for centuries. That's how *gianduia* paste or Giandujot came about—a hard block made up of cocoa, sugar and hazelnuts from the surrounding hills. My grandfather called it the *pastone*, the mash. It was the forerunner of Nutella, its ancestor from about seventy years ago. It came wrapped in straw paper, the yellowish paper used in drugstores in those days, and you had to slice it like salami. It had a unique taste and creamy texture and the price was fair.

"But this was just the beginning; less than a year later, in 1947, the name was changed to Cremino and the product became a single-portion pack of *gianduia* paste at the reasonable price of five liras. It was an intelligent solution: they wanted to offer people an excellent, affordable product."

Supercrema arrived two years later in 1949. Giovanni's grandfather Pietro had died a few months before at the age of fifty-one and it was up to his grandmother Piera, his uncle Giovanni and his father, Michele, who was just twenty-four, to launch the new invention.

It was presented in the stores as a high-quality product that would appeal to Italy's best housewives. Giovanni still proudly recalls the target of their invention: "Signora Valeria" the classic wife and mother who played an active role in the family and felt it her responsibility to choose a product that was good for all of them. Delicious, natural, authentic, nourishing, but above all one that wouldn't break the budget; it came in a reusable glass as well. The Ferreros had understood consumer needs perfectly, and along with their great product they launched a marketing campaign that was simple but spot-on.

"Now Giovanni, do you mind explaining how the Giandujot for slicing became a spread? Was it serendipity?"

"It might be more accurate to talk about opportunities, guided by an enlightened pragmatism and the ingenuity of an innovative businessman. Serendipity can have a place in the search for perfection, where important 'discoveries' happen not while you're looking for something else, but when intelligence and an instinct for innovation turn what looks like a defect into an opportunity and create that need even before it's perceived by the customer.

"The simple, spreadable Giandujot was invented by adding new ingredients, varying the quantities, tasting innumerable formulations and every day giving substance to the saying, 'We learn by our mistakes.' That's how our spread remains unique, still a star in its own right fifty years after it first appeared."

There's a story his father used to tell. Back in 1949, when he visited the bakeries and grocery stores in Asti, he would see his blocks of Giandujot going soft on the counters. At first he was unhappy and saw it as a problem, but as he continued doing the rounds of the grocery stores, inspiration struck. The "structural defect" that caused the block to start melting at room temperature led to the creation of a new product, a new interpretation of a need and a new form of consumption.

Giovanni continues: "That triggered a journey in pursuit of perfection leading to the launch of Nutella by Michele Ferrero in 1964, fifteen years later." The "nuttiness" of the hazelnut combined with "creaminess." Genius!

"The obsessive hunt for perfection is what inspires our innovative and ambitious approach to our business, even as we face the challenges of today.

"At Ferrero, our values are closely tied to the fact that we're a family business, committed from the get-go to looking after the consumer with authenticity and integrity."

Their approach has been handed down from one generation to the next, "perfectly in tune with the new cohort of millennial employees," as Giovanni says. "Young people expect cohesion between the company's values and their own, and they want to use their talents in a business that has the ability to act and grow in a fair and sustainable way."

Like his father before him, he has the well-being of his coworkers at heart. I still remember those buses painted the color of hazelnuts that used to ferry Ferrero's staff to and from work free of charge. In my mind I still see them tootling along the narrow streets of the most remote villages in the Langhe. That somehow symbolizes the recipe they feel they must remain faithful to—respecting people's skills and doing their utmost to provide them the opportunity to apply those skills to the best of their ability. It's each person's individual skills that have made it possible to bring to life some history-making products, from Nutella through to their newest creations.

"We 'Ferrerans' have a mission: to create unique and memorable consumer experiences, leveraging our passion for research and our position as entrepreneurs who can challenge preexisting paradigms without losing sight of our strong connection to people and the area where we operate. I like to remember that for us, tradition and all the values it involves are represented metaphorically by a bow: the more the string is pulled the further we can shoot the arrows of modernity and innovation."

At this point I think we're finished. But one last question comes to mind, and it's about their marketing strategy. Because it's so captivatingly simple it is effectively the antithesis of a model in the landscape of today's businesses. Yet it works, and some Ferrero products have defeated classic expectations of the life cycle of commercial products to become eternal and ageless. What does Giovanni think about this? Absolutely true, but something that hadn't occurred to him.

"I think the answer is in the deep roots of our products and their value as archetypes. We create responses to universal and everlasting needs of the human condition. If Nutella has something extra it's that universal human truth. Let me explain myself better: Nutella is not only the most delicious breakfast spread there is, but also part of the emotional phase preceding breakfast, the ritual of waking that marks the passage from the night aspect of our psyche to the day aspect, the critical time when we want more 'cocooning' and as much comfort food as possible. Metaphorically speaking, the powerful taste of Nutella is that affectionate embrace."

"So Nutella is an optimistic product?" I suggest.

"Well yes," Giovanni replies, "because optimism is what makes a positive difference in our lives, or generates it. And that's exactly Nutella's 'universal truth for all.'"

32

THE PANETTONE
Toni's bread

WITH ALBERTO BALOCCO

To understand the story of the panettone we need to take ourselves back to late-fifteenth-century Milan, in the transition period between the Late Middle Ages and the Renaissance. Milan, Rome and especially Florence were centerstage. At that time Milan was the wealthiest and most important city in Europe. It was a coveted destination for artists and financiers from all over the continent, and was ruled by the Sforza family, in particular Ludovico Maria Sforza, known as Il Moro, who was reigning as regent. He'd recently become a duke, at last.

This was the kind of man who loved to organize memorable banquets and grand events for his guests. It was at one of these, Christmas dinner to be precise, that the panettone was invented—by accident, of course.

Ludovico Il Moro liked to surround himself with great artists and architects; he wanted to make Milan an even more beautiful city with new buildings, churches and frescoes, and he had a plan to improve the network of canals people used to get around the city. For this he called on Leonardo da Vinci, and also used the brilliant architectural plans by Bramante.

What those two managed to do with Santa Maria delle Grazie is worth noting. Bramante finished Solari's earlier design, changing it radically in the process, and came up with a new tribune and the grandiose dome. Da Vinci painted what might be considered the greatest masterpiece in the history of humanity on the northern wall of the refectory. But we shouldn't forget Montorfano, by all accounts an excellent painter but an unlucky one, because the duke chose the southern wall of the refectory for him to paint his wonderful *Crucifixion*, directly facing Leonardo's *Last Supper*.

Back to that grand Christmas dinner arranged by Ludovico. Most likely the artists were there as well as nobles, financiers and families who mattered. I picture Leonardo with his contraptions—those machines he invented to astonish everyone with magic tricks and liven up the duke's sumptuous banquets. Meanwhile in the kitchen, the best cooks to be found in the area were at work and the dishes were numerous and rich: game, fish, vegetables and heaps of cakes and desserts. The head chef personally placed the main dessert in the oven, and because all his cooks were busy putting the finishing touches to other dishes, he asked a scullery boy to check it and take it out when it was ready. The scullery boy was called Toni, the Milanese diminutive of Antonio.

*

Now it's time to hand over to Alberto Balocco to finish the story. In my view Alberto is one of the leading connoisseurs of the panettone today. I've chosen him because when he talks about the panettone his enthusiasm is infectious. "I'll get to that shortly, dear Oscar. But first let me tell you in a few words about a much earlier case of serendipity, because without it we wouldn't be able to make our Christmas specialty, and it's leavening. We're told that in ancient Egypt someone left a piece of dough for unleavened bread out in the sun and it started to ferment and swell. The Egyptians tried cooking it, and lo and behold, they got a lighter, more fragrant and better bread. There you have it!

The first bread leavened with the starter."

I know there are many legends around the birth of the panettone, but this is not only the most famous—its etymology also makes it the most credible. Alberto tells me that Toni, the young scullery boy, really wanted to become a cook, and that day, during preparations for the banquet, he'd been working on a new mixture of flour, butter, egg, citrus peel and raisins.

He did it partly as an experiment, but also because with the approach of Christmas the poor were allowed to make a special bread with wheat flour, which normally only wealthy families could afford. There was no shortage of ingredients in that magnificent kitchen, and since they were there he put lots of them into his mixture. He took some of it home to cook the following day for his parents, so the story goes, and gave some to the other scullery boys working with him. But let's go back to Toni in front of the wood fire, busy checking the progress of the dessert as the master chef had ordered.

"Probably he fell asleep!" Alberto continues. "Or perhaps he was just distracted. A strong smell of burning spread through the kitchen and the cake was ruined. Toni was in despair, and the chef was beside himself with rage.

"Then the scullery boy had an idea. He showed the chefs his mixture and offered it as an alternative to the burnt cake. There was general skepticism: the citrus peel and raisin mixture had risen in the meantime and looked a bit strange. But there was no alternative and no time to make another dessert. The chef poked his finger into the mass of dough and raised it to his mouth. It wasn't so bad. They divided it into sections, shaped them into cylinders and thrust them straight into the oven. As soon as they were cooked they were served, still warm. All the diners were enthusiastic and so was the duke. He called the chef to find out about this delectable new dessert. The master chef didn't want to lie and told him the story, calling Toni out of the kitchen to present him to the noble audience. Imagine the embarrassment of the boy from Milan who a moment earlier was considered a mere scullery boy."

That's how "Toni's bread" or *pan del Toni* was born. The name evolved naturally into *panettone*, but it would be a few centuries before the panettone became Milan's official dessert. Alberto tells me that at the end of the eighteenth century the Cisalpine Republic (the state created by Napoleon in 1797 incorporating the former Duchy of Milan) began singing its praises, promoting the skills of the Milanese artisan bakers, and then in the nineteenth century, under Austrian occupation, the panettone became the ubiquitous symbol of Christmas festivities and began its spread throughout Europe.

The story of the Balocco family started around this time with Alberto's great-grandfather who was coincidentally also named Antonio, and whom everyone called Toni Balocc.

In the mid-nineteenth century Antonio had a grocery store in Narzole, in the Province of Cuneo, and his passion was baking cakes at the back of the shop. "Later it was my grandfather Francesco Antonio's turn (the destiny of the Tonis, it seems): he opened his first pastry shop in Piazza Castello in Fossano, and then another in Via Roma. In 1950 the first factory was set up and my father, Aldo, who'd just turned thirty, decided to focus on a different and original product: a tall panettone like the Milanese one, but with a glaze like the flatter Piedmontese version, covered in toasted almonds and sugar crystals. That's how we created the Mandorlato Balocco. But it's not us I want to talk about. We have to thank Toni, the distracted but brilliant Milanese scullery boy: if not for him, you and I wouldn't be here talking about panettone."

Today, Balocco is the leader in the panettone market with a 19 percent share. In 2018 it produced 27 million items between the panettone, the pandoro and *colombe pasquali*, the dove-shaped yeast cakes made for Easter.

I understand Alberto's modesty, but I'm curious to know what it means to make panettones in provincial Cuneo rather than in Milan. Cuneo is the fourth-largest province in Italy and hence known as *La Granda.*

"We've become '*grandini*' because we're not from Milan, but we've never sacrificed the artisan quality my family started out with. We're still passionate about high-quality ingredients and respecting processing times. It runs in the veins of the people who live in the Granda."

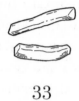

33

CHIPS

Respect for the humble potato

WITH ANTONIA KLUGMANN

In Italy, we use the term *"patatine fritte"* to mean two different things: French fries and potato chips, or crisps. Both versions are now found everywhere and loved by young and old.

I've chosen Antonia Klugmann to chat with about them. Antonia has become more popular than ever after appearing as a judge on the TV program *MasterChef*, but those in the industry have known and admired her since way before that—we're talking about one of the greatest Italian chefs.

After a year in television, Antonia decided to retreat to her Michelin-starred restaurant, L'Argine a Vencò, in the Collio area of Friuli near the Slovenian border. The way she cooks the local produce is amazing, and that includes the potato.

"So, Oscar, let's start with the primary material, which is just an extraordinary tuber you can cook a thousand ways, assuming it comes out of the earth sound and healthy."

Indispensable as they are today, potatoes haven't always been part of the Italian culinary tradition. They were discovered in relatively recent times by the conquistadors near Lake Titicaca, on the border of what are now Bolivia and Peru. More than a hundred wild species can still be found in Italy, and about four hundred varieties are cultivated.

"After they were imported into Europe," Antonia goes on, "they weren't widely used until the eighteenth century, and you know why? Because at first the Spanish tried eating them raw as they'd done with the tomatoes that came from the same area, but of course the taste was horrible. It took them a while to understand that cooking them turned them into a delicacy. It was around the mid-1700s when chips first appeared. Street sellers would often have buckets of boiling lard, and somebody thought of cooking slices of potato in it. Around 1830 these fried potato crisps became very popular—they were mentioned in novels and plays and a few songs. In the same period the thin slices were replaced by longer cuts, so they didn't need to keep stirring the fat to prevent the crisps from sticking together."

But there are two different things: the thin slices (about which cooks are less competitive) and the short cut potato sticks fried as needed. With the second case it was less serendipity and more a contest between two countries, Belgium and France.

As Antonia points out, these two nations have never agreed on who was the first to fry cut-up potatoes: "The Belgians claim there's a 1781 manuscript that makes it quite clear. The Walloons liked to fry the small fish they caught in the river Meuse, but in winter they couldn't because the river iced over. So as a substitute they sliced potatoes the same way as they filleted the fish, and fried them. The French on the other hand trace the birth of fries to Antoine-Augustin Parmentier, who started a big campaign for wider distribution of the potato. Listening to them you'd think it was one big fry-up under the bridges of Paris."

But now let's talk about chips: potatoes finely sliced, fried and packed for fast and informal consumption. A global manufacturing success. We know for certain they originated in the United States.

There's a lovely, serendipitous story attributing their invention to an African American cook named George Crum. "We're in Saratoga

Springs around the middle of the nineteenth century," Antonia explains, "at Moon's Lake House. One day George saw plates of French fries sent back to his kitchen again and again by an unpleasant customer who said they were too thick, not crunchy enough, and tasteless. In a rage, he sliced the potatoes very thin, threw them into the fryer, sprinkled them with copious amounts of salt and ordered the waiter (who was understandably reluctant) to serve them to the disgruntled customer. He was preparing for a brawl when complimentary sounds reached his ears: the customer was thrilled with this new version of potato chips. From that day on George Crum never stopped cooking potatoes that way, and his restaurant became famous for them. Behold the birth of potato chips: pure serendipity.

"In 1920, their popularity went through the roof when Herman Lay, creator of the eponymous company, invented a machine to produce them on an industrial scale. A short time later in Monterey Park, California, Laura Scudder replaced their tube packaging with the little sealed bags that enabled them to stay fresh over time, and above all retain their crunch. 'Laura Scudder's potato chips, the noisiest chips in the world' was her slogan. And then there were ..."

I stop her there. Antonia really does know it all. She tells me the Italian *fritto* has a special place in her memories of childhood. "I used to go and eat at my paternal grandmother Marisa's house after school three times a week, and she'd often make a mixed fry, always varying the ingredients. We called her Nonna Mimma. She was from Ferrara, and she'd moved to Trieste for love. There her cooking incorporated lots of dishes in the Central European tradition, but she still made some of the great classics like fresh pasta and the *fritto*. She'd sometimes use meat and sometimes fish, but there were always potato chips. I never saw a fryer in her kitchen—it was always an iron pot that was never used for anything else."

Now there's only one more thing to find out: how Antonia cooks them.

She said the best French fries they've made at L'Argine a Vencò began with a potato typical of Friuli Venezia Giulia: the village of

Godia in Udine is famous for growing a white-fleshed kennebec potato. She and her team of cooks put a potato on the electric slicer, cut it very finely and fried it after rinsing it under cold running water to remove the starch. "You need to know that the frying changes a lot depending on the degree of ripeness, and we chose a new potato, which has a very different flesh from a riper one. In general, 'old' potatoes are used for gnocchi."

For cooking matchstick potatoes they conducted another experiment, working on the idea of a potato constructed from a puree. "This technique is normally used to make chips commercially, and often other ingredients are added, so it's not the potato in its pure state, as I like it. They use a mold to create the typical shape of a sliced potato. Before, when I was in Venice, I used to serve a dish of calamari with a boiled potato that had been crushed, put into a mold, pressed, dried out and finally fried. The result was a chip very crisp on the outside and very soft and moist on the inside."

Yum. I can already feel it melting in my mouth after the first crunch.

Antonia has genuine respect and admiration for the potato. And the reason, she reveals, is because it's seen as food for the poor that for centuries has fed people who couldn't afford more expensive meals. She has the same respect for all the "poor" foods, but that's not all: she also admires such a simple product that can form the basis for fabulous and important dishes.

The greatness of the great chefs lies in their ability to transform what seem like the most ordinary ingredients into dishes bursting with flavors, and it's why they deserve our respect—even when what we're talking about is only a small potato.

34

THE CHILI
Provoker of unhealthy intentions

WITH SERGIO FESSIA

A while ago I went into Eataly in Milan and came upon an enormous counter filled entirely with chilies. I counted seventy-two different types.

There were crowds looking at it, intrigued by the multi-colored miniature peppers, most gleaming red but some green and a few yellow ones as well. Lots of people were buying them; many were taking photos. One of our saleswomen, attentive and very well informed, was explaining the features of the different varieties and cautioned against touching the two hottest varieties. "Those are so strong," she said, "that just brushing them with your fingers will make your fingertips red hot." But how many varieties of chili are there? And what's the story behind the chili?

I had to talk to Sergio Fessia. That counter full of chilies was his idea, as manager of Eataly's produce sections from the very beginning. We jokingly call him "the jeweler"—Sergio is fanatical about quality, and that doesn't come cheap. For each type of vegetable or fruit, he seeks out the best producer in the most suitable growing region in the country. He knows them all and has been studying them for years. I consider him the most authoritative connoisseur of marvels when it comes to vegetables, and not only Italian vegetables. He is constantly studying, learning and researching. Sergio is a wonderful person and we need lots more like him to get involved in food. My first question to him is why did he create such a large counter with chilies and nothing else?

"Because it's the spice of the poor people that has now taken the fancy of the rich as well. Normally, you know, the opposite happens—it's the dishes of the rich that are passed on to 'the common people' over time. To think the chili was brought to Europe for the nobility and aristocrats, but for some reason they didn't like it! It's an incredible tale."

It all began in Mexico and Peru more than nine thousand years ago. The indigenous populations were already picking wild chilies for various uses, and about five thousand years ago they started growing them. To the Aztecs, the Incas and the Maya, the chili was a sacred plant, so important that it was even used as currency.

Sergio tells me they used it to add flavor to foods and also as a preservative; they recognized its aphrodisiac properties, and they used it as a medicine but also for torture. Imagine all those poor souls forced to swallow huge amounts of very hot chilies! It would surely have killed them.

When Columbus arrived in 1492, he was impressed by the power of the chili: he'd never seen anything like it in nature. The natives called it *axi*, and that's the name he used when he first enthused about it in January 1493.

"Was he the one who took it to Europe?" I ask.

"When he got back to Spain, the chili was one of the first specialties he unloaded from the caravel. The first delivery was to the royal family, complete with a grandiloquent description and a tasting. Word of this rare 'Indian' delicacy spread quickly, and the nobility and the wealthy initially liked it so much that massive hype and speculation built up around it, expeditions to collect it were financed and funds invested in it. There were some who put all their savings into it, and the chili came to represent a dream of huge future profits. At the end of the fifteenth century, Spain was gripped by chili fever."

In effect, the sacredness of the chili was transferred from the cult of the Maya to that of the Spanish financiers, with appropriate adjust-ments. But it didn't take long for the bubble to stretch, Sergio explains, or rather burst. The story goes that some people went bankrupt and there were even suicides. So what was a star in the commercial firma-ment became the financial tomb of unwary investors.

The reason for this was simple: "They soon discovered that if they put a few seeds in any old pot the chilies would grow and flourish. You know, Oscar, it's one of the easiest plants in the world to replicate. Importing it in large quantities was pointless. Later the Church entered into the fray. A Jesuit named José de Acosta first called the chili the 'pro-voker of unhealthy intentions' and other prominent prelates followed. The wealthy class, notoriously sanctimonious at that time, banned chili in their kitchens."

Sergio tells me the rest of the story, beginning with the name: "The original name *axi* was changed to Indian pepper, and its scientific name became capsicum (from the Greek *kapto*, to bite). In Italy it only took on the name *peperoncino*, meaning little pepper, in the twentieth century. During the eighteenth and nineteenth centuries its spread was remark-able. However, it doesn't rate a mention in either of the foundation texts for French and Italian cooking. Brillat-Savarin in *The Physiology of Taste* and Pellegrino Artusi in *Science in the Kitchen and the Art of Eating Well* both ignored it: there's not a single trace of chili in their recipes. That stuff was for the poor. Today there are three thousand varieties of chili, from the unbearably hot to the very sweet. Some great cultivars have been selected in Italy as well. The southerners in particular love it but, like the migrating populations, it too has traveled north. Here in Milan we now have seventy-two types of *peperoncino* and soon that will rise to 120. The customers at Eataly are big fans of my new counter."

So there we have it. Today the chili is found on every continent and is the second most widely used seasoning after sea salt.

*

After all this talk about chilies, tonight I'm going to treat myself to a lovely plate of *spaghetti olio e peperoncino*. I'll cut a fresh medium-hot chili from Battipaglia into very small dice and add it to the pan where I'll have started frying (very briefly!) three Vessalico garlic cloves (halved so I can discard the green germs) in extra virgin Taggiasca olive oil from the latest harvest. After draining my Gragnano *spaghettoni* before it becomes al dente, I'll finish it in the pan for two minutes with a little of the cooking water added. In the bowl, I'll pour over some more extra virgin olive oil (just a smidgeon!) and add a pinch of Cervia salt. I'll have it with a glass of young Barolo—ah yes, a 2016 from Serralunga, because it has just the right structure to support the heat of the chili.

I tell Sergio about this and he smiles: "Oh, in that case I'll come too, Oscar! I'll bring the garlic, and of course the chili, okay?"

35

POPCORN

Crazy edible bomb

WITH FABIO COSTA

"Who said popcorn is only for eating at the movies?"

Fabio Costa would like to see popcorn on the tasting menus of Michelin-starred restaurants. He's thirty-nine and lives in Turin, and in 2014 he and a few friends set up a company called Fol which makes popcorn. In the dialect of Piedmont, *fol* means crazy or mad.

The decision to set up a "gourmet" popcorn production center in Turin and open shops in Italy and abroad specializing in that alone might indeed have appeared crazy. But the idea of exporting Piedmontese popcorn to the very place where the kernels of "exploded" maize originated—Central and South America—must have seemed even crazier. Nevertheless, four young men managed to do just that, and when they needed a name, Fol seemed very fitting.

Fabio talks about popcorn the way Veronelli, the well-known Italian wine critic, talked about wine. In the beginning it's a bit strange, but listening to him you realize that the story behind any product can't be underestimated. Even the most common products, or the cheapest and simplest to make, hide a world of wonders and fascinating details.

So I ask him what was mysterious or fortuitous or legendary about the birth of this little corn bomb, or what mistake or misadventure might have been behind it.

"Nobody knows exactly how the story of popcorn began, but we do know where the relationship between humans and maize began thousands of years ago. It was in Central America, in a region of Mexico probably between Yucatán and the capital. Maize was something completely different then from what we know today: there was no wild plant bearing any resemblance to those soft starchy kernels arranged along a stem. Its ancestor was *teosinte*, something much closer to a traditional fruit-producing plant, but by experimenting with cross-pollination, the Mexican farmers eventually came up with the cob shaped like an airship.

"So it was there, between Chichén Itzá and Teotihuacán, that the first fortuitous explosion took place about ten thousand years ago, probably when someone accidentally tipped the primordial kernels into burning ashes. Imagine the astonishment, the stunned looks and even the fear as some of the onlookers no doubt jumped at the noise. The Spanish conquistadors may have disembarked in Central America to the crack of rifle fire, but the locals were not to be outdone and surprised them with corn bombs in burning ashes or scalding terracotta pots. Columbus himself had noted that the indigenous people used exploded corn kernels to make headwear, vests, necklaces and garlands: edible ornaments, given that they ate them as well."

That's more or less how things went. However, behind these small bubbles lay a very interesting physical reaction, and Fabio tries to explain it to me as simply as possible.

We know now exactly how the once-mysterious explosion happens. Like other cereals, each kernel of corn contains a certain amount of water consisting mainly of starch. But unlike other cereals, the natural protection of the corn's kernel is impermeable to moisture. This means that every time a kernel reaches a temperature above 212 degrees Fahrenheit, a natural pressure chamber is created and starts converting the water in its interior into steam.

Since the external wall of the nucleus is impermeable, there's no natural mechanism for releasing the moisture. The extra volume created within the kernel translates to increased internal pressure, and when this exceeds the structural resistance of the nucleus itself a small explosion occurs. "The result of course is popcorn," Fabio continues. "The shape depends on the type of corn: the one we're familiar with is normally called butterfly because of its shape, but there are other types as well, like the spherical one and the mushroom."

Fabio certainly knows a thing or two about corn. He tells me that after the Spanish invaded Central America, and the English and French invaded North America, maize cultivation spread across what would become the United States. "In the beginning the kernels had been marketed with grandiose names like 'pearls' and sold in the east coast area. Large-scale use of corn only emerged in the early nineteenth century, and in 1848 the term 'popped corn' appeared for the first time (including in John Russell Bartlett's *Dictionary of Americanisms*). Popcorn was still exploded manually, and in that form it became the world's first commercial snack. The main company making and distributing it from 1896 onward was Cracker Jack in Chicago."

Industry quickly muscled in, as tends to happen with products that work. The market took off in a big way when Charles Cretors invented the use of steam to pop the corn and launched his famous carts in Chicago early in the twentieth century. Yet it was the Depression that helped popcorn become a symbol of American culture. Because it was cheap, consumption was high, especially in cinemas, and this made an important contribution to the farming sector economy at the time. The sugar shortage of World War II consolidated the role of popcorn as a mass-consumption snack.

"The end of last century saw innovations in processing," Fabio continues, "first of all using air to produce the explosion, similar to the way a hairdryer works at high temperature, and then adding a coating of various kinds of molasses in a controlled process. In other words, the introduction of technology facilitated a radical change in the popcorn scene, and we saw 'gourmet popcorn' emerge."

He explains that unlike the classic exploded popcorn with butter or oil, the gourmet variety can and should be eaten cold. In fact, the corn needs to return to room temperature before it can be covered with various sweet or salted molasses.

Fabio is not a cook; he's an engineer with an MBA from Washington. This invites the question: how did he get to where he is?

"The story starts in 2009 in Washington. A Mexican friend of mine, Gabriel, persuaded me to go to Dallas to help out a young American named Paul who had opened a gourmet popcorn shop. Paul was making a good product, but he had some technical issues. We were able to set a few things right in that original shop, and I fell in love with popcorn and its amazing antioxidant properties generated by the polyphenols.

"Back in Turin, in 2013, I sat down with a good friend—another Fabio—to talk about potential innovative ideas. We got two other pals from Turin Polytech involved, Alessandro and Alberto, and together we decided it was time to take the plunge into a career as entrepreneurs."

So these four crazy young men decided to launch their popcorn: gourmet, yes, but reinvented Italian-style with fewer fats and sugars and no artificial preservatives. In 2014 they set up A2F2, a combination of their initials. Fabio's Mexican friend Gabriel joined them soon after. As the project gradually grew and their ambitions with it, creating the Fol brand came naturally.

"Whenever we told people about our idea of taking Italian gourmet popcorn out into the world, and mentioned that we were looking for funding, they'd look at us as if we were mad. But we got there in the end. After a few months of traveling and experimenting we set up our first artisanal laboratory in Venaria where our terrific cook, Simone, invents exclusive recipes. Now there's a second branch in Mexico City as well."

Fabio is clear about the problem and their mission: "Europe still associates popcorn with the idea of fast food—a snack to eat at the cinema—and Fol wants to change that perception and teach people that it's a food to be enjoyed in its own right and not simply an element of entertainment."

They opened their first shops in Italy and then around the world as evangelists of a new understanding of popcorn. High-quality corn of the mushroom type, not genetically modified, and grown in Europe. Air-popped to retain its nutritional properties, with no fats or oils added in the popping phase, and then covered with molasses made with artisanal ingredients from Piedmont and around the world.

It's wonderful to see young people starting from nothing and building up a business, and in a way Fol is serendipitous too. An engineer from Turin Polytechnic looking for a career found himself successfully selling popcorn on two continents. Bravo.

There's one final question: why is corn that comes from Mexico called *granoturco*, which means Turkish grain?

It seems that question is still unresolved. Most linguists maintain that the adjective *turco* was applied in the sixteenth century to anything colonial or exotic; in other words, any foreign product. According to other reliable sources it came from a mistranslation of the English "wheat of turkey," or turkey food. At the end of our long chat Fabio simply shrugs his shoulders: "I guess we should hold onto at least one mystery."

36

RAVIOLI OR AGNOLOTTI: ACTUALLY, *RAVIOLE AL PLIN*

Serendipity unknown

**WITH PIERO AND UGO ALCIATI
AND PIERCARLO GRIMALDI**

Don't fret over which name to use. In reality, the term "ravioli" is used all over Italy and agnolotti only in Piedmont, while in the language of the Langhe hills this form of pasta is given the feminine tag *raviole*. In short it's a mess, just like tortellini and *cappelletti*, arancini and *arancine*. But this too is part of the beauty and diversity of Italian cuisine.

When I was a child it was pretty rare to be able to enjoy a long stretch of your life with your grandmothers, because life expectancy was a lot shorter. But I was quite lucky. The first sixteen years of my life were shared with my paternal grandmother, Teresa. She was an extraordinary woman, widowed before she turned thirty and left with two children, no property and no money. Teresa lived with us and raised me, since my parents were always at work.

Pina, my mother's mother, was a very different person. She lived longer than Teresa and by the time she died I was married. She came from a wealthy family. Pina raised four daughters of her own, plus my grandfather's two sons, who came with him when he married my grand-mother as a young widower.

I could go on for ages about the differences between the two women. But one significant difference stands out: their way of making *raviole al plin*. I'm talking about the unique agnolotti, hand-sealed by pinching, the main party dish in the Langhe region (where *plin* is the word for pinch).

Nonna Teresa made them with deft hand movements every two or three weeks and on feast days. Nonna Pina, on the other hand, prepared them with equal speed and mastery every Sunday, not to mention all the designated feast-days. Similar in size—quite small—and the same sealing technique of pinching very quickly with both hands at once.

The big difference was in the ingredients.

For a start, Pina's *plin* were yellower because she would add at least ten eggs to the dough per kilogram of flour. Teresa could only afford two at most, so she used a lot more water. Then there was the filling: Nonna Teresa would put in all the week's leftovers, kept aside specifically for the Sunday *plin,* including leftover cooked meat of any description, cooked and raw vegetables, a whole egg and lots of rice, boiled in large quantities for Saturday's dinner so there'd be enough left over. Teresa cut everything up by hand using a half-moon chopper, and prepared the filling in no time because it was a mixture of ready-made ingredients.

Nonna Pina would create the filling from scratch every time. She put good-sized chunks of pork and veal into a saucepan and browned them slowly in a tasty *soffritto*, while nettles and endive were boiled in a separate pot. Then she'd cut it all up finely in the Tre Spade (a popular brand of mincer), turning the handle manually. I still remember that miraculous little machine, which she guarded jealously in a shoebox in her little storage room full of wonderful things. Lastly, she would mix it all with at least four egg yolks, salt and pepper and a pinch of nutmeg.

Back then I couldn't discern the differences in taste as I do now; Nonna Pina's *plin* were better without a doubt, but I must confess I preferred Nonna Teresa's "poor" version.

I asked my mother who had taught my grandmothers to make *plin* and she answered without hesitation: "Their mothers."

But who invented them? And when? Square ravioli are made all over Piedmont and we call them agnolotti, while in the Langhe (and a few towns around Monferrato) they're only made in this rather odd way, pinching the pasta, and we call them *raviole*. There must be a reason that explains the different names.

I consulted Piercarlo Grimaldi, Magnificent Rector of our Pollenza University of Gastronomic Sciences (he's now retired). His research into the origins of *raviole al plin* took him to the valley of the Belbo, a slender stream of water crossing the Langhe from San Benedetto (native town of the writer and partisan Beppe Fenoglio) to Santo Stefano (birthplace of the novelist and poet Cesare Pavese).

Piercarlo is certain they were first made in one of the many *osterie* or taverns along the banks of the Belbo and in Val Bormida, in order to assemble the leftovers into something delicious. The epitome of poor cuisine yet good enough to be served without sauce, simply boiled and presented on a coarse cotton napkin. Sublime. They're still served that way in many of the *osterie* that have managed to stay in business from one generation to the next.

However, even Grimaldi wasn't able to identify a precise location, or even the name of their inventor. He reminded me that in 1678 Charles du Fresne, lord of Cange and an erudite French scholar and foodie, wrote about a filled pasta sealed with pressure from the fingers, but didn't explain where or by whom he saw it done. Nobody knows who had the bright idea of giving that stuffed pasta a *plin*! Nobody knows what fabulous serendipity is hiding in there! But Grimaldi remains an incurable researcher and keeps looking, and he's promised me that when he finds the answer I'll be the first to know.

*

I visit Piero and Ugo Alciati's fabulous restaurant, Guido, where *plin* occupies the throne of the grand tradition begun by their grandmother

Pierina and reinvented by their mother, Lidia, during the visionary reign of their father, Guido. Now that tradition is carried high—in fact, very high—by chef Ugo, who is strict, sophisticated and kind, and Piero, the elegant and cultured maître d'.

Piero gets straight to the point: "The thing is nobody looked into it at the time; perhaps it was a random thing. We prefer to call them agnolotti. The Savoy army's cook, Angelòt, might have given the name to the entree he created to feed the troops during the siege of Casale, perhaps looking for a one-dish meal incorporating pasta, filling and seasoning. But equally it could be derived from *anolòt*, the tool housewives used for cutting pasta. Or perhaps the Duchess of Parma's cook, Vincenzo Agnoletti, 'slipped up' with a *cappelletto* and then described the new shape in a book he wrote in 1814 as 'Piedmontese-style agnellotti.'"

In short, amid these and many other half-truths it could indeed have happened accidentally, when someone was looking for a different way to economize on pantry supplies or a way of providing a complete meal in one dish.

I ask chef Ugo for his thoughts. "*Agnolotti al plin* are still the focus of the main meal of the day in Piedmont, whether they're dressed with the juices from a roast, with meat sauce, wine sauce, served plain on a napkin or with butter and sage. I'm ready to bet, though, that it was a woman who invented them, a Langhe housewife. She grasped the evolutionary legacy of opposable thumbs—the first intelligent gesture distinguishing us from the animals—and interpreted it in an artisanal gesture, sealing the agnolotti with two simple pinches. That anonymous woman also intelligently reduced the sides to be cut by the pasta wheel to three: less time, more aesthetic appeal. A stroke of genius."

What is 100 percent true is that behind great stories, other stories come to light. That's what happened for Ugo and Piero's parents, Lidia and Guido, who began their personal gastronomic journey in Costigliole d'Asti in the late 1950s. They realized from the start that they needed a signature dish, an item on the menu that would stay in people's minds and inspire nostalgia and the desire to come back and eat it over and again. So the *plin*, which in the postwar years had become a useful vehicle for recycling leftovers, might be just the recipe for a resurgence.

"My mother, Lidia, had learned how to make them from Nonna Pierina," Ugo tells me, "but it took the combination of her skill and my father's grandiose ideas to make the agnolotti a sumptuous dish: first and foremost they had to be very fresh, with thirty egg yolks in the dough (thirty!). The fillings had to be expressly cooked every time with no compromises, using the best parts of veal, pork and rabbit roasts, Parmigiano suitably aged for the particular stuffing, and no nutmeg because it covered the other flavors. The pasta was rolled out a bit thicker than usual to protect the filling during the boiling in salted water or broth, and to retain a bit of bite as well. Then they thought of dressing the *plin* with the cooking juices from the roasts used in the stuffing, with the fat skimmed off, to make them even more aromatic and to harmonize with the taste of the filling. This meant the ravioli had to be quite a bit bigger, and my parents noticed that changing the ratio between pasta and filling also improved the taste."

Once the rules were laid down, all that remained was to learn to implement them, and luckily Lidia had soft hands for kneading the dough and strong fingers for pinching it. In the Villa Reale di Fontanafredda, where they're now based, Piero and Ugo are still making their customers smile.

Well, this is the story of serendipity not found. But you'll have to forgive me for including it because it's such a good story to tell. Sometimes even an unfinished tale is worth telling.

37

MILANESE RISOTTO
A blank sheet

WITH DAVIDE OLDANI

There's a chef, a friend of mine, who not only has formidable skills with pots and pans but also knows how to use his head—he never tires of studying, questioning and inventing. He works hard—very hard—and he's launched a new cuisine without losing the respect for tradition and authentic ingredients. He's given it a name: Pop. It's not easy to get a table in his Michelin-starred restaurant, D'O, in Cornaredo, and you always have to book well in advance.

I'm talking about Davide Oldani.

He was born in Milan, a city he loves, and that love was reciprocated when, in 2008, he was awarded the Ambrogino d'oro, the city's highest honor. I couldn't have chosen anyone else to talk about *risotto alla milanese*.

"Your turn now, Davide."

"In the town where I grew up, at the entrance to the city, rice was what we usually ate. In our house, even when our mother put pasta on the table I remember it inevitably ended up looking like rice, short and creamy in the Milanese style. Saffron rice is the symbol of Milan's culinary tradition and gastronomic art, and its history is full of anec-dotes and legends."

One story suggests that the recipe goes way back to the traditions of medieval kosher cuisine, but there's another story about a Sicilian cook who moved to Milan: he couldn't find all the ingredients needed to make the stuffing for arancini, so he made do with a slightly differ-ent version, and that's how the first plate of yellow risotto was created.

But Davide's preferred version, and the one that most represents the serendipity of Milanese risotto, is the story that it emerged in 1574 from an artist's palette.

"At the wedding of the daughter of Mastro Valerio of Flanders, a Flemish painter working on the windows of Milan Cathedral, his assis-tant (who was nicknamed Zafferano because he mixed saffron with his colors to make them brighter) added a little saffron powder to the risotto, either accidentally or as a joke. This was a marvelous surprise for the guests, who not only feasted on a delicious new taste but also feasted their eyes on the spectacular gold-colored rice. What I like about this 'accidental origin' of the recipe is that it brings together two icons, the rice and the cathedral, to create a third: a dish that's ended up on tables all over Italy."

And, I would add, all over the world.

On the occasion of Expo 2015, as Milan was preparing for a big inter-national meeting, Davide dedicated a recipe to the city: *D'O saffron and rice alla milanese*. For the event he had the idea of rejuvenating a rec-ipe that most people may have considered set in stone and impossible to alter.

Here is the great chef's thinking: "When I studied it, I realized I could respect tradition and still move it toward something more mod-ern. So I chose the method of dry toasting the rice in a saucepan, which releases all the rice's natural fragrance: that's why there's no *soffritto* or preliminary sautéing, no wine and no broth; it's why I wanted to give the dish a different name and do away with the term 'risotto' (which I regard as a cooking method), replacing it with the name of the ingredient. I added 'saffron' at the beginning of the name because that's what gives the dish its taste, and I wanted to give it prominence. It's made with the traditional rice but dressed with a swirl of saffron as a symbol, sort of saying, 'Here we are in this dish, different but fantastically together.' A spiral intended as a journey that never ends but starts over and over. That's also how I imagine the ingredients coexisting, balancing each other with their contrasts: each with its own character but all of them harmonizing on the palate and continually transformed with new pairings."

It's clear that since the time his mother used to cook rice at home, Davide has never ceased loving and celebrating its enormous possibilities.

He calls it "my blank sheet" because it can enhance the specific qualities of the ingredients paired with it, which vary according to the season and their capacity to bring out the best in the rice.

"A blank sheet to color in, giving space to all those who, like me, want to experiment in the kitchen. And there's no doubt saffron is the color of colors. With the rice I'm fanatical about quality, and that starts in the fields. I use Carnaroli aged for twenty months, and I've found a producer who uses the traditional old Milanese techniques. The saffron is the result of our careful selection as well: to begin with it's Italian, from Lombardy, and it's grown with great care by a friend of mine I call 'the peasant' in recognition of how hard and how delicate his work is."

Davide tells me he loves rice so much, and always has, that he's made six different versions of saffron and rice so far. It's like anything we become really attached to: it accompanies us through life and changes along with us. The first really big change came with the idea of Pop cuisine and his decision to lighten the classic recipe without sacrificing its traditional taste. Here's how he did it.

"As I said before, I chose toasting as a taste factor—no more inevitable coating with fats; then, because I didn't want to mistreat a delicate and expensive ingredient like saffron that requires such care and attention from the farmer, I replaced the lengthy cooking with infusion to bring its unique characteristics to the fore. Saying goodbye to the preliminary sauté, the wine and the meat broths also meant the ingredients remained separate, and for me that's another important taste factor. Like many innovations in cooking, my most recent version has its roots in the past and reinterprets an old tradition. I remember when we were kids we'd rush to scrape the risotto saucepan and eat the crust that formed during the cooking. So I had this idea of bringing the crust to the surface. These days my saffron and rice retains the basic steps in the preparation, which I believe are still valid, but there's a clearer separation of the ingredients. The diluted, infused saffron is separate from the creamy white rice, and then there's the crust made with rice flour. To serve it I spoon the saffron sauce onto the plate first, then the rice, and the crust on top. Together they make up a 'blank sheet' rice that goes with other quality ingredients, without any one taking precedence over another. Because I've asked myself many times whether we really get the perfume of the saffron with the classic risotto—*soffritto*, wine, meat broth, and saffron cooked for twenty minutes. If we explored the taste further we might find that what we think we're tasting is really the color we're seeing."

So here it is: Davide Oldani's recipe.

═══════════════

INGREDIENTS:

Rice

1-3/4 cups carnaroli rice	3/4 cup grated Grana Padano
3/4 tsp salt	1/2 tsp white wine vinegar
5 tbsp butter	

Crust

1/4 cup rice flour	2 pinch saffron threads
1-1/3 tbsp vegetable oil	

Sauce

1/4 tsp sugar	1/2 tsp cornstarch diluted
1/4 tsp salt	with cold water
1/4 tsp white wine vinegar	1 pinch saffron threads

METHOD

Rice

1 Toast the rice in a saucepan.

2 Cook it in boiling salted water, remove from the heat, stir in the butter and grated cheese and finish with the vinegar.

3 Divide the rice among four small steel pots.

Crust

1 Whisk all the ingredients together with 1 cup water and cook in a preheated nonstick pan on both sides to form thin discs.

Sauce

1 Put 2/3 cup water and the sugar, salt and vinegar in a saucepan and bring to a boil.

2 Add the cornstarch, remove the saucepan from the heat and add the saffron threads. Leave to infuse.

To serve: Spoon the sauce onto the plates and serve the rice separately in the little pots with the saffron crust.

38

RUM

Contemporary serendipity

WITH LUCA GARGANO

In April 1789, when George Washington made his famous inaugural address, he climbed onto a cask of Barbados rum to make sure everyone could see him clearly.

On October 21, 1805 Admiral Horatio Nelson won the Battle of Trafalgar. The British fleet sank twenty-two French and Spanish ships without losing a single one of their own. Unfortunately, the victory was tarnished by the admiral's demise: he was fatally wounded by a musket and scarcely had time to rejoice over the sensational battle before he expired.

Nelson's body was immersed in a barrel full of rum, which was then resealed to preserve the body on the voyage to England. When it arrived and the barrel was opened, they found not a single drop of liquid. Some of the rum had penetrated the body during the voyage, but the sailors had made a hole in the cask and quaffed most of its contents, thus drinking the blood of their legendary commander at the same time. In England since then rum has been known as "Nelson's blood."

This and numerous other stories, some true and some not, have elevated rum to the realm of myth. There are fascinating stories behind all the major distillates, but none that reach the epic levels of the one about *ron*, as it was known to the Spanish settlers who took the original sugarcane plants to the East Indies.

There are many types of rum, distilled either from sugarcane molasses or directly from the juice of the cane. It would be easy to lose your way in the geography, the history and the politics of the English-speaking colonies (where they call it rum), the French (where it's spelled *rhum*) and the Spanish colonies (*ron*, as above). Each type has a different backstory, and in all of them it's possible to discover intriguing cases of serendipity—stories that take us back to the Caribbean through the sixteenth and nineteenth centuries, around the small and large Antilles, and to New South Wales in Australia as well.

But I'm going to focus on a story of rum that's much more recent. The main character is Luca Gargano, a man of about my age who doesn't own a mobile phone, a watch or a driver's license but is always on the move, traveling the world to find unique products to import and sell in Italy. Luca has created Italy's leading import company, Velier, dealing not only with distillates but also champagne, tonic water and cigars. He's the man who invented the Triple A trademark, which stands for *agricoltore, artigiano, artista* (farmer, artisan, artist) and represents a network of small producers of "real wines," as he calls them.

Velier, based in Genoa, is virtually the only importer of Caroni, a very important rum from Trinidad. Caroni has reached legendary status and its bottles go under the hammer for stratospheric prices. Since the Rum Auctioneer website was set up for rum auctions, the Caroni rums have monopolized the top positions. Some bottles change hands for thousands of euros.

I reached out to him to tell the serendipitous story of his personal Caroni experience.

"Even in my dreams I couldn't have envisaged what fate had in store for me. I'd decided to spend the years from 2001 to 2004 documenting all the distilleries in the Caribbean photographically. My traveling companions were my fiancée, Urska, who's passionate about wines and a terrific cook, and Fredi Marcarini. Fredi is one of Italy's best photographers, and we'd met a few years earlier when the two of us and Andrea Molinari set up the Diadema company, the first independent Italian importer of Cuban cigars. So Urska and Fredi and I made two or three trips a year to the different islands of the Caribbean, recording and photographically documenting the production processes of all the rum distilleries.

"Our final visit was to Trinidad, the southernmost island just a few thousand kilometers from the South American continent. We arrived at Piarco Airport on December 9, 2004. We knew there were two active distilleries on the island: Angostura, which also makes the well-known bitters and exports its rums all over the world, and Caroni, which mostly sells rum in barrels for British Navy Rum blends and keeps its bottled rum just for Trinidad. There was hardly any existing information on Caroni and I was curious to find out about it, so we decided to go there first.

"We took a taxi and were there in a few minutes. I'm pretty sure all three of us had the same initial thought: this isn't possible—the taxi driver must have got the wrong street. 'Excuse me,' I said, 'we want to go to the Caroni distillery, where is it?' His answer was: 'This is the Caroni distillery.'

"We were in front of a gate. In the distance, the tower housing the distillation column was in ruins and leaning like the one in Pisa; there was wreckage everywhere and the rails used for transporting the molasses to the distillery were covered in tall grass. We were shocked. What a disappointment! This was the only distillery in the Caribbean I wasn't familiar with and I couldn't wait to discover it, and now?! I was dumbfounded. I walked through the gate feeling like an intruder, scrambled over debris and bushes and ended up with my foot wedged in a rail covered by the grass, nearly dislocating my ankle in the process. There wasn't a soul in sight.

"But after a few moments I could make out a woman way off in the distance next to a small house. She was busy hanging out washing. I shouted to get her attention and she heard me and came toward me.

"'This isn't the Caroni distillery, is it?'

"'Sure it is.'

"'But what's happened?'

"'What's happened? You don't know what's happened?' She was almost indignant. I confessed that no, I had no idea what had happened. So the woman explained that the previous year the government had decided to close the last sugar factory operating on the island, putting the thirteen thousand canegrowers and cutters out on the street. Hence no sugarcane, no molasses, and no rum. The Caroni distillery was forced to close. I was getting more disappointed by the minute; I asked if by any chance they had a few casks of the rum that was distilled in 2003. She looked at me wide-eyed in amazement: 'Come with me!' It was an order.

"This woman knew more than I could possibly have imagined. We made our way through rubble, garbage and weeds till we came to an old warehouse. She opened the door and I just couldn't believe my eyes. There were hundreds of casks full of rum in that warehouse. I asked her if these were the 2003 distillates.

"'Of course not, they're 1983, 1984, 1974 ...' I was speechless. I was like a hungry cat in a mischief of mice. Finding hundreds of casks of rum twenty and thirty years old that nobody knew existed is something inexplicable for a dealer and rum buff. I remember pinching myself to make sure I wasn't dreaming and it took me a bit of time to recover, but then I went straight into action.

"The first thing I did was persuade the woman to put me in contact with Rudy Moore, the Caroni distillery liquidator, and then I convinced Rudy to let me taste those rums. They were sensational! As we consumed one shot after another, Rudy and I became friends as you can well imagine, and I bought all those casks without discussing the price. I wanted them whatever they cost, and I already had my new 'Caroni project' clear in my mind. On April 1, 2005 the barrels left for Europe, and I began bottling them using a carefully calibrated criterion according to the 'readiness' of the vintages. For the labels I used the beautiful photos Fredi Marcarini had taken during the Trinidad trip. Fifteen years later we're still bottling the last of the barrels. That rum has become the legend it deserves to be. I've gotten up to all sorts of things in my life, but this Caroni adventure might be the best. I went there to take a few photos and fate changed every bit of the plan!"

Last year Luca gave me a gift: he bottled one of the last casks of Caroni exclusively for Eataly. It produced just on two hundred bottles and I asked him if I could put them on sale for a fixed price of 150 euros each and make a special event of it. He let me do that, but with one condition: no more than one bottle per person. They all sold in a single afternoon in our Italian stores. That day I happened to be in Bari and I saw a customer, obviously a lover of rum, hand the lady behind him 150 euros to buy him a Caroni, and 100 more euros as a tip. He really wanted to take two bottles home. I smiled at him and thought about Luca and his incredible Trinidad adventure.

39

WORCESTERSHIRE SAUCE

That measure in the Bloody Mary

WITH JOE BASTIANICH

Worcester is a city in the UK about 125 miles northwest of London, and the main city in Worcestershire County, with a population of approximately 100 thousand. In 1835 it was obviously a lot smaller, but it was already a major center of the Industrial Revolution in Britain, for porcelain in particular. These days Worcester is famous not for crockery but as the birthplace of the world's best-known and most-used barbecue sauce.

To tell its story we need to go back to that fateful year, 1835. Lord Marcus Sandys, ex-governor of Bengal, had just returned to his home city of Worcester with lots of memories and souvenirs from his lengthy sojourn in the colony. They included the Indian recipe for a sauce he was crazy about: malt and spirit vinegar, molasses, sugar, salt, anchovies, tamarind extract, onions, garlic, various spices and flavorings (probably including soy sauce, lemon, pickles and capsicums). This sauce wasn't available in the West, so he asked pharmacists John Lea and William Perrins to replicate it.

The two got to work straight away and made a whole barrel full of the sauce, but it was far from satisfactory: they didn't like it and neither did Lord Marcus. Months passed and the two chemists forgot about the barrel in the cellar of their pharmacy, until one day when they were tidying up to make more space, they decided on the spur of the moment to taste the sauce again before throwing it out. It was fantastic—very different from the dreadful concoction they'd tasted with Lord Marcus. Time had worked its magic. Apparently all those ingredients needed to be together for some time before they found a balance. The two pharmacists told Lord Marcus what had happened, but he was no longer interested in his discovery and agreed to let John and William develop the original idea themselves. Lea and Perrins Worcestershire sauce began production in 1838, and the rest is a story of overwhelming success. Serendipity!

*

Joe Bastianich is a serious food connoisseur. Some people think he's a chef because he was a judge on the US *MasterChef* series, where all his colleagues were skilled cooks. Actually Joe is a great maître d': "a pretty good waiter" as I call him teasingly. These days, with all of his restaurants, Joe is first and foremost an entrepreneur. He doesn't greet clients in person anymore, only because it would be impossible given that his restaurants host thousands of guests a day, but that's where his vast experience began.

Anyone who's in the dining room as head of the business has the same degree of responsibility as the executive chef, if not greater. It works a bit like the tires and the chassis in Formula One—they're as important as the engine, but more often the deciding factor. Transferring the power of the engine to the road requires great equilibrium; without that your restaurant won't work even if you have the best chef in the world. You need harmony in the dining room and a thorough knowledge of the raw materials, the wines and the traditions. You need the competence to correct mistakes, the capacity to welcome guests and make them feel at ease, and above all the ability to understand what your customers want so that you can work with the chef to create the right menu. Well, Joe's a champion at all of that. I ask him to tell me about his relationship with Worcestershire sauce.

"I even remember the date, June 14, 1985. I was about to turn seventeen. It was 9.30 a.m. when I went into a restaurant that was still in darkness. The air was thick with smoke. The pungent, sickly sweet smell of spent cigarettes and alcoholic residues hit me, and I could still feel the energy of the music from a few hours earlier and the vibrations of a wild night on the dance floor. I was living my dream, leaving the world of our family restaurant to get behind the counter in a bar—a real bar. It was my first big opportunity to show I could go it alone.

"Wall Street was flourishing, hip-hop was booming and New York was alive. I wanted to be cool, get ahead, be part of the change, get away from the Upper East Side and my parents' restaurant and move downtown to the heart of the city. Thanks to a few family friends I was given an opportunity to get into New York nightlife. On June 14, 1985 I started work in a new trendy restaurant in Tribeca and it was my first real experience away from my parents. I'd be starting as a barback, the guy who has to clean and prepare the bar, but in my heart I was sure I had a brilliant career ahead of me and I was moving into the fast lane.

"So the first day, I turned up to the job ready to clean up the chaos from the night before. There was nobody to guide me, just a napkin left on the counter where the boss had written a list of things to be done: clean the bar, refill the fridges, prepare the mixes (those ready-made concoctions a few places use to speed up the orders). Polishing the counter from top to bottom was nothing new for me; my father had been training me for this all through my teenage years and I was quite familiar with buckets of water and bleach. So I gave everything a thorough clean and then I filled all the restaurant's fridges to the brim. Then it was time to look after the mixes.

"In the '80s, daiquiris and margaritas ruled, but in the last container I found a red mixture that must have been the Bloody Mary. As a lover of beer and having grown up in a family devoted to wine, I've never understood the appeal of tomato juice pumped up with vodka. Who in their right mind would drink tomato juice? That's what I was thinking as I tried my hand at preparing it. I did have a vague idea of the recipe because every now and then somebody would order it in our family restaurant. Sam, the bartender at Felidia, had once given me a taste of it behind the counter and I remembered the ingredients were lemon juice, horseradish, Tabasco and Worcestershire sauce. But as for the proportions, I was groping around in the dark. I added some of the Worcestershire sauce and took a taste because I had no idea how much to put in. In its pure state it conjures up flavors of cooking and food, and at first blush you'd never think that combination of acid, spicy and sweet-and-sour notes could be added to a drink. It was a familiar taste, but a very long way from the realm of cocktails, I thought.

"At eleven o'clock sharp I heard the door bang and Steve, the head barman, came in, red-eyed and looking sleepy but with a broad smile. He made straight for the mixes without even saying hi. Well, in that moment all my certainties vanished into thin air along with my ego. He mumbled that the daiquiri mix was too sweet and there wasn't enough Triple Sec in the margarita mix. Then he looked at me as he took a sip of the Bloody Mary—by that point I must have appeared pretty terrified—and pronounced it literally perfect. Those were his exact words. It was July 14, 1985 and Steve, my fabulous head barman, was drinking a Bloody Mary for breakfast, prepared by yours truly with the perfect measure of Worcestershire sauce. I'll remember that confidence boost for as long as I live."

Joe opened his first restaurant a few years after that in New York. It was 1991 and he was twenty-three. At the time, he tells me, the city was starting the process of upgrading the Theater District, and the area around Times Square was having a renaissance. It was crammed with adult shops and a far cry from the tourist attraction everyone knows today, but the first entrepreneurs were opening new businesses, renovating the theaters and cleaning up the area.

"There I was, right in the middle of all that excitement," Bastianich continues. "I was opening my very first restaurant with a loan from my grandmother. I'd decided to call it Becco, and it was just an old three-story building in what later became Restaurant Row. It was the perfect opportunity to fail, but I was ready to take risks and have my moment. For the first time every decision I made and every action I took would have an impact, positive or negative, on my life, my name and my image."

So Joe decided the restaurant would reflect his personality in every detail, from the service to the décor, but especially in the food. The inspiration came from his disco days, the years he'd spent living in the world of barmen and the New York night scene. The idea was to recreate that same atmosphere in the food as well. How did he do it? It pretty much came naturally.

"I chose to serve a classical version of steak tartare, but with a touch more Worcestershire sauce in memory of those mad joyous nights behind the counter making Bloody Marys. Our guests loved it from the start and it still has a permanent spot on our menu nearly thirty years later."

It's common enough these days to find ingredients that can be used either in the world of mixology or in the kitchen, but it wasn't so simple back in the day. Bastianich says Worcestershire sauce was a precursor of this trend, and I think he's right. But there's something more when he talks about it—nostalgia.

"It always takes me back to my memories of New York City as in *The Wolf of Wall Street*," he says with a smile. But while Leonardo DiCaprio juggled stocks and shares and ended up ruined, Joe juggled everything divinely among the tables at Becco and built an amazing career. With Worcestershire sauce.

40

THE PANINO

The Italian sandwich

WITH ANTONIO CIVITA

The sandwich was invented by a man named John Montagu, Fourth Earl of Sandwich, and he was Britain's First Lord of the Admiralty for fifteen years in the mid-eighteenth century. It appears he was at the center of various scandals, both political (corruption) and private (loose morals), and had two wives, six children and countless lovers. His life was frenetic; he was always in a rush and unwilling to stop even to eat.

One day he had a special request for the cook, who had made some excellent roast beef with various delicious sauces. Lord Montagu summoned him and told him to put it all between two soft bread slices, preferably buttered. The cook shuddered, but of course he couldn't contradict the earl. So the strange new dish duly arrived at the table and Lord Montagu showed that he could go on playing cards even while eating first-class meat with sauces, simply by using one hand. Naturally everyone at the table followed suit and the despairing cook was obliged to make many more of the same. But what was this thing to be called? It was natural to choose a name linked to the inventor, and so we have the sandwich. All the earl wanted was to find a way of continuing his card game uninterrupted, and he unwittingly invented a new recipe for the world.

*

Antonio Civita heads the Italian restaurant chain Panino Giusto, and in the space of a few years has accumulated thirty-three restaurants serving panini. I approach him to check that my story about the serendipity of the sandwich is correct.

He confirms that's exactly how it happened. But actually, as Antonio explains, the panino, understood as "bread with something," seems to have been around hundreds of years before John Montagu, Earl of Sandwich.

"Going back in time to imperial Rome, people ate *panis ac perna* in the streets and at the markets. The name is Latin for 'bread and ham,' and this forerunner of the ham roll even had a street named after it. In Milan, much later, Leonardo da Vinci tried a sort of reverse sandwich: what the Renaissance genius wanted was a slice of bread between two slices of meat, but he had no idea what to call it. It's a curious fact that much later Milan became the homeland of the panino and Rome the home of the sandwich.

"Moving on to the nineteenth century, when class divisions became very clear, the path of the panino took two directions: bread with onion or with a cheese crust was the food of the poor, while guests in the elegant parlors of the bourgeoisie were served small panini with rich fillings, in the form of canapés and sandwiches. The earliest recipe collection to include panini is Alberto Cougnet's from 1911, which distinguishes sandwiches from the typical Italian 'pregnant' panini packed with fillings."

The most recent turning point came in 1968. People were spending more time out of the house for both work and leisure, and the panino became what we might call a new urban food. Antonio tells me this "dish" in its new life outside the home, came in two diametrically opposed forms. One was modern and accessible and so disruptive that it gave rise to the Paninari movement (the only youth movement ever to originate from a food!). The other was a much richer, almost opulent, sophisticated version where luxury ingredients such as foie gras, caviar, salmon, game products and French cheeses were associated with the trend toward informality. The panino took napkins and crockery off the table and people ate with their hands, but the food was fit for kings.

Now we get to the debut of the modern panino, in the "Milano da bere" or "drinking Milan" of the early 1980s. The panino took over in those years and became something to build a business around: a bona fide commercial product with symbolic meaning in terms of social mores, and something that could be marketed.

Antonio continues, "At that time I didn't understand anything about panini; in fact, I didn't eat them at all. I lived in Rome and I was eating *spaghetti all'amatriciana* and grilled lamb cutlets. In terms of work, I was doing something quite different. But as luck would have it, one day I stumbled upon the panino. I was visiting Milan often and thinking of moving there because Elena, who's now my wife, lived there, but also for the dynamism and the vibe I got from the city. Panino Giusto already existed and Elena was a fan. At lunchtime she made me stand in exhausting queues that to me were incomprehensible. As we waited forever for a panino, a sad excuse for a meal, I wondered if the Milanese had gone mad. But one mouthful changed my mind. I think it was while we were in one of these queues outside the restaurant that I first realized the potential of the panino. Elena and I got married and decided to set up a company to develop the Panino Giusto brand as a franchise. After we'd opened about ten restaurants, we put together a proposal to buy the whole business, and in 2010 we refined it with the goal of focusing on new ideas for the panino and what it could offer after the splendor of the '80s."

It worked. Now the company is making Italian-style panini in Paris, London, Tokyo and many other cities. Meanwhile, in Milan you'll find a Panino Giusto wherever you turn.

But the greatest satisfaction lies elsewhere. Antonio set up a cultural foundation to protect the heritage of the Italian panino, and he's still supporting it. "I think it's a fundamental expression of our country, like pizza and pasta. I see the fondazione Accademia del Panino Italiano as our legacy. The Foundation is run by a young team and guided by an advisory board of twenty professionals—experts in food, design, history, media, publishing and retail. We have a manifesto setting out our values, plus a standards manual and an app, the 'Panino map,' covering twenty-five hundred restaurants in Italy and Europe. Our next goal is to take it to the rest of the world."

Antonio tells me the Foundation also has a digital magazine and a printed yearbook, organizes and chairs events, and facilitates interaction between cooks, foodies, researchers and artisans.

I ask Antonio about the adjective in the name of his business: *giusto*, meaning "fair."

"When we acquired the brand in the '80s it already had that name, and *giusto* was a figure of speech that meant 'being fashionable or trendy.' But the meaning of the word has changed too. Now we want to return to the original meaning: *giusto* in the sense of proper respect for people and animals and the environment."

"I know the mission we've set ourselves might seem utopian, but we really do want to improve the world through panini."

One of the projects they're focusing on is "Cooking for a new start," set up for children who have found refuge in Italy and want to give something back by working. They've created a training program with internships and employment in their restaurants and the restaurants of all their partners who participate in the program every year.

Before we part, Antonio reminds me that they've called the panino they launched last year to celebrate their fortieth birthday *Lo sbagliato*, "the mistake," in honor of all those mistakes that once reinterpreted have led to better panini. Serendipity.

41

SAUTERNES

When mold becomes noble

WITH ANGELO GAJA

Angelo Gaja turned eighty in 2020, but don't go round telling people. Not because he doesn't want anyone to know—that's not it at all. The thing is he looks at least fifteen years younger, so nobody would believe it. Genes probably play a part, but it's largely due to his lifestyle. He works a lot and constantly travels around the world, but he has always been careful with his diet, rides a bike and has never smoked.

Then there's his mind, even fitter than his body. When I have doubts about my work as a winemaker (which is often), I seek him out. But it's not only wine I like to discuss with him.

Every morning Angelo reads at least seven newspapers, underlines the most interesting articles and then likes to discuss them. I feel privileged to be one of his conversation partners. We talk about politics, history, books and especially the future. It seems paradoxical that someone who comes from five generations of a family that lends its name to the most prestigious wine brand in the Langhe region, someone with such depth of history behind him, would rather talk about the future than the past.

In 2008 I'd just bought two quite important wineries, Fontanafredda and Borgogno, and the first thing I did was read a book on the history of Bordeaux. It included an interview with Baroness Philippine Mathilde Camille de Rothschild, owner of the very famous Premier Cru Classé Château Mouton. "It's an excellent business, winemaking," said the baroness, "and it's only the first 250 years that are a bit hard." This was disappointing. I was already fifty-four, so what should I do?

"Study! There's no other way but to study wine diligently. In the countryside, in the cellar, in the markets and in books."

I did that, and I did get somewhere. Partly thanks to him.

Years later, when I came across one of the most interesting cases of serendipity in the wine world, the renowned French sweet wine called Sauternes, I immediately thought of Angelo.

"Way back in antiquity, sweet wines already had a big reputation. The Egyptians, Etruscans, Greeks and Romans had realized that sweet wine keeps better, and consequently has a longer life, if it's made with grapes dried in the sun to concentrate the sugars. Another method was boiling the must to reduce the volume and concentrate the sugars that way. And we believe the Romans applied torsion to the peduncle of the grape cluster to produce the wine they called falernum and bring about drying. Another common practice was to add sweetening substances, especially honey, to give a richer and more pleasant taste. From the twelfth to the sixteenth century, Venice had a monopoly on the sweet wines coming from Sicily, Cyprus, Greece and Crete. As the demand for sweet wines grew, the Venetians supported new vineyards in Veneto and Friuli, so there was more Recioto made by drying the red grapes intended for making white wine. Then in the first half of the sixteenth century, the Portuguese introduced vines from Crete into Madeira. Gradually, sweet wines were made all over Europe, in northern Germany, on the Mediterranean coast of Spain, in Sicily. From the end of the sixteenth century Dutch merchants had a big influence, buying white wines and adulterating them with sugar and syrup to satisfy contemporary palates. They were the ones who asked the farmers in Barsac to make wine with sugary residues.

"Barsac is a small town in Gironde, twenty-five miles south of Bordeaux, with a population of just over two thousand, but it looks like a city compared to Sauternes, six miles farther south with 730 inhabitants. Barsac and Sauternes between them have the world's best producers of sweet wines affected by noble rot."

This noble rot first occurred due to an unintentional delay in the grape harvest. At that time nobody knew about its beneficial effects, and the first bottles of Sauternes emerged by accident in 1847. That autumn, the Marquis de Lur Saluces, owner of Château d'Yquem, was coming home from Russia when he had a setback that delayed his return. He'd sent instructions from Russia that the harvest was not to begin until he got back, and his staff respected their master's wishes, even though they were worried about the grapes looking sicker on the vine. When the marquis finally reached Sauternes and started the harvest, the rot had damaged all the vines. The workers picked the sémillon and sauvignon blanc clusters with heavy hearts, but when the time came to taste the wine from this harvest it was so good! It exceeded everyone's expectations: no longer was it just sweet, it had acquired a rich bouquet and a complexity never encountered before.

Angelo explains the reason for this: "It was all down to the action of a microscopic fungus, *botrytis cinerea*. It appears on the vines in September, and in specific conditions it creates what is known as noble rot. Producing grapes affected by noble rot requires particular weather conditions as the grapes ripen, a mixture of foggy mornings every day and some wind, with autumn sun in the afternoon. These conditions are found consistently only in very few places including Sauternes, Tokay and some areas along the Rhine and the Moselle.

"Producing wines from *Botrytis*-infected grapes is demanding, risky and expensive. It's only in the best and most successful vintages that the alternating weather conditions allow noble rot to reach all the grape clusters with equal speed, but this level of homogeneous ripening is not always achieved. The producers need to have a large group of pickers available to come back again and again to pick the clusters as and when needed—or even just fully ripened individual grapes."

But sweet wines today aren't as popular as they once were, and they take a lot of effort to make. Wine production from grapes affected by noble rot has slowed down considerably for a number of reasons.

First there's climate change, which in some vintages means the grapes can't be harvested because of high production costs that only the most successful companies can afford. Another reason is the arrival of substitutes competing for the market, such as ice wines and wines obtained through cold maceration. Finally there's the trivial but true fact that at a certain point things go out of fashion. That's what happened with consumers in the developed markets in relation to the intensely sweet wines.

But Angelo is an optimist and insists that quality producers must not give up. "It's not a funeral. The great sweet wines made around the world will always find their place, even if the market remains limited and unlikely to grow. Unless there's an education campaign to win new markets ... Africa? Asia?"

In the meantime, he reveals that in all the areas famous for sweet wines it's becoming more common to make dry wines from the same grapes. "Trends don't grow out of the whims of consumers. It's not as if the high-end chefs pampered by the food writers create their dishes with a perfect wine match in mind. The sparkling wines benefitted from that in the past when they were consumed separately from meals and for celebrating, whereas now they've won a place at the table because they can be drunk cold and they go well with all kinds of food. Climate change is forcing producers more or less everywhere to make still, dense and concentrated wines with more body and more alcohol. The easy-drinking spumantes with moderate alcohol content like rosés or elegant medium-bodied wines are coming up trumps."

"So in the wine world do we need to be prepared for a new dimension?" I ask. I'm a bit worried. "Now don't make it such a big deal, Oscar.

Change has affected every aspect of human history from the year dot. The climate changes, consumer tastes change and producers adapt accordingly. Some can interpret the change quickly, some don't move an inch, and some go too far. As usual, in the end intelligence will win."

42
___

SPAGHETTI BOLOGNESE

A mischievous prank?

WITH BRUNO BARBIERI

"Do something for me, Oscar: split that name in two so there's no connection between the two words. Spaghetti is one thing, Bolognese sauce or ragù is another. Both have something to do with Bologna but not together, except on the menus of restaurants outside of Italy, and in a few touristy Italian cities."

This is Bruno Barbieri, one of Italy's most renowned chefs with no fewer than seven Michelin stars to his name, across four restaurants. As well as cooking like a god, Bruno is a brilliant communicator who's appeared in major TV shows and is a highly respected name. He comes from Medicina, a small town in the east of metropolitan Bologna toward Imola. His restaurants are spread around the provinces of Bologna, Ferrara and Ravenna, and one has strayed a little to the north, near Verona. So when I wanted to talk about spaghetti Bolognese, I had to call on him as someone I know well and admire a lot.

This is not a case of serendipity. Everyone knows it wasn't born by accident, but it's equally clear that it was created to achieve a mistaken aim, and it ended up riding to world fame on a tradition that had never existed. In 2010, when we were creating the menus for the different Eataly restaurants in New York (due to open a few weeks later), we came to the pasta restaurant and a young, serious and well-qualified American chef spoke up: "We should start with spaghetti Bolognese and *fettuccine all'Alfredo*," he suggested in blissful ignorance. My associate Joe Bastianich looked at me mortified, and I shot a withering look at the misguided cook. But I immediately regretted it, because the young man was an excellent chef and fortunately still works with us.

He only meant to remind us of the two most famous Italian pasta dishes in the Big Apple at the time. What he hadn't fully grasped was that we wanted to bring the true regional specialties of our country to America.

In any case, the mystery remains: we don't know exactly who first wrote "*spaghetti alla bolognese*" on a menu. I've often wondered about it and pictured the scene in my mind.

I thought it must certainly have been outside Italy: in New York, I like to imagine, at Manhattan's first Italian restaurant, Barbetta, opened in 1906 by Sebastiano Maioglio. The same family runs it today, in the Theater District on 46th Street. It's a lovely, historic place and the food is good. Obviously I have no proof that it's the birthplace of spaghetti Bolognese, and with all the Italian restaurants there are in New York it was more likely someone else's mischievous prank. But knowing how historic this restaurant is, I like to imagine it was the Barbetta chef who first put the dish on the menu. I'm determined to believe he wasn't being a smart aleck but did it because he had a good meat ragout on hand, and since he liked putting it on his own spaghetti he offered it to his customers as well, and invented a pompous-sounding name for it. And he was right. The dish brought together two very famous names recognizable to the sizeable Italophile public: spaghetti, the icon of pasta, and Bologna, known as "the gluttonous."

But Bruno knows all about it and I don't, so he tells me what Bologna has to do with spaghetti.

"Word is that the people of Bologna, mainly the less well-off, were eating dried pasta as far back as the Middle Ages because it was ready for use and cheaper, as it didn't contain eggs. What's more it didn't require the women to knead and roll out the dough: that took a great deal of effort, and it meant pasta was made by hand mainly on holidays or for special events. There were different types of dried pasta, one being vermicelli, or *vermizi* as it was called then.

"The dried pasta usually came from Genoa or Puglia. But eventually, as consumption increased, the Senate in Bologna decided to support the opening of a pasta factory locally, with the aim of reducing the huge transport costs that were having an impact on the price of the product. The Bologna Chamber of Commerce, the ultimate authority, approved a tomato and tuna sauce as the dressing most commonly used for vermicelli. That's credible enough, but I tend to believe other types of sauce were used as well, not written down in recipes because they were made from leftovers."

Barbieri admits they might also have used the ragu left over from the holidays, possibly enriched with a *soffritto* of celery and onion. Very likely peas were added when in season, because there are ancient texts proving that the people of Bologna loved peas. Bruno explains that it was very common to use leftovers. "So it's plausible to say there was meat in the vermicelli sauce, but you can't say it was the true Bolognese ragu because that was much more of a luxury."

Bruno tells me the Bolognese ragu has a relatively recent history and only began appearing in recipe books in the nineteenth century. One of these of course is Pellegrino Artusi's timeless *Science in the Kitchen and the Art of Eating Well*.

The use of the ragu in Bologna isn't all that old, and given the high cost of the ingredients it was quite likely used to dress the rich pastas made by hand for feast days and holidays: tagliatelle and green lasagne. Chef Barbieri reminds me of the fact (not a given) that the tomato only reached Europe after the discovery of America, but it wasn't used in cooking before the eighteenth century. There's also another reason why it couldn't have been the everyday sauce. The Bolognese ragu needs watching over for a long time, and time is something these working women didn't have. "So the conclusion is that spaghetti had a worthy place at Bologna's tables, but mainly on meatless days and dressed with onion, tuna and other sauces using leftovers—certainly not with the true Bolognese ragu. That was a noble sauce reserved for equally noble handmade egg pastas. Tagliatelle and green lasagne with five or six or seven layers."

Bruno is kind. He explains that *spaghetti alla bolognese*, that is to say with a meat ragu, is purely and simply a marketing invention. But he doesn't put the knife in and curse the exploitation of noble Emilian traditions or rail against an insolent form of "Italian-sounding" cuisine that alters the historical characteristics of Italian tradition. Let's say that some in Bologna take a much stronger view, like the former mayor Virginio Merola.

Whenever "Bologna the gluttonous" was mentioned, Merola grasped the opportunity to remind everyone that spaghetti Bolognese has nothing to do with the city. On social media he wrote: "Dear residents, I am collecting photos of *spaghetti alla bolognese* from all over the world (speaking of fake news). Here's one from London. Please send me yours." And many people did. So there were images of the famous Knorr *spaghetti alla bolognese* with a mixture of Austrian spices, and a woeful plastic packet of cooked pasta from Utrecht, not to mention a can of Heinz spaghetti sauce sold by online supermarket Ocado in the UK, and a blackboard in Moravia offering "*Bolonske spagety.*" As he told *The Telegraph*, "It's strange being famous all over the world for a dish that isn't ours. Of course we're happy for it to draw attention to our city, but we'd rather be known for the high-quality food that's part of our culinary tradition."

Well, if even the former mayor says it we can only fall into line. On the one hand I'm horrified when I see *spaghetti alla bolognese* served in the umpteenth tourist restaurant on the Venice canals with the pasta obviously cooked in advance, but on the other hand I'm not ashamed to admit I absolutely love a plate of Gragnano artisan spaghetti cooked al dente, with a ragu made with long-cooked top-quality meat. But don't go around telling people that.

43

THE WHITE TRUFFLE

Blessed be that gift

WITH BRUNO URBANI

Throughout the world the white truffle is called by the same family name: "d'Alba," of Alba, indicating that it comes from a specific place. Alba is the capital of the Langhe, located thirty-seven miles south of Turin, and in the Cuneo province even though it's closer to Asti. I was born there, so I know it well. It's a small city with a population of around thirty thousand. Alba is the heart of a wine and farming economy based on Barolo and Barbaresco wines, chestnuts and many other specialties. But it's probably most famous for the white truffle. If you go to the Four Seasons in New York or the Mandarin in Hong Kong you'll find "*Tartufo bianco d'Alba*" on the menu.

And yet less than 10 percent of Italian white truffles are dug out of the soil in the hills around Alba. There are other places where you can find them in greater numbers, like Acqualagna in the Marche and the hills around Savigno in Emilia. Not to mention Monferrato (in the provinces of Asti and Alessandria), which produces more than twice the quantity grown in Alba. So why does everyone refer to it as "d'Alba"?

While Alba only grows a small proportion of the total white truffle production, it markets more than 60 percent. The little perfumed nugget from other areas of the world, such as Croatia, Serbia, the Czech Republic or Slovakia, has to go through Alba to be sold at a profitable price. For many this is a mystery as to why but the people of Alba know the reason, and now I'll share it with you.

Often it's the heroes born in a place that bring it fame, and Alba has had one truly special hero, Giacomo Morra (1889–1963). That's the first serendipitous thing.

It's our good fortune that Giacomo Morra was born in Alba. In 1928 he set up the first company to market the truffle. He also bought the Hotel Savona, where he established a restaurant that could feed up to a thousand people, and feed them well. In 1930 he started the Alba Truffle Fair and transformed some kennels in Roddi, a little town perched above the Langhe hills, into a university for truffle dogs where the first simulated searches were conducted for journalists and tourists.

In 1938 he found an enormous truffle weighing nearly a kilogram and presented it as a gift to Prince Umberto of Savoy. In 1942 he did the same for King Victor Emmanuel III, and in 1949 he decided it was time to go international and sent a splendid truffle to Rita Hayworth. But the major coup came in 1951, when a *trifulau*, a truffle hunter, found a specimen in Serralunga d'Alba weighing an unbelievable five pounds. He took it straight to Giacomo Morra, who had no doubts about where it should go. The package was sent to President Harry Truman at the White House, and apparently the president's chef had already put the water on to boil when he phoned the Savona asking for Morra, because he wasn't sure about the cooking time. Fortunately Morra answered straight away, thus saving the chef from ruining the jewel he had in his hands. Second serendipitous moment. The news was published with great fanfare in all the American dailies, and of course the Italian newspapers.

In the 1950s, Asti, jealous of Alba's success, decided to launch its own truffle fair. On the opening Sunday, Giacomo Morra arrived at the market at 6 a.m. with several colleagues and a suitcase full of money. He offered more than the market value and bought all the truffles. So the first Asti Fair opened without a single truffle, and that was the first and last truffle fair in the Monferrato capital.

We are still enjoying the legacy of that amazing man and we're thankful he was born in La Morra, a charming town nestled into one of the lovely hills around Alba. But credit is also due elsewhere, including to successive administrations which have managed that legacy very well.

Back in 1852, before Giacomo Morra was born, there was another family destined to go down in history courtesy of the truffle trade: the Urbanis, in the charming village of Scheggino in the Valnerina, Umbria. Just over four decades ago the Urbani family bought the Giacomo Morra company. Can you imagine what that means? The company founded by the man who essentially invented the Alba white truffle is in the hands of an Umbrian family. Dammit! I would be throwing my hands up in horror, but the Urbanis are good people, and savvy enough to realize that nothing about the Morra truffle should be changed, including the celebration of it as a legend belonging to Alba.

"My dear Oscar, as you know even the strongest oak starts off as a tiny seedling. No end of miracles take place beneath the soil, and the truffle is surely the most beautiful! It's born hidden in the silent darkness of the earth, and it forms in silence from white molds that attach themselves to the roots of particular plants to create a unique kind of symbiosis, where the truffle takes all the substances for itself and sucks the life out of others to increase its beauty and fascination."

Bruno Urbani, boss of Urbani Tartufi, reminds me it's no coincidence that Molière's comedy about a swindler is called *Tartuffe* (*The Imposter*). As he tells me the full story of the company sale negotiations, I can only imagine Morra's heirs must have been biting their lips while Urbani was signing the agreement. "In every person's life, fate adds a few unusual and unexpected turns, but the one that united the destinies of the truffle king Giacomo Morra and the Urbani family really is surprising. Giacomo and his beloved wife, Teresa, had four sons, none of whom wanted to take on their father's business. So one day I called one of them, Mario, and offered to buy the Alba company. The conditions the Morras set were far from simple, but I wasn't discouraged. I had to make the journey over to Alba countless times before the deal was finalized."

It was by no means an easy settlement. It seemed as if the Morra brothers would never reach a decision, but the courtship from Umbria was intense. Bruno held his nerve. He clearly remembers the last of his endless trips to Alba. "That day we were negotiating until three in the morning. We were exhausted, but in the end we sealed the deal. Now I want you to understand what kind of person Mario was—the third of Giacomo's four sons."

This was more or less the situation, he tells me. Mario was the only one who could type out the text of the contract and he was happy to volunteer. He started tapping away on the Olivetti typewriter but after only a few lines he asked if he could go out for a minute for a pressing need. We waited ten minutes, an hour, several hours … but he'd actually snuck off to bed to get some sleep! The next day the typing went on until seven in the evening because every line triggered fresh discussion. In the end we got to the signatures, and we were utterly exhausted all over again. At that point Mario showed a generosity and cheerfulness that were never on display during the negotiations, inviting us to dinner to celebrate. I remember that evening Piazza Savona in Alba was packed for a rally where the communist Giancarlo Pajetta was speaking. He was a phenomenal speaker, and we stopped to listen. At a certain point we went searching for Mario all around the piazza, but he'd disappeared. At first we were laughing, but then we realized how difficult and painful it must have been for him giving up what had been the throne of his father, Giacomo, the truffle king."

Perhaps he really needed to be alone to start digesting the tremendous decision to sell not just a business, but a piece of Alba's history to an ordinary man from Scheggino in the country outside Perugia.

But it all went well. Urbani was able to maintain both the identity and the legend, leaving the headquarters and the workers in their native city. It wasn't just out of kindness (although hopefully that was part of it), but of necessity: the value of the Morra company lay in the story of the Langhe, and still does. So Bruno and his people operated respectfully from the start and entrusted the management to people from Alba. These days Tartufi Morra is run by the Bonino family: Gianmaria and his brother, Alessandro, and daughter, Carlotta, natives of Alba.

Bruno Urbani represents the fourth generation of the most important truffle family in the world. With his brother Paolo, another great man sadly no longer with us, he took it to half the world in an extraordinary way. Together with Paolo's daughter, Olga, and his own sons Carlo and Giammarco, he operates in seventy-five countries. They control the largest slice of the world market for both fresh and preserved truffles. However, what I admire in them is not the power they have, but rather their passion and humanity.

44

TOFU

When a population falls in love

WITH SHIGERU HAYASHI

In the West we use the Japanese name, but tofu originated in China with the name *doufu*, more than two thousand years ago. It arrived in the Land of the Rising Sun hundreds of years later, and the Japanese became more enamored of it than any other population in the East, where tofu is made just about everywhere. It was the Japanese who first brought it to Europe, where it now has plenty of admirers.

These are the stats provided by my friend Shigeru Hayashi: around 80 percent of Japanese eat tofu at least twice a week, raw or cooked in a variety of ways. They consider it a food to eat for longevity, and it's the jewel in the crown of *shojin ryori*, the traditional vegetarian cuisine of the Buddhist monks. Studies have shown that their community includes countless centenarians, and the average lifespan has increased thanks to their diet.

Shigeru lives in Tokyo. I finally managed to catch up with him using tofu as an excuse, but our friendship goes back a good fifteen years. He's the leading Japanese expert in Italian wines, and in 2013 we wrote a book on wine together. The title of the Italian edition is

Storie di coraggio, and the English title is *Vino, I Love You*, but it has been translated into other languages too, including Korean. It's been quite successful, in other words, and we became good friends when we were writing it, traveling the length and breadth of Italy and visiting some of the most important wine families.

Shigeru is not only a sommelier but a great gastronome as well. He knows the story of the age-old Japanese cuisine as few others do. One day he told me the inhabitants of his country have intestines about six-and-a-half feet longer than ours in the West. Why? Centuries of eating legumes, cereals and vegetables, food that's more difficult to digest and thus calls for a larger intestine. We're the same age, but he looks at least ten years younger. Whenever we meet at his home I watch him gorge on tofu while I'm busy with the last pieces of my Kobe beef. So I decided I should try to like this blessed tofu, and maybe a chat with him would help.

"My dear Shigeru, tell us about the origin of tofu. It seems to be a case of serendipity."

"First, Oscar, I'll tell you what tofu is and how it's made. It's obtained from soy milk by a process like the one used for some animal milk cheeses. You can do it all at home quite quickly, and we like to make it because we've been doing it for centuries, from generation to generation; we've improved bits of the process here and there, but the basic procedure has never changed."

Shigeru describes what seems to be a simple process.

You start with soybeans. In Japan you can get very good natural ones, GMO-free and organic as well. You steep them in water for about six hours in summer or twelve in winter. My friend recommends quality ingredients. "You need pure fresh water. In Japan we have the best fresh water in the world, and plenty of it." I want to tell him there's no shortage of good water in Italy either, but I restrain myself.

After soaking, the beans are blended to a puree and cooked in boiling water (four liters for every five hundred grams of soy) for ten minutes. Attention: when the water reaches 185 degrees

Fahrenheit—that's to say when the first bubbles rise—it's time to add the *nigari*, a natural rennet consisting of magnesium chloride. You need four grams for every liter of water you put on to boil, and first it must be dissolved in a glass of hot water. After it has boiled for ten minutes you turn off the heat, and it's lovely to watch the first flakes already starting to form. Let it rest for another ten minutes.

Shigeru explains that every Japanese home has special tofu molds, but you can use an ordinary container ten centimeters deep. Before pouring in your mixture you line the mold with linen gauze or cheese-cloth, then pour in the mixture and fold the cloth over the curdling milk until it's completely covered. Place a weight on top and wait for one hour minimum. Your tofu is then ready.

If you want to save time you can start with ready-made soy milk from the shop, but making it yourself at home is another thing entirely.

"But I'm curious to know who invented it, when and how," I tell the Japanese master.

"Don't rush, Oscar. I still have to tell you why tofu is good for you and how to eat it. We call soy 'meat of the fields' because it's very rich in protein. Even richer than meat. A hundred grams of pork has 19 grams of protein, beef 16, and soy 25. But the best thing is that there's almost zero cholesterol, and soy also has many amino acids that are good for the health. In short, it's got the beneficial qualities of meat but with very low cholesterol content. I can't do without tofu in my life. I eat it almost every day, at home and in the restaurant I often go to for work. In summer I have *hiyayakko*, cold tofu, and in winter I order the hot one, *yu dofu*."

He tells me that Tokyo has many izakaya, informal pub-like restaurants that offer a large number of dishes, including tofu. Shigeru is so crazy about tofu that even when he goes to a more generic restaurant or one that specializes in other dishes he still orders tofu. "For instance, it's excellent in miso soup and perfect between courses of sukiyaki, and it's indispensable in *shabu-shabu*—the richest dish in our cuisine, where various ingredients are dipped into broth one at a time. What you should do, Oscar, is dip in less meat and more tofu."

But let's get back to the history of tofu. Even if we can't be entirely sure this is how it happened, the date couldn't be more precise: it's 164 BC, in China.

It appears the scion of the Han dynasty, Prince Liu An, was much happier cooking and eating than governing. One day he was making a soybean soup, very common even back then, and he added some dirty sea salt. It must have contained calcium and magnesium, because soon he saw with dismay that the mixture was coagulating. It was the start of the process generated by the chance formation of rennet. Not to be discouraged, the prince waited until it cooled and then took a taste of the soy cheese that had formed. It tasted good, but that wasn't enough for him. Realizing the phenomenon was due to the dirty salt, he got a large quantity of it and repeated the operation a number of times until he found the best method. The new dish was well received in the Han dynasty court and, as written in the sixteenth-century book *Honso-Komoku*, where the story was first told, this *doufu* soon became the new food for the nobility in China.

Later on it gradually spread to all social strata.

There are other stories about the origin of tofu, Shigeru reveals, but they're not nearly as appealing as this one. What's certain is that from the second century AD, tofu, or rather *doufu*, was consumed regularly all over China. Stories and poems from the Song and Yuan dynasties describe methods of making it that are very similar to today's. It arrived in Japan eight centuries later, in the Nara period between 710 and 784 AD.

"We don't know for certain whether it was brought in by a Japanese diplomatic delegation returning from an official visit to China, or by monks," Shigeru says. "I lean toward the second hypothesis because it all seems to have started with their *shojin ryori* diet. We Japanese have been hopelessly devoted to tofu for more than twelve centuries and we've managed to slip it into a lot of our traditional dishes. I remember when I came to Milan over thirty years ago to run Italy's first major Japanese restaurant, Suntory. I wanted to introduce tofu straight away, and initially we imported it, but later we made it in-house. Getting Italians to 'digest' it was no easy task, but we did it in the end. Besides, what could be more digestible than tofu?"

Pasta, I'd like to say, but I don't. Otherwise he'd start explaining to me how pasta came from the Orient as well.

45

CAPRI CAKE

A scrumptious scare

WITH ANTONINO CANNAVACCIUOLO

If you haven't been to Capri, walked around the island, paused to breathe in the air and take in its views, make haste to Naples as soon as you have the time and opportunity, get on one of the frequent ferries, and in just over half an hour you'll find yourself on one of the world's most beautiful islands.

Capri smashes the definition of utopia. In 1516, Thomas More wrote *Utopia*, where he described an island as a "non place," from the Greek *ou-topos*, a place that doesn't exist because it's hard to get to, and if you ever do get there you don't leave.

Visiting Capri, inhaling its perfumes and being moved by its enchanting panoramas is an easy way to get to utopia. Go the length and breadth of the island, stop in a café—but perhaps not right in the Piazzetta along with the rest of the world. Take a walk through the narrow lanes and climb up to the center of the island, where you can look down over the gulf and appreciate the wonder of the Tyrrhenian Sea in this truly blessed piece of Italy.

Now let's talk about the Capri of the 1920s. It was already famous as a tourist destination, and probably even more beautiful than it is now. The visitors were mainly people who'd had the time and the means to read about the wonders of the island—an odd mixture of intellectuals: anarchists and socialists escaping from the mainland, artists, poets, Futurists, philosophers, writers.

But there were others there as well, of a different breed. The *Mafiosi* certainly weren't short of the means to enjoy a summer holiday on Capri. One morning in May 1920, three of these shady customers from the other side of the Atlantic landed on the island. They were well known around Naples and their behavior was unmistakable. In reality this was more a mission than a holiday.

The story of the *torta caprese* starts here. But I'm not the one who should tell it. Someone who knows a lot more about it than I do, given his origins and his profession, is Antonino Cannavacciuolo. He's a fantastic cook, and an intelligent man with a deep knowledge of his home territory, and the attachment remains despite the fact that he has had to leave it for work. He was born in Vico Equense, a charming seaside town on the Sorrento coast, and from there you can see Capri on the horizon. One of his first jobs after graduating from the hospitality school where his father taught was on Capri, at the restaurant in the Grand Hotel Quisisana. Imagine how many Capri cakes he must have put in the oven as a young cook at the Quisisana. In 1999 he became manager of Villa Crespi on Lake Orta in Piedmont, and from there his career took off. He has two Michelin stars and a high profile as a TV personality.

These days Antonino lives in an equally spectacular part of Italy, but I can imagine how much he misses the little beach at Vico.

"The *torta caprese* is the result of a mistake, right?" I ask him.

"The pastry chef who first made it by accident was called Carmine Fiore. In 1920 he was considered Capri's best pastry cook. One day three thugs sauntered into his restaurant and looked around contemptuously. They were obviously underworld figures. Can you imagine? American *Mafiosi* in Naples for business, and visiting Capri to buy gaiters for their boss, Al Capone! Apparently the best gaiters at the time were on the island.

"As it happened, in that moment Fiore was busy making an almond cake, and probably due to a combination of fear, emotion and too much haste, he left out the main ingredient: flour. When he took the cake out of the oven he was stunned to find it soft in the center and crisp on the outside. You see, Oscar, the *torta caprese* is a hymn to simplicity. It only has five ingredients: almonds, cocoa, butter, eggs and sugar. There are variations, but those are the ingredients in the original recipe. The secret is in the preparation—how to put them together, how to cook them and for how long. On that day in 1920 everything turned out perfect for Carmine Fiore. Scared witless, he unwittingly created perfection. An even bigger surprise was to see the cake winning over the palates of the Americans it was made for. They even asked him for the recipe. The *torta caprese* or Capri cake is an example of how, throughout history, 'errors' or absent-mindedness in the kitchen have led to dishes that symbolize our tradition and go on to worldwide success." An exceptional cook like Antonino knows you can never assume you've done it all. Every day you can try new flavor combinations, a new cooking technique or new food pairings that generate fresh textures and pleasant surprises.

"I've loved mixing different ingredients since I was young, and now with experience and maturity I'm still experimenting with the same enthusiasm as when I was trying things out at my mom's house in the afternoons after school. I don't like talking about errors when it comes to a mistake in the kitchen: I'd rather talk about trials and research and new opportunities. As the proverb says, we learn by our mistakes. When you learn from a mistake, that's an opportunity. And what teaches us this is the story of human evolution and improvement—it's not just in the kitchen."

"Are you still making the Capri cake, Antonino?"

"Of course!" He seems almost surprised at the question. "The *torta caprese* is on my menu every day. At Villa Crespi we've been offering it to our guests every morning for twenty years, and now it's in my bistros in Novara and Turin too. The absence of flour gives it lightness, and the exquisite taste makes it perfect for people with dietary restrictions due to food intolerances and allergies. When Carmine Fiori made that mistake, he not only created a great dessert but also discovered a cake that's still enviably relevant a century later. I also feel honored and duty-bound to offer a dessert from a tradition my family and I love, and that's not to be underestimated."

Here is Antonino's recipe for the *torta caprese*.

===

INGREDIENTS:

3/4 cup butter	1 egg white
1-1/8 cups powdered sugar	1/3 cup granulated sugar
3 eggs	3 cups almond meal
1 egg yolk	1/3 cup cocoa
	slivered almonds, to taste

METHOD:

1 Cream the butter with the powdered sugar in an electric mixer.

2 In a separate bowl, beat the whole eggs with the yolk and add to the butter mixture in a thin stream.

3 Meanwhile, beat the egg white with the granulated sugar, and mix the almond meal with the cocoa.

4 Remove the butter and eggs from the mixer, add the egg white, and finally the almond meal and cocoa mixture.

5 Butter the cake rings and place them on baking sheets covered with baking paper, spread slivered almonds over and pour the cake mixture on top.

6 Bake at 350°F for about 40 minutes.

===

If you find yourself lucky enough to be in Capri, don't forget to have a large slice of *torta caprese*, and while you're eating it think of Carmine Fiore the pastry cook and how lucky he was to make that mistake!

46

YOGURT

Genghis Khan's energy drink

WITH ANA ROŠ

Ana Roš was voted the World's Best Female Chef in 2017, by The
World's 50 Best Restaurants, a worldwide organization that uses a thousand or so of the best independent food and wine experts to rank the
best cooks. I imagine April 5, 2017 was a big day in Melbourne, Australia, where they officially declared her the number one woman in
the kitchen: suddenly everyone knew who Ana Roš was, and she truly
deserved it.

Ana's restaurant, Hiša Franko, is in Caporetto, Slovenia, in a farm-
house she moved into with her husband, Walter, in 2002, armed with
a degree in Diplomatic Studies. Yes, that mythical Caporetto every Italian knows well, in the Karst region; it has moved its borders too often
over the past century, and it's the place where the Italian army suffered
its worst-ever defeat in October 1917, with the retreat lasting almost a
month. However, in that world war Italy was among the victors, and
Caporetto flew the Italian flag for about twenty years, until it became
a Yugoslavian city after World War II. It didn't become part of Slovenia again until the 1990s.

Ana is proudly Slovenian, and her cooking comes from her strong and determined character. When the time came to tell the story of yogurt, I remembered Ana telling me about the milk produced in the valleys around her home and how much she enjoyed starting yeasts.

"I love yogurt. I often skip breakfast, and sometimes lunch as well, but I'm always thinking about yogurt. It makes me happier than any other food."

Ana lives in an area where dairy products are key: unpasteurized milk cheese, butter, kefir and sour milk. Milk rules. Always raw, with no added sugars. In the restaurant, she tells me, they're currently serving natural yogurt marinated with roasted coffee, vanilla, figs, sage and foie gras. But she likes yogurt because of the character it gives to a dish: rich, with a mineral taste in the mouth that's almost ferrous.

This is another extraordinary product apparently born by accident, a bit like the others derived from fermentation.

The Mongolian people have long been big yogurt eaters, and Genghis Khan's warriors believed it could give them strength and even beauty. And the serendipity of yogurt is found in a legend circulated among the Mongolians.

"It comes from a story often told at night around the fire. One of Genghis Khan's soldiers had to do a long desert crossing and stopped in a village to rest. He encountered an enemy warrior there, who pretended to be a friend by filling his water bottle for him. But he filled it with milk, believing that would ruin it and Genghis Khan's soldier would be poisoned, so he wouldn't be leaving those dangerous steppes alive. However, exactly the opposite happened: the milk started to ferment. Since there was nothing else available the soldier drank it, and that primitive form of yogurt gave him the necessary strength to reach his destination safe and sound. The incident convinced Genghis Khan of the power of yogurt, and he personally urged all his warriors to eat it."

There's a much more modern story relating to Ana and her childhood in her grandmother's house. Nonna Iva had nine grandchildren. One day Ana, her cousin Duško and her sister Maja were eating at their grandparents' house—a day Ana remembers well. "There was the classic consommé followed by meat stew, potatoes, and salad from the kitchen garden. Instead of dessert my grandmother brought us a few tubs of natural yogurt. My sister and I were used to eating whole-milk yogurt as is, but my cousin Duško asked for some sugar. This puzzled me: sweet yogurt? My curiosity got the better of me and I copied him. I thought it was horrible. After the first teaspoon I couldn't bring myself to take another mouthful; the combination of slight natural sweetness and pleasant acidity that I loved so much was gone. My grandmother got very angry: in our family nobody was allowed to waste food. 'You don't leave the table until you've finished your yogurt!' she ordered. Cartoon time on TV came and went and I hadn't touched it. We were still there after the news, sitting opposite each other: me with my head down sulking, and my grandmother watching the television and peeping now and again to see if I'd give in. Then there was a terribly boring film, and finally the late-night news. Yet there I was, still at the table sitting in front of the tub full of that horrible sweetened yogurt. In the end my poor grandmother was falling asleep, so she went off to bed shaking her head. The drama was over and I'd held on."

Our approach to a food can be an indicator of our lifestyle: "That's how I am. It's not being inflexible, it's being consistent. And that's what I try to bring to my cooking every day. In any case, let me say—please don't play around with yogurt!"

47

VERDIGRIS

Don't steal my grapes

WITH ATTILIO SCIENZA

Attilio Scienza is an agricultural scientist, and in particular works with wine. It's quite amusing that a man whose surname is "Science" is a scientist by profession; he's also hugely successful, with numerous publications to his name.

Attilio has been a professor of viticulture at the University of Milan since 2004. One of the most curious cases of serendipity is verdigris, the blue mixture sprayed on vines to prevent and cure some diseases, so I went straight to him to find out more about it.

He began by explaining that copper is an ancient metal, dating back to the fifth millennium BC. It was easy to come by and to process and was used mainly in Central and Eastern Europe for making tools and weapons. In more recent times it has been used to kill algae, bacteria and fungi, and has really boomed with the arrival of downy mildew on grapevines, potatoes and tomatoes.

Attilio reminds me that copper can turn from a solution into a problem: "With the rise of organic farming it was used more and more in the fight against parasites. Eventually, the European Community brought in a new set of rules limiting its use in wine growing to four kilograms a year (twenty-eight kilograms in seven years, about sixty-two pounds), to avoid the biological damage the heavy metal does to the soil. A study of the soil in French vineyards from 1998 to 2010 showed very high levels of so-called bioavailable copper in some areas like Bordeaux and the Languedoc, above the limit of fifty parts per million considered toxic for the soil microbiome. We have to remember that copper in the form of the Bordeaux mixture has been in use since the mid-1800s, and it's a metal that doesn't break down over time."

So verdigris in large quantities can become a problem for the health of the land. But when it was invented it was welcomed as the perfect remedy for downy mildew. An ampelographer named Alexis Millardet discovered it by a fluke, when the parasite came from America into a Europe already in crisis through damage from another harmful insect, the grape phylloxera. On a visit to the Château Ducru-Beaucaillou in Saint Julien, in the Bordeaux region, Millardet noticed that the disease had not attacked vines growing close to the road. The man running the business, Ernest David, told him there was a simple and rather curious explanation for that. He'd had enough of people constantly stealing the grape clusters in the first few meters of the vine rows nearest the road, so he'd invented a solution of basic copper or blue vitriol acetate, mixed with lime, to smear on the grapes of the first vines in each row. The objective was to discourage the grape thieves with the blue color.

The man had invented verdigris, but only because he wanted to put off marauders! Then he realized something strange was going on. The smeared bunches were healthy and weren't being attacked by the downy mildew, unlike all the others. Verdigris was the right medicine.

"They started applying it in 1883," Attilio tells me. "They would brush the plants with heather brooms steeped in the solution, but it turned out to be a long and laborious operation, and costly as well: it took twenty workers twenty days to treat an area of fifty hectares. But the industry is always moving forward and they refined the technique.

The first distribution was in 1886 when they used the powdered mixture in a pump carried on the worker's back, and then after a few years they moved to spraying the verdigris from a cart pulled by a horse."

He adds that a great chemist named Ulysses Gayon created the famous Bordeaux mixture, and it was both easy to prepare and cheap. "At last we had a natural antidote to the vine disease and the right method of spraying it. But unfortunately the winegrowers used the magic mix in much higher doses than the experts recommended. In the '50s they got to forty or fifty kilograms a year per hectare. An ethnologist, André Lagrange, wrote on seeing vineyards covered in the Bordeaux mixture: 'Blue is now everywhere, as if all the blue of the sky has descended to the earth.'"

As you will have gathered, Scienza is no big fan of verdigris. Yet it's the only remedy the organic rulebook gives for vine diseases, which makes me wonder what can be done. Do we have to go back to the chemicals?

"Not the ones that damage our health and the soil, that's for sure. In the meantime, we need to improve the way these treatments are done. Generally more than half misses its target, so we have to work on 'precise viticulture' approaches. There are technologies that can limit the distribution of the verdigris to where it's needed, and others that can calculate the right timing via a system that supports those decisions with monitoring and information. We can foresee 'recovery panels' being used to drastically reduce dispersion in the environment, and already anti-rain screens have been developed to cover the vine rows. The reality is that for financial and landscaping reasons, these new technologies are not being used. The chemical industry is working hard to create pesticides to replace verdigris, but it's not simple. There are multiple requirements to meet before they can be used successfully in organic farming: no artificial chemicals, a prolonged efficacy over time, environmental sustainability, adequate toxicology profile, a favorable environmental future, absolute indifference to the qualitative properties of the grape and therefore the wine, and tolerance by the vine.

Finally, of course, we can't ignore the financial aspect. At present, only mixtures based on orange essential oil are registered, and a few Tuscan companies are trialing those. The scientific community has been actively searching for new molecules for a long time and tapping into natural compounds, but they're still in the study phase and some prerequisites seem impossible to achieve at the moment. In my view the fastest, safest and cheapest way is to work on the genetics."

I ask Attilio if he intended to create genetically modified vines; his answer is no. Transgenic modification, which we know as GMO, involves combining genes of various vegetable and animal origins that change the natural sequence of the original plant.

Instead, what Scienza is talking about is the possibility of working on combinations of genes from plants of the same genus, *Vitis*, and even the same species, *Vinifera*; their function is to make the vines produce substances to counter the fungal diseases. He explains it further: "The European vines have a large number of disease-resistant genes, but because of their evolutionary history they can't do that job. They might be able to in the future, but it would take a very long time—too long. In the 1980s and '90s our research led us to what's known as decrypting the grapevine genome, the starting point for all future applications of genetic improvement techniques for the vines. Today there are two technologies that can change the genome of a grapevine, belonging to the NPBT (New Plant Breeding Techniques) group. One is very recent, linked to the discovery of a protein called CRISPR/Cas9, which can bring about genome editing through a kind of molecular scissors that cut the DNA at a predetermined point when they recognize a particular base sequence. We could describe this operation as producing 'clone' plants, because the genetic mutation is minimal and only affects a few bases (the same thing happens spontaneously in nature through mutations). This genome correction is a kind of microsurgery carried out on so-called 'susceptibility' genes, and means the vine is no longer susceptible to the disease.

"The other technology is cisgenesis, introduced in 2006, with the aim of overcoming the public's fears and resistance to GMOs. Cisgenesis differs from transgenesis (GMO) in that it uses disease-resisting or quality-control genes that are not modified and come from sexually compatible plants. In GMOs the inserted genes come from plants that are very different genetically, or even from animal organisms. The unique aspect of these technologies is that the modifications are targeted, as opposed to other systems such as physical or chemical mutagenesis or crossing, which generate an undefinable number of random modifications that may or may not be positive. The final result is the same as what we can achieve with more traditional approaches like crossing, but with greater efficiency and respect for the quality of the wine, so as to maximize the value of our native vine stock and the Designations of Origin."

The new appreciation of winemaking without synthetic chemistry has accelerated this innovative research approach, and Italy is taking the lead. The University of Udine, working with ten of Friuli's wine-producing companies, has obtained ten vines with the traditional crossing technique, using American and Asian vines resistant to downy mildew and powdery mildew. And recently the Edmund Mach Foundation in San Michele all'Adige was granted permission to cultivate new resistant varieties. Can we say we've found the ideal grapevine? Not yet, there's still some way to go, and we need to resolve bureaucratic problems and ideological resistance around the concept of genetics to distinguish our work from the world of GMOs. At the moment, creating resistant vines with genome editing and cisgenesis is made difficult by a decision of the Court of Justice in Strasbourg approving the grapevines obtained by these technologies for GMOs.

But things are changing on this front too, and the Council of the European Union has asked the European Commission to present a study on the review of the 2018 directive.

What could make this project successful, and Italian viticulture research a world leader, is a major effort in terms of organization and funding, Attilio says. "We need to create a network of Italian research

bodies and wine producers, possibly through a dedicated foundation that would operate via effective lobbying. It also requires money,
because without it research stops—something like 15 million euros a
year for five years. It would only take less than one cent for each bottle of wine produced in Italy (around 2.5 billion a year), a trifling figure
for the winemakers but crucial to develop the research. Also it's not yet
clear how the European Community will approach the classification of
these plants and subsequently the use of the 'clones' in the DOC wine
specifications. In a nutshell, we can do it in five years, believe me!"

48

HUMANKIND

Absolute serendipity

WITH TELMO PIEVANI

I'd like to finish off with the most important case of serendipity in the history of our planet—in other words, us. Yes, I mean human beings. Regardless of your thinking about our origins, nothing in the world has been created or autonomously formed in a more accidental or imperfect way than humans.

If you believe in God the Creator, you must nevertheless admit that He probably would've hoped for a species very different from the flawed *sapiens* that start wars and are capable of racism and selfishness. In the first chapter of the Book of Genesis, verse 26, we read: "And God said let us make man in our image and likeness." But the Bible is even more explicit in chapter 5, verses 1 and 2, where we find: "When God created man, He made him in His likeness. He created male and female and blessed them."

We might think that even He imagined this man as something better, a bit more like Himself at least in terms of values. But He saw it wasn't so. Very soon (in chapter 3, verse 17 to be exact) Adam and Eve were stained by Original Sin and God was so angry that He threw them

265

out of the Garden of Eden. A very different result from the expected one, hence a perfect example of serendipity.

If, like Charles Darwin, you believe humans are the product of natural selection, studying this will show you how much chance, unpredictability and fate are behind our "being" as we are today. At the start of the third millennium this is more or less the situation: there are about eight billion of us. We belong to 195 different recognized nations, speak over seven thousand languages, and practice roughly fourteen major religions. But the scenario could have been very different if other things had happened in the three-billion-year arc of human development. Whichever way you look at it, serendipity is involved.

It's a long story and it began even before life emerged on our planet. Many scientists agree it all started about fourteen billion years ago with the Big Bang. It's not to be imagined as an explosion, but the moment the universe began to expand, due to the particular density and heat conditions. This phenomenon led to the birth of space and time, matter and energy. After that came ten billion years of crazy cosmic activity. Gaseous nebulae flattening to become protoplanetary disks, star formations, exploding supernovas, planets colliding, meteorites crashing. Around four and a half billion years ago one of these accidental disruptions generated the solar system, which includes Earth. This was about when our history began.

Earth at the start was not as we know it today. It was smaller, and in its first two billion years it copped just about everything. There was a tremendous collision with another slightly smaller planet and then millions of frozen comets breaking against the Earth's crust, carrying vast amounts of water that created the oceans.

And water is where life emerged. We don't have an exact date, but it was somewhere between 3 and 3.7 billion years ago. However, with all these comets and meteorites raining down, life was probably born and perished a number of times in those billions of years.

At some point a molecule playing around in the water managed to replicate itself. After that it joined other like particles, for reproductive purposes and to coalesce with polymolecular organisms. It seems bacteria developed first, followed by fungi, plants and animals. And by animals we mean fish, but not as we know them today. Those who've studied the genesis of life in depth imagine the first visible animal beings as a kind of sea sponge, more or less. But by gradually adapting to their environment, with billions of trials and errors, these creatures became actual fish.

At some point there was a scarcity of oxygen in parts of the sea along the coast, so some of these marine creatures learned to raise their heads out of the water in search of it. In time this became their normal behavior, and as they came in closer to land they began to adapt their fins to support themselves. It's quite exciting to think about this billion-year process taking us from the molecule to dinosaurs.

In fact, 230 million years ago the ancient dinosaurs were the first to separate from their reptile ancestors and thus became the rulers of the Earth. A few of them even learned to fly. This was what we call the Jurassic era. A single continent had emerged called Pangea, and about 180 million years ago it began the long, slow process of separation that would lead to the current configuration of the planet, with the Americas moving west and Eurasia east.

But let's go back to sixty-six million years ago. A catastrophic event changed the course of history forever. An enormous meteorite about 6.2 miles in diameter fell onto our planet just off what is now the Yucatán Peninsula, generating such devastation that two-thirds of life on Earth was destroyed. Nearly all the dinosaurs died, but in the following millions of years a few vertebrates began very slowly propagating again.

Now it was just a question of time. The general conditions on the planet favored life, from the right mixture of nitrogen, oxygen and carbon dioxide to the ozone curtain protecting it from ultraviolet rays. Diversification among mammals included a monkey in Africa we might describe today as like the chimpanzee, which some scientists believe is the evolution of a small mammal like a shrew.

We're not entirely sure why some of those monkeys began standing upright and why their brains gradually increased in size. But it happened. From two million years ago we can begin to classify a group of these monkeys—that walked upright, had opposable thumbs and could probably communicate with each other in some primitive way—as almost Homo.

The decisive turning point came about one and a half million years ago, when one of these apes invented fire. From then on exponential growth occurred that led to humans ruling the planet unopposed, achieving the community of more than 7.5 billion people who today can communicate with each other in real time from all corners of the Earth. A million and a half years is only an instant by comparison, just 0.01 percent of the time separating us from the birth of the universe.

Even the invention of fire can be classified as serendipitous. It happened for a practical reason: to tackle the wild animals that came into the caves to eat whatever they could find, including humans. At the sight of fire they took fright and fled. The apes with their superior intelligence noticed that fire spread from tree to tree, so they tried isolating it; by transferring it from one branch to another, they found they could carry it into the cave. Then they fueled it with more wood, thus solving the biggest problem of all: preserving life. Only many centuries later did they learn to light it themselves by vigorously rubbing two twigs together.

At the same time they realized that this thing they'd created to solve a problem could lead to something much better. Life, once preserved, could be improved.

In terms of creations, after the invention of fire there was no holding back. That was just the first invention establishing the superiority of humans over other animals, at least in adaptability and survival. They were no longer afraid. They became more and more curious and started exploring the world, reaching just about every corner of it over the next million years.

After the apes there were various categories of hominids, each different in appearance and intellectual awareness. These crucial transitions can be dated to around three hundred thousand years ago. For example, some believe Neanderthals and Homo sapiens never met, but recently scholars have found proof that their paths crossed. And while the extinction of the Neanderthals remains a mystery, Homo sapiens survived and generated humankind as we understand it today.

So here we are about twelve thousand years ago, at the end of the last glacial period, in a geographical area more or less corresponding to the Middle East and in a spot on the border between Iran, Iraq and Syria, on the plain between the Tigris and the Euphrates. It's known as the Fertile Crescent. A small group of people settled here, giving up their nomadic life and with it the constant search for new wild fruits and game. It's likely this decision was made in various parts of the world due to an abrupt change in the climate. Once again a chance event changing human destiny. They tried planting seeds in the soil to replicate the naturally growing cereals that were their food: it worked. They tried breeding a few animal species for milk and meat: that worked too. This group expanded over the centuries and so did the species they cultivated. Agriculture was born: another huge qualitative leap for humankind.

It was natural that these parts of the world would see the first form of organized society emerge. Around six thousand years ago the Sumerians perfected methods of cultivation, irrigation and harvesting and started making beer, wine and olive oil with quite good results. In the next three thousand years the Egyptians and the Greeks further improved techniques in agriculture, animal breeding and the processing and preservation of raw materials. They invented more efficient fishing equipment and even learned to breed a few species of fish. In the following centuries, knowledge of these practices spread farther and farther north until they finally reached the most fertile peninsula in the world. It found the ideal environment in Italy and exploded.

The Romans refined the principles of modern agriculture and became the best-nourished of all populations, and consequently the most powerful. A story of growth and conquests lasting over five hundred years. Then toward the end of the fifth century AD it all came to an end.

So we come to the Middle Ages, a long and varied period hard to sum up in a few words. For agriculture it was certainly a dark time, as if we'd taken a step backward and, I have to say, the central role of the religions played a large part. Yet paradoxically it was the monks, in the shelter of their growing number of monasteries, who preserved the sound agricultural practices and sometimes even improved them. Innovation in farming gained momentum early in the medieval period, and with the Renaissance everything took off again. We'd arrived. This was six hundred years ago, just eighteen generations before ours. A new way of thinking pervaded our country and Italy was once again important in the world. Humans were at the core of this cultural model and they gained faith in themselves and their abilities, with consequent growth in the economy and general well-being. If I had to name the greatest thing to come out of the Renaissance I'd say it was faith, a potent natural engine that propels humanity toward harmony, beauty and well-being. Unfamiliar fruits and vegetables being brought in from the New Worlds to the West and the East brought a change of gear to the biodiversity of the Old Continent. In the following centuries national and regional cuisines emerged, and the products transformed by agriculture became progressively better and healthier.

With the Industrial Revolution at the end of the eighteenth century, food and drink essentially took on their current characteristics, and while agriculture was becoming less important in the economy it was starting to benefit from powerful technological innovation that gradually reduced the need for manual labor. The Industrial Revolution came somewhat late to Italy—at the time we were going through the Risorgimento. This was the mid-1800s, and a new sentiment emerged called patriotism. Previously it hadn't featured among this country's values, but now it led to Italian unification, promoting integration and transforming it into interaction. Needless to say it brought a thousand problems with it. Nevertheless, behold Italy!

But unfortunately, in a Europe where internal borders were still a new phenomenon, it was the start of a dark time affecting the entire world. Two world wars, massacres and destruction: there had never been so much atrocity concentrated within a few decades. The delusions of a ruler capable of taking his people toward blind egotism and racism can do enormous harm to humanity.

With the post-war economic miracle the Italian population, then predominantly peasants, changed radically. A smaller number of people could produce much more, but the main player in the miracle was industry.

The invention of that period par excellence was courage. Courage spreading contagiously through the Italian people, who in twenty-five years of dedicated work became the fifth most powerful population in the world. Meanwhile, in agriculture and stock breeding, attention was increasingly focused on quantity, and not just in Italy. In addition to the rapidly developing mechanical technologies, chemistry came to the fore with the aim of eradicating disease, but also reducing human toil and exploiting the energy of the Earth using artificial means.

In the last two decades of the twentieth century, first at CERN, the European Organization for Nuclear Research in Geneva, and then at MIT in Boston, a young English researcher named Tim Berners-Lee invented the World Wide Web. The internet was born. It came on the heels of another invention perfected by another young man, in this case Bill Gates, in a garage in Seattle: software that was inserted into a small machine with a keyboard and a monitor to create a kind of artificial intelligence. This was the first personal computer. And let's not forget someone else about the same age who was building these machines in another garage at the same time, in the vicinity of San Francisco. The great Steve Jobs.

The combination of artificial intelligence and the internet, in a whirlwind of (often serendipitous) research and perfecting, generated what we know today as the digital economy, although digital society might be a better term. For me it's the greatest invention of all, along with fire. And like fire it was destined to change humanity's fortunes for the better. But like fire it also has to be tamed. At the moment we're still burning our feet a bit, and sometimes burning forests. The application of digital innovations destroys workplaces, and in a socioeconomic model where each of us is employed as a generator of the salaries that are the basis of consumption, that creates disasters. And as if that wasn't enough, digital relations seem to have fostered an exaggerated language mainly about grievances, mistrust and insults.

I don't think that's quite how the young Americans imagined it when they invented all this.

Alessandro Baricco in his book *The Game* maintains it began as a revolutionary gesture of protest against the twentieth-century elite, an attempt to eliminate brokers with the dream of enabling everyone to understand (or at least access) the truth, and offering each individual the possibility to grow and to fight economic inequities through connection. What emerged within a few years was an incredible machine, beautiful on the one hand and concerning on the other. I think even the inventors (who in the meantime had left behind the fairytale of their garages and become the richest people on the planet) were a bit spooked by developments that were pretty much impossible to foresee.

Now we're all grappling with the very urgent problems of climate change and pollution. And I'm just as certain the inventors of plastic, the internal combustion engine, and the production of electrical energy with hydrocarbons wouldn't have imagined that along with their amazing mechanisms they'd built the future disaster of the planet. We could call it an unintended kind of serendipity with unforeseen negative effects, but the fact remains that we're now in the midst of a very serious emergency.

Climate change has suddenly made us all aware that the end of human life on this planet may be closer than we could have imagined, and we need to reset our relationship with land, air and water; in other words, with what believers call "creation" and the secular world calls "nature."

The mission of consumer society, invented by humans nearly two centuries ago, was enjoyment. Ever-increasing enjoyment, eating better, dressing better, owning better houses, better cars, having more convenient equipment, living warmer in winter and cooler in summer; living better.

Despite many positive effects (to name just one, the average lifespan has increased by twenty years), in the search for ever-greater enjoyment, consumption has in many respects degenerated into consumerism. We've seen and continue to see overproduction; waste is increasing, and often respect for the environment is diminishing—in industry and agriculture and in our domestic lives. All this while part of the world remains without food twelve thousand years after agriculture was invented.

From one case of serendipity to another we've steadily grown and improved, with enormous capacity to adapt to events and changes. Now we must overcome this new great obstacle, and let's hope our ability to manage imperfection will come to our aid once again.

When it comes to research into human imperfection, in Italy we have one of the world's finest minds. Telmo Pievani is a young scholar teaching Philosophy of Biological Sciences at the University of Padua. He's written a book that can help us better understand humans as the result of a series of successful imperfections. The title is *Imperfezione: Una storia naturale (Imperfection: A Natural History)*.

"Dear Telmo, after a brief history of human serendipity as inter-preted by a food and wine entrepreneur and history enthusiast, now it's your turn."

Telmo Pievani

It's true, we are the quintessential children of serendipity in every sense. You mentioned that we don't know why we became bipeds. We don't know because walking on legs can serve many different functions, and above all because the upright stance is one of the most imperfect adap-tations we know. People with back pain, lumbago, sciatica, scoliosis, hernias and other aches and pains know what I mean and suffer the consequences. Besides, taking the bending spine of a quadruped and making it vertical, dumping all the weight on very fragile feet, is not the ultimate in efficiency. The spinal column curves and the vertebrae are subjected to undue pressures. Nerves and muscles have to readapt. Why on earth did we do that? And our neck with that swinging ball on top is another weak spot. It was so easy for the felines that once used to eat us to sink their teeth into the carotid. And even our soft abdomen with all its internal organs is exposed to all kinds of trauma. It makes no sense. The force of gravity pushes down the peritoneum and that causes terrible prolapsing tendencies. We pay the price in our faces too. Our maxillary sinuses have drainage channels directed toward the nasal cavities above—in other words, against gravity. That's another terrible idea; yet in a quadruped the opening of the maxillary sinuses faces forwards and works perfectly well. We ex-quadrupeds stood up and put our faces in a vertical position and the result is frequent bad colds, sinusitis, etc. Not to mention the pain of childbirth and lots of other malfunctions. A collection of imperfections.

However, being biped has also given us great advantages in terms of survival and reproduction: otherwise, our peers more accustomed to living in trees would have prevailed. We can imagine them perched on the branches looking on puzzled and amused as their cousins lurch along below as if walking on trampolines. But in the processes of evolution innovation takes unpredictable paths.

The upright posture enabled us to run long distances and gave us more flexible mobility. As bipeds we could still climb trees, walk, run or wade across a river and, most importantly, rise above the grass to get a better view of predators lying in wait.

Then, of course, the upright posture freed our hands and arms so that we could use them to handle tools and carry food and children. In that regard it opened up vast possibilities in technological and cultural evolution in the long term. It's a pity we've only recently discovered stone tools at Lake Turkana dating back to seven hundred thousand years before the genus Homo emerged. It means someone else was making them when the upright posture was yet to be established. The story of becoming biped to free the hands doesn't add up. Then comes the surprise: maybe these advantages were just unforeseen and serendipitous collateral effects? One of the problems for species like the Australopithecines, our ancestors who lived in Africa on the border between forests and grasslands, was keeping the temperature of the body within physiological limits. And the brain in particular, because it doesn't tolerate overheating. Maybe the solution was to reduce the surface area exposed to the sun and guarantee control of body temperature. How? By standing upright. At the same time our ancestors may have gradually lost their fur and developed sweat glands. If that's the case, a heat-regulating adaptation might have triggered the series of advantageous uses that made bipedalism a good strategy, despite the high cost in terms of structural imperfections. That's how evolution works: by creatively reusing what's there.

In short, bipedalism is a very imperfect compromise, but after lots of trial and error it began to work. Let's forget the tale of human evolution starting with the heroic "descent from the trees" to conquer the savannah on foot. We only became complete bipeds in the early days of the genus Homo, between 2 and 2.8 million years ago. Before that we'd regularly go back to the trees for shelter.

Genetic mutations are transcription errors in the DNA, and often they're detrimental, but without them there'd be nothing to fuel any evolutionary change. In nature, errors are generative. What's even more interesting is that sometimes evolution serendipitously stores its surplus embellishments. Our genome, for example, is full of superfluous repeated sequences and deactivated genes. If they cost too much it jettisons them. If not it keeps them where they are, because you never know; it's like the odds and ends people keep in the garage ready to be repurposed.

I'm sure you can sing the praises of the onion in terms of biodiversity and gastronomic versatility, Oscar. Well, the onion's DNA is four times longer than ours! But with all due respect, it's a bulbous plant and it's hardly four times more evolved or more intelligent than we are. Wherever possible, nature is lavish.

In fact, we recently discovered that some important stages in our evolution happened as a result of reusing genes that were doing other jobs or were temporarily unemployed. That's serendipity too: you find yourself with a gene that does one thing and you discover it can be used to do something else entirely.

The point is that evolution always proceeds serendipitously, and we are the ultimate confirmation of that rule. In nature a structure evolves in relation to a function, like the wing that allows an insect to fly, for example, giving it advantages in terms of survival and reproduction. So we say the wing evolved for flying, but we need to be careful because often in nature a given feature turns out to have multiple uses: serendipitously that wing can become very handy for camouflage or protection, creating shade, seducing females with its flamboyant colors, or sending out signals. In the end it's hard to know what that wing evolved for originally. Nature is full of imagination and feeds on diversity. There's never a predetermined norm because evolution explores the possible case by case, feeding on the inexhaustible variations and uniqueness inherent in every single individual.

We only believe birds' wings evolved to fly because we always think in terms of an end, a plan, a story that went the way it did by necessity. But that's wrong. Wings, like all complex structures, were not suddenly born between sunset and dawn: it took thousands of generations of natural selection and individual sacrifices. So we must assume that in the beginning there were drafts of wings, attempts at wings. And at every stage those strange drafts must still have been useful for something, otherwise they'd have been discarded straight away. You try standing on a cliff and attempting to fly with a draft wing: it doesn't work! That's the point—the wings of the first avian dinosaurs had other functions: sexual attraction, regulation of body temperature, or balance while running. Then a few learned to use them in gliding, launching themselves at their prey from tree trunks. Much later they were co-opted for full free flight through the air as well: a marvelous discovery (which we humans only managed to emulate a century ago).

This is the serendipitous greatness of nature: natural selection leads you to a result and within that result are a host of other possible stories. A characteristic evolves for a certain purpose but is reused for something quite different.

We humans are world champions at this creative tinkering; we've made a virtue of necessity and thought up alternatives that seemed impossible. Woe betide anyone who says there are no alternatives! That's why imperfection is so important. If we were perfect everything would be in its place. We'd be highly specialized for a particular environment and that's it. With the first major ecological shock we'd be extinct. Our secret weapon is flexibility; in other words, ingenious adaptability, malleability. Darwin said nature is overflowing with futility, and that's why it's so innovative—because there's always material to work on: excesses, imperfections, chance variations.

Only our brain has tripled its size in two million years, exploding in our heads, pushing and expanding in every possible direction. That large brain has certainly given us great advantages in managing ever more complex social relations, but it's also very costly and imperfect. It has forced us to enrich and diversify our diet with vegetables, fruit, seeds, a bit more animal protein and lots of cooked tubers. Our brain is the child of serendipitous tinkering. As it grew it put together old bits and new bits as best it could, and they're still interacting with each other today. Sometimes the oldest areas, associated with the emotions and instinctive reactions, conflict with more recent ones—the prefrontal cortex and the parietal lobes associated with reasoning, language and a lot else besides.

The brain is the champion of creative recycling: it's an imperfect gadget but it has marvelous potential. We read and write and converse using parts of the brain that evolved to do something quite different, and for that matter our opposable thumbs would never have thought they'd be used for compulsively pressing keys on a smartphone. There is virtually no area of that gray matter allocated to the same function today as it was created for. Serendipity in its pure state.

Consider the magic of it: that serendipitous brain is now cognizant of itself, asks questions about the universe, builds spaceships, studies natural phenomena, and very often in the process goes looking for one thing and finds something completely different! So now our mind, the child of serendipity, realizes what it still doesn't know and explores the unknown letting itself be carried along by chance.

The serendipity of nature created us, and now we use serendipity to understand nature. As a great forgotten Nobel Prize winner, George Wald, said, given that our body and our mind consist of heavy elements synthesized in the nuclei of the stars, humanity is the method invented by a star to get to know itself.

In science, then, serendipity also means humility.

We thought we understood the universe, and instead we find that putting together energy and dark matter we know less than 10 percent of it. So the adventure of discovery continues.

We were certain of being the only humans on Earth, and instead we realize that until fifty thousand years ago our planet was inhabited by at least five different human forms, all together in Africa and Eurasia: an apotheosis of diversity. In my opinion it's wonderful to know there have been many ways of being human, and ours wasn't the only one possible.

Besides, as befits serendipity, the answer to a question in science unleashes many other questions. For instance, now we are wondering how it is that we're the only ones left, if we were in the company of other humans up until a few thousand years ago (we don't know, but we suspect Homo sapiens has been an interfering species for a long time). Science is that awesome human enterprise where instead of diminishing over time the number of question marks grows. The more you know the more you realize you don't know. In fact, you realize you didn't even know you didn't know, and that's the most fascinating form of serendipity.

It's no accident that as soon as we became bipeds, and as our brain was beginning to grow, we started migrating and we've never stopped. Several times we left Africa, the continent where all of us originated, and dispersed around Eurasia. Whether out of curiosity or reacting to the vagaries of climate, we've been migrants for two million years, although some people think of migration as an emergency or (worse still) a recent invasion.

On the contrary, we are human because we're migrants.

The flexibility of our brain, our remarkable adaptability and our diversity largely come from cultural evolution and the constant tendency to move; we always want to see what's on the other side of the hill. Homo sapiens is the migratory species par excellence: we started coming out of Africa 130 thousand years ago and we've never stopped. We were also the first to go to Australia, around sixty-five thousand years ago, and to the Americas twenty-five thousand years ago.

From a small original stock of African pioneers (fifty to sixty thousand people at most—a small township today) the whole marvelous diversity of peoples, languages and cultures of the world fanned out. "Unity in diversity" should be the world's motto.

Migrating is serendipitous behavior too: you set out to look for something—say, new lands and resources—and you might find something totally different—for example, another human species descended from earlier migrants out of Africa that you have to live with. Sometimes we got really lucky: there's genetic data showing that the human population was drastically reduced more than once due to sudden climate changes, huge volcanic eruptions or the difficulty of living with certain viruses. But every time we got through it and the serendipitous adventure resumed.

In migrating and in adapting to all the Earth's ecosystems, from the Arctic to the tropics, the *sapiens* explorer groups soon revealed their contradictory nature. They were capable of extraordinary creativity (ritual burials, musical instruments, body ornaments, rock paintings) but they were also invaders, aggressors and predators. As far back as forty thousand years ago, wherever Homo sapiens went environments were altered and often depleted. The limited sustainability of our environment is an old story.

You've explained how fire was a crucial and serendipitous discovery. It literally allowed us to change the world around us to make it more comfortable. This is the secret of our evolutionary success: rather than passively adapting to the world we change it, and then we must adapt to the changes we've introduced. Fire allowed us to feed ourselves with more chewable, more digestible and more nourishing cooked foods. But there's another important detail. Now our digestive system is dependent on cooking and we can't really survive on raw foods alone, so our physiology has changed. Even our cousins the apes will prefer a cooked meal to an uncooked one if given the choice. To me this is a marvelous example of serendipity: a cultural and technological invention like the cooking of food has changed our genetics. It's the world upside down—first culture, then biology.

It was the same with the digestion of milk and milk products in adults, and metabolizing alcohol, but in other cases that mechanism didn't work. Too many fatty and sugar-rich foods are bad for us because our biology hasn't yet adapted to urban environments where those high-calorie foods are always available in large quantity. But the process continues, albeit slowly. The microbiome (the ecosystem of bacteria, fungi and other microorganisms we host in our intestine, in our mouths and on our skin that enables us to live) is much healthier and richer in hunter-gatherers and rural dwellers than in people living in cities and industrialized areas. This is not good news. Besides, what's climate warming if not large-scale transformation of the planet's regulatory mechanisms? It's due to human activities that have also brought well-being and progress for part of humanity, and it's a transformation we now have to adapt to.

Our evolutionary serendipity has made us contradictory. Adapting to rapid changes we ourselves have introduced, warming the Earth and impoverishing its ecosystems (we've already wiped out a third of the biodiversity on the planet) could be a dangerous game because of the multiplying effects. For instance, the environmental crisis exacerbates already shocking global inequalities, fuels wars and forced migrations, and increases the likelihood of pandemics.

Anyone lucky enough to have been born in Italy should be especially sensitive to this question. We're a transit country, and too often we forget that despite decades of insane over-use of the land and over-building on the coasts, our peninsula is still the most richly biodiverse region in the whole of Europe. At the same time (for partly analogous reasons that merit scientific investigation) a human, linguistic, cultural and gastronomic genetic diversity without equal has evolved in our country.

In a nutshell, what I'd say is that an imperfect and serendipitous species has great power. But unlike the dinosaurs, we know it and we realize it would be truly absurd (and not very *sapiens*) to let our species die out. Apart from anything else, life on Earth would continue perfectly well without us and indeed would quickly prosper again. We're not indispensable. Commitment to the environment, in my view, is ultimately a humanist commitment to respect for ourselves and even more for future generations.

Besides, after all the lucky accidents that have brought us this far, it would be a real waste of good fortune to exhaust the only planet we've got.

Thinking about it gives you goosebumps. At the start of it all there's the infinitesimal fluctuation in the quantum vacuum, the original imperfection; then matter prevailing over antimatter; matter distributing unevenly so that in the densest areas the furnaces of the stars are lit; the fact that on the periphery of a random galaxy, but in a region filled with heavy elements, a star is born that's not too big and not too small; chance collisions between the rocky bodies orbiting around it create a planet of the right size at the right distance. The rest is the story of life you've summarized well, including the entirely accidental turning point sixty-six million years ago that saw the sun set on the rule of the dinosaurs and delivered Earth to the mammals that are our ancestors. Nowhere was it written that things had to happen like that, a fact we need to recognize: we're only here by a lucky chance. A serendipitous chance.

Most likely it happened elsewhere, too, on one of the numerous extrasolar planets the astronomers are identifying, but with what results is anyone's guess. As for our cosmic neighborhood, the most we'll find is some exotic bacterium that loves the extreme. I don't like going along with the pessimism of the Fermi paradox, but maybe the physicists are right to speculate that aliens don't come and visit because by the time any extraterrestrial civilization reached a stage of evolution to allow interstellar travel, it would already have exhausted its planet's resources and collapsed. It would be torn to pieces in wars. In short, an alien intelligent enough to come and pay us a visit is an alien that's extinct. The message is more for us than for them, obviously. We'd do well not to go in that direction.

To get out of this evolutionary trap I think we should cultivate the serendipity of our intelligence. By that I mean we should support basic research purely out of curiosity about natural phenomena. It just happens that those phenomena trigger revolutionary and unexpected applications, like the ones you mention in the introduction to this book.

I'll add another recent one. The most powerful biotechnology we use today, gene editing, was discovered "unwittingly" several years ago by a few microbiologists who were studying the defenses of bacteria against viruses, with next to no funding. Now huge new companies listed on Wall Street are working on it.

Serendipity is not pure chance: it means having a mind open to change and surprise and the irruption of the unexpected. You ask a question of nature via an experiment, and nature responds with something totally different. The genius lies in understanding immediately that within this "totally different" there's something important.

Promoting pure and disinterested research means being open to generative error, knowing we're still very ignorant, being farsighted and not expecting immediate returns; not being stubborn but prepared to take a different path if the evidence points to it. We need to understand that true innovations must be accessible to everyone, for the common good, because without social justice we're not going to save the environment.

Besides, we Italians are very strong internationally in this sophisticated qualitative research, and if only our leaders understood that we could see a fantastic return from it.

After all, the serendipitous mind is the opposite of the fundamentalist mind, which is obfuscated by false certainties, convinced it understands the rationale of history, and always ready to categorize others as friend or enemy and feed on fears, self-interest and resentments.

The serendipitous mind is also the opposite of the tribal mind obsessed with the profits of its corporation, its sect or its party—the mind of those who'd rather win their own backyard squabbles than think about the common good. Unfortunately many recent scientific studies show that these deplorable human attitudes are very successful at conquering our brains. They persuade us and they come easy: they're reassuring, instinctive shortcuts.

This is exactly what's happening with the internet. After the first phase when we enthusiastically explored its emancipating and information-sharing possibilities, now the digital universe is becoming populated with tribes, with bubbles where we only look for confirmation of our prejudices, and with chatter and fake news. But we're in web prehistory, and I agree civilizing it will take time. All the more reason then to work at cultivating the spirit of criticism and serendipity, especially in young people. I see them discouraged at times and resigned to fatalism, which is nonsense. We have great resources in the areas of innovation and surprise.

Up until now we've always got by thanks to serendipity, and that's how it will be in the future too. If we come together and set ourselves a long-term goal, nothing will be out of reach.

Recently we celebrated the fiftieth anniversary of the moon landing. Today if you look at the "prehistoric" materials and technologies they were using then, you realize the risk they took was madness, and yet they got there in spite of everything. That collective undertaking led to cascades of serendipitous technological applications. Our grandchildren, who'll be born into climate warming and the damage and opportunities we have created, will look back with affection at the "prehistoric" technologies we're using in these first decades of the twenty-first century.

Human serendipity is a story without an end, in the sense that it doesn't finish and in the sense that it has no hidden goal. Homo sapiens were born two hundred millennia ago in Africa, and that's only eight thousand generations ago—the blink of an eye in evolutionary time.

I like to think our exploration of the possible is only in its infancy.

EPILOGUE

I wish you lots of serendipity!

Here we are at the end. We've had a great trip around the world, from Turin to Naples, Milan, Buenos Aires, Mexico, New York, Chicago, San Diego, Trinidad, Paris, London, Mongolia and Japan. We've traveled between different eras, from the discovery of fire to modern medicine. We've heard about the experiences of amazing people and chatted with some truly special individuals.

I hope you've enjoyed reading these stories as much as I've enjoyed telling them. We now know quite a bit more about some of the products we eat and drink, and undoubtedly it will help us enjoy them more.

I'm convinced good lessons can be found in each of these stories using the examples of people who, at the most disparate moments in history and faced with problems large or small, have found solutions and managed to get through thanks to passion, perseverance and courage.

I'd like to add that the most important lesson these stories together may have given us is that doubt can be more valuable than certainty. We've learned that thanks to doubt, many "mistaken" products have turned into products of excellence. We've witnessed the capacity to change direction, to retreat, to learn from mistakes, to never be completely certain one thing is right and the other wrong. Having doubts doesn't mean being uncertain—far from it. In fact it's doubt that can lead us not to give up, but to change our minds and look for a new path.

Enjoy life! I wish each and every one of you an excellent and serendipitous journey.